KOREAN STUDIES OF THE HENRY M. JACKSON
SCHOOL OF INTERNATIONAL STUDIES

Clark W. Sorensen, Editor

THE SHAMAN'S WAGES

TRADING IN RITUAL
ON CHEJU ISLAND

KYOIM YUN

UNIVERSITY OF WASHINGTON PRESS
Seattle

THE SHAMAN'S WAGES WAS PUBLISHED WITH THE GENEROUS SUPPORT OF THE
INTERNATIONAL CENTER FOR KOREAN STUDIES, KOREA UNIVERSITY'S CENTER FOR
RESEARCH, PUBLICATION, AND DEVELOPMENT IN KOREAN STUDIES. THE CENTER
WAS ESTABLISHED IN 2003 TO SUPPORT SCHOLARSHIP AND EXPLORATION OF
KOREA IN THE HUMANITIES AND SOCIAL SCIENCES, AND TO PROMOTE NEW
RESEARCH IN KOREAN STUDIES TO A WIDE INTERNATIONAL AUDIENCE.

ADDITIONAL SUPPORT WAS PROVIDED BY THE ASSOCIATION FOR ASIAN STUDIES
FIRST BOOK SUBVENTION PROGRAM AND BY THE KOREA STUDIES PROGRAM OF THE
UNIVERSITY OF WASHINGTON IN COOPERATION WITH THE HENRY M. JACKSON
SCHOOL OF INTERNATIONAL STUDIES.

UNIVERSITY OF WASHINGTON PRESS
www.washington.edu/uwpress

LIBRARY OF CONGRESS CATALOGING-IN-PUBLICATION DATA
Names: Yun, Kyoim, author.
Title: The shaman's wages : trading in ritual on Cheju Island / Kyoim Yun.
Description: Seattle : University of Washington Press, [2019] | Series: Korean studies of the Henry
    M. Jackson School of International Studies | Includes bibliographical references and index. |
Identifiers: LCCN 2018059844 (print) | LCCN 2019015882 (ebook) | ISBN 9780295745961 (ebook) |
    ISBN 9780295745978 (hardcover : alk. paper) | ISBN 9780295745954 (pbk. : alk. paper)
Subjects: LCSH: Shamanism—Korea (South)—Cheju Island. | Economic anthropology—Korea
    (South)—Cheju Island. | Shamanism—Rituals. | Cheju Island (Korea)—Religious life and
    customs.
Classification: LCC BL2236.S5 (ebook) | LCC BL2236.S5 Y865 2019 (print) |
    DDC 299.5/7—dc23
LC record available at https://lccn.loc.gov/2018059844

For my mother and father,
Kim Chaeyŏl 김재열 *and Yun Chŏngch'ae* 윤정채

CONTENTS

ACKNOWLEDGMENTS

Over the many years that it has taken to bring this project to fruition, I have been extremely fortunate to receive generous support from many individuals and organizations in South Korea and the United States. First and foremost, I thank the people of Cheju Island for their warm hospitality and invaluable assistance with my research, without which this book would never have been born. I have used fictitious names for shamans and their clients, except for public figures, to protect their privacy. They have my deepest gratitude. Mun Sunduck provided me not only with unflagging friendship but also with important books about the island. I am indebted to Cho Sung-Youn of Cheju National University for nurturing my scholarly growth with his warm heart and magisterial knowledge of the island. Intellectuals on Cheju impressed me time and again with their vigorous pursuit of knowledge of the local history and culture. I am grateful for their willingness to share their findings and insights with me.

Many scholars helped with my intellectual enrichment. Song Hyosup and the late Kim Yŏlkyu inspired me to appreciate the aesthetics of language and the rich world of mythology. Song encouraged me to pursue an academic career, and Kim was the first to introduce me to Cheju mythology and shamanism. At Indiana University, Gregory A. Schrempp, William Hansen, and John McDowell furthered my interest in mythology in a broader context. Richard Bauman opened my eyes to the power of words in getting things done in a range of communicative events in both the secular and sacred realms. I am obliged to Michael Robinson for his scholarship and mentorship. Roger L. Janelli taught me to discreetly observe the intricacies of human interests and desires for power exercised structurally and situationally as expressed explicitly and implicitly. I owe him more than I can ever express for the constant encouragement and extremely helpful counsel he so generously provided for more than two decades. His unfailing faith in me and my work was a remedy during periods of despair.

This book benefited from conversations with and comments from a range of scholars from different disciplines. An Mi-jeong (Mijŏng) generously shared her insights into the culture of the diving women and their popular religion. Kelly Chong, Michael Foster, Danille E. Christensen, and Kathy Roberts read earlier versions of the manuscript and offered valuable feedback and encouragement. Marsha Haufler, with her long-standing connections to and love for Korea, coached me on how to strengthen an authorial voice and winnow essential components from criticism. I appreciate Andre Schmid, Seo Young Park, and the late Nancy Abelmann for their constructive criticism and moral support at the 2011 Rising Star Conference organized by the Korean Studies Institute of the University of Southern California. Different versions of each chapter were presented at several academic venues, and I appreciate those audience members who gave me helpful feedback. An earlier version of chapter 5 was published as "The Economic Imperative of UNESCO Recognition: A South Korean Shamanic Ritual," in the *Journal of Folklore Research* 52, nos. 2/3, in 2015.

At various stages of the project, I received generous institutional support, financial, logistical, and otherwise. The General Research Funds and the Center for East Asian Studies' International Travel Grants at the University of Kansas, as well as the funds provided by the Center for East Asian Studies and the Society of Friends of Korean Studies at Indiana University, allowed me to write and to conduct both library research and extended periods of fieldwork. Librarian Vickie Doll at the University of Kansas has never failed to furnish information and resources with remarkable alacrity.

Both the Kyujanggak Institute for Korean Studies at Seoul National University and the International Center for Korean Studies at Korea University hosted me for my library research and the writing of this book. At Seoul National University, I benefited from discussions with Kim Sunkyoung, Kim Nam Yun, Lee Wook, Jisoo M. Kim, and Hilary Finchum-Sung, all of whom I would also like to thank for their kindness. Sem Vermeersch provided very helpful comments on an earlier version of chapter 1. The warm collegiality and friendship of my office mate Youngju Ryu during my fellowship year at Kyujanggak helped me cope with both academic and personal challenges. At Korea University, the sagelike scholars Jang Sookpil and Chang Chungsoo taught me that scholarly and personal growth are inextricably entwined.

I am grateful to the editors at the University of Washington Press. Clark W. Sorensen saw a book in my manuscript and helped me both sharpen my focus and broaden the relevance of this study to different disciplines.

Lorri D. Hagman guided me with marvelous patience and efficiency at several stages of the production, and Caitlin Tyler-Richards assisted me with uplifting and helpful communications. I cannot help but compare the editorial team with the secretaries of King Yŏmna of the otherworld, who changed the destiny of the protagonist in the myth of Saman by editing the record of his life span to his very considerable advantage. Two anonymous readers enhanced the quality of the book. Any shortcomings of this work are of course mine.

Ji-Yeon Lee was the most supportive and reliable colleague and comrade that anyone could hope for. Ron Odle has never stopped cheering me on with his wisdom, humor, and steadfast support. I will forever be grateful to my dear grandmother Park Munja, who passed away before seeing this book's birth, for all the love that she showed to me and my siblings, Minho, Younghee, and Yangho. This book is dedicated to my parents, who have always trusted me even when I doubted myself and who provided me with everything that they could.

AUTHOR'S NOTE

Romanization of Korean terms and names in the text follows the McCune-Reischauer system, with the exception of familiar names such as Seoul, for which I have adopted the standard English spellings. Korean and Japanese names in the text and the bibliography are written according to native traditions (surname first, without commas), except for those authors who have published primarily in English. For Korean authors using different romanizations for their names, I have provided standard romanization in brackets in the bibliography and on first occurrence in the text. For public figures such as presidents, conventional romanizations are used. All Korean names in the text are pseudonyms, except for those of authors and public figures. When "Cheju" is rendered "Jeju" in English-language titles of publications, I maintain that romanization. All transliterations, transcriptions, and translations are mine unless otherwise noted. The exchange rate between the Korean won and the US dollar has fluctuated over the years, but I use a rough estimate of 1,000 won to US$1 throughout the text.

THE SHAMAN'S WAGES

INTRODUCTION

IN OCTOBER 2001 SEVERAL *SIMBANG* (NATIVE SHAMANS OF CHEJU Island) conducted a three-day ritual at a family home. The group included two primary practitioners (husband and wife) and three assistants (two females and one male). I accompanied them as an observer. The lead *simbang*, Yang, had told me beforehand that the main purpose of the ritual was to console the household's son, who had died in a car accident when he was only twenty-six. Had he still been alive, he would have been my age. I naturally felt compassion for the family and was somewhat apprehensive both about witnessing "lamentations of the dead" (Kim Seong-nae 1989a, 1989b) and about what was expected to be the *simbang*'s consolation of the living and the dead in a "sacred" séance. I was also eager to hear the ritual specialists' live recitation of the oral repertoire, particularly *ponp'uri* (mythic narratives) of Cheju, a place known by scholars and romantics as the "island of myth."

The three-day event, however, unfolded rather differently than I had expected. After an exchange of greetings, the household head, Mr. Cho, passed an envelope containing the ritual fee to Simbang Yang. Upon counting the bank checks (*sup'yo*) in the envelope, the *simbang* asked cautiously, "Wasn't it six?" (meaning "Hadn't we agreed on 6 million won [US$6,000]?").[1]

Mr. Cho replied, "It was five."

The two parties did not come to an agreement even after an extended discussion. An assistant *simbang* who had been folding the white paper that would be offered as pseudo-money during the ritual chimed in, "He wouldn't make a mistake about such a thing."

But then Cho's wife, Han,[2] who had visited the *simbang* couple earlier to request the ritual and to arrange the ritual preparations and fee, came into the living room from the kitchen. Countering the assistant's claim, she assured the *simbang*, "It was five, and you said you would do *aengmaegi* [a ritual sequence for forestalling misfortune] for free." Her firm assertion wrapped up the discussion, and the tug-of-war between the two parties seemed to be over.

This scene, which reminded me of bargaining in the old-style open-air markets in Korea, caught me off guard. I was well aware that shamans do not perform gratis. I also knew of the ethnographic depictions of the keen interest some ambitious urban practitioners took in fame and gain (e.g., Chungmoo Choi 1987, 191–200; 1989; 1991) but thought them exceptional. In retrospect, I naively expected *simbang* on the island to be rather less practical-minded than media-savvy urban practitioners. The process of deciding the ritual fee was not then in my research purview despite the fact that shamans are service providers. In addition to the initial dispute regarding the service fee, I later observed a more subtle tug-of-war associated with cash offerings immediately following an emotionally heightened séance in which the dead and the living wept together. This time, the shamans had the upper hand (see chap. 4). Over the course of my fieldwork, I encountered more of these contentious situations involving fee negotiations and monetary offerings. During these disputes, I felt awkward, a bit embarrassed, and generally tried to appear as if I were paying no attention to the haggling, although the negotiators themselves did not seem to be uneasy. Moreover, Cheju residents, including those who sponsor *kut* (large-scale shamanic rituals), who I had thought would welcome shamanic services without question, gossiped outside the ritual context about the extravagance of ritual expense and the practitioners' greed.[3]

Witnessing shamans actively pursuing their own interests in such intimate settings as Mr. Cho's household presented a dilemma to me as someone who was eager to learn about the *simbang*'s verbal talents and spiritual power. Persistent demand for shamanic services testifies to their social value, yet ritual expenditure draws heated commentary. Critics have often dismissed practitioners outright as swindlers. What I was observing seemed to agree with this prevailing prejudice against shamans, a prejudice I had earlier simply ignored in defense of shamans.

The particular reactions of researchers in the field can "serve as significant clues to any buried assumptions or beliefs we might have" (Chong 2008, 385). Even seemingly idiosyncratic reactions can reveal much about the scholarship and the social norms to which we adhere and thus help us identify blind spots in our thinking. Ethnographic studies conducted in Seoul have related the prevailing ritual materialism of contemporary practice to the spirits' demands, to socioeconomic changes, and to practitioners' adaptability.[4] However, ritual expenditure has been a concern of the social elite in Korea since the thirteenth century. Confucian elites, Christian missionaries, and modernist reformers dismissed ritual consumption as an utter waste of resources and shamans of course, not the deities, for manipulating gullible people. However, in defense of the subjects of their studies, scholars have little explored the contentious nature of ritual consumption and distrust of shamans that manifest in real-life situations and is of consequence to practitioners and their clients. In particular, proponents of Cheju shamanism, including scholars, have portrayed the practitioners as epic poets removed from material concerns and characterized the earthy vernacular religion as the epitome of the indigenous spirit (Kim Seong-nae 2004; Pettid 2000a, 2001). Given that the controversy over ritual consumption and the practitioners' alleged exploitation is an age-old issue, still very much alive today, how can we understand it in a respectful way without dismissing the value of ritual consumption? Tackling the issue head-on seems more useful than pretending that public denigration does not exist or dismissing it as merely an invalid stereotype. I found the terrain ethnographically sensitive and complicated by matters of money, but a new topic of inquiry gradually emerged and became the primary subject of this book: the ritual economy of Cheju shamanism.

MONEY MATTERS

Money is central to practitioners and clients. Patrons invest a significant portion of their household budgets in attempts to resolve pressing problems, including financial matters, by resorting to shamans (Chongho Kim 2003, 5).[5] In contrast to the stereotype of naive patrons being preyed upon by shamans, they carefully consider their investments and negotiate skillfully with *simbang*. As do other Korean shamans (e.g., Hogarth 2009; Kendall 1985a), *simbang* perform rituals for their livelihood and are genuinely interested in bringing about benefits for their clients; achieving desired outcomes is also essential to their business success—no money, no ritual, and vice versa. Both *simbang* and clients deal with ritual matters as rationally as they would other personal financial affairs. However, monetary issues often become the reason patrons distrust shamans, even though the laity seeks shamanic services in the hope they will be efficacious.

From the clients' point of view, there are good reasons for discontent with shamans. They find it difficult to appraise the value of shamanic services and "products," which engenders doubt about the cost-effectiveness of ritual expenditures. After investing a substantial amount of personal capital, clients can be profoundly disappointed and even angry when their investments do not prove fruitful, that is, if expensive rituals do not generate the desired results. In the 2009 feature film *Fortune Salon* (Ch'ŏngdam posal),[6] an erstwhile client calls a male fortune-teller a "fraud" (*sagikkun*) because the man, acting on the fortune-teller's advice, spends 10 million won (US$10,000) sponsoring a ritual and ends up going to jail despite his outlay. Enraged, he grabs the seer by the collar and demands the return of the fee he paid for the ineffectual ritual. This sort of dispute is not limited to the fictional world. After sponsoring several rituals in vain for her mentally ill son, a disgruntled woman told an anthropologist, "I would consider it [*kut*] if the shaman gave me a money-back guarantee" (Chongho Kim 2003, 171). Patrons also sue, albeit rarely, shamans that they have hired.[7] Although I heard of no lawsuits involving *simbang* during my fieldwork, some islanders did not hesitate to express, to me and among themselves, their doubts and suspicions regarding some *simbang* when the shamans were absent. *Simbang*-managed rituals are not always efficacious, especially from the client's perspective, and after an unsuccessful ritual, a patron may look for another *simbang* or turn to a migrant shaman from the mainland. While emphasizing success stories, practitioners often attribute the misfortunes that occur after a ritual or its lack of efficacy to their clients' failure to follow instructions on post-ritual behavior.

Along with food and cheaply purchased clothes and straw shoes, substantial amounts of money, both imitation and real, are offered at *kut*. Offering legal tender is frequently a source of contention. As many scholars have demonstrated, things are imbued with a cultural significance that varies in accordance with the social and historical context.[8] For instance, human organs—parts of one's own body and self—were not accepted as socially appropriate items of exchange in the United States until advocates for organ transplants made considerable efforts to validate them as a "gift of life" (Healy 2006). Less intimate objects might be assumed to be more suitable for exchange but harder to sacralize. However, even money, construed by social philosophers such as Georg Simmel, Max Weber, and Karl Marx as the catalyst of heartless instrumentalism, is not culturally and socially barren (Truitt 2013, 106–9; Zelizer 1994, 6–10). Far from being an absolutely impersonal instrument, it is often used to initiate and nurture relationships, not only between humans, but also between humans and other beings (e.g., spirits, ancestors, and deities). Indeed, this utilitarian medium of market exchange or its imitations have served as popular offerings in many Asian ritual contexts; money does not index impoverished religiosity.[9] As they do with other goods, *simbang* transform the impersonal real cash into personalized offerings infused with ritual meaning. However, cash offerings depart with the shamans, unlike other items: most of the food is consumed by the ritual participants, although *simbang* take some with them, and the clothes, straw shoes, and imitation money are burned at the conclusion of the ritual. Moreover, assessing the "proper" amount for an offering is a delicate matter. These issues add to doubts about the purity of the practitioners' motives.

The fact that shamans deal with monetary issues directly, without an institutional buffer like a church or a temple, also heightens these doubts. Knowing full well that the public distrusts them, one *simbang* claimed that a shaman's patrons (who sponsor rituals only occasionally) are better off economically than Christians who tithe throughout their lifetimes. Nothing comparable shields the shamans from the handling of money, making them ready targets for accusations of avarice.[10] Despite the fact that ritual transactions are fraught with considerable ambiguity, clients spend copiously for rituals. What then is their view of ritual consumption? How do the *simbang* fashion ritual exchange as distinct from secular forms of transaction, such as barter, purchases, bribery, and gift giving? Entertaining these questions encourages a discerning view of the social forms required by different relationships, appreciation of participants' viewpoints, and a careful assessment of the *simbang*'s ritual roles.

OFFERINGS THAT COME WITH STRINGS ATTACHED

In spring 2010, after collecting cash offerings from a range of participants at a public ritual, a *simbang* dedicated them to the gods by reciting the following couplet:

> Please eat and bless in return. (Mŏgŭmyŏn mŏgŭn kapsŭl hapsŏ.)
> Please take and give in return. (Padŭmyŏn padŭn kapsŭl hapsŏ.)

Her words demonstrate a transactional interaction between the human and spirit worlds, whereby sacrifices are presented in the hope of supernatural assistance. This mode of exchange has been observed in many religious traditions across time and space. One Vedic principle, for example, holds that "sacrifice is a gift that compels the deity to make a return: *Do ut des*; I give so that you may give." Likewise, in reference to Greek practice, Plato wrote, "Is not sacrifice a gift to the gods, and prayer a request?" Sociologist Rodney Stark has gone so far as to argue that the "basis of all religious practice involves exchanges with the supernatural" (2006, 49). Anthropologists have also described the critical role that the gift of commodities and money has played in contemporary religious practices in the wake of economic transition.[11] Indeed, this form of reciprocity is central to shamanic rituals on Cheju and elsewhere in Korea.[12] My experience also suggests that people sponsor costly rituals and make lavish offerings in the expectation that the recipients would bestow something of value in return.

The belief in reciprocity is explicit in the word the islanders use when referring to offerings made in shamanic rituals. In a move that is both metonymic and euphemistic, they use the term *injŏng*, rather than the standard Korean *chemul* (literally meaning "ceremonial goods"), to refer to all kinds of offerings dedicated to the invisible at shamanic rituals, such as food, clothing, cigarettes, and currency (both legal tender and pseudo-money) (Hyŏn P'yŏngho et al. 1995, 475).[13] They call them neither "gifts" (*sŏnmul*) nor "bribes" (*noemul*) within the ritual frame. Referring also to *human* feelings, especially empathy, compassion, and kindness, *injŏng* suggests the moral quality of relations that mitigate the harsh righteousness of the gods, who are believed to be strict and just but can be moved by the ritual sponsors' sincerity (*chŏngsŏng*) and the shamans' petitions. Sharing Chinese characters (signifying "human" and "feelings") with the Chinese term *renqing* and the Japanese *ninjō*, *injŏng* is etymologically a human trait. People who lack *injŏng* are considered inhumane, callous, cruel, cold-hearted or heartless, and unfeeling. This word has enjoyed pervasive usage in East Asian social life outside ritual contexts, in both the past and the present and in urban and rural settings.[14] In Cheju as well as in the more general Korean shamanic tradition, the nature of the gods is believed to mirror that of humans (Bruno 2007a, 57–58). *Simbang* and the laity construe gods as compassionate and subject to emotional manipulation. Choosing to designate offerings as *injŏng* underscores the similarities among actors, contexts, and motivations in both worlds and highlights the immaterial nature of material objects dedicated to supernatural beings.

Although the concept of *injŏng* emphasizes uncalculating benevolence, the discourse and practice of *injŏng* are not based entirely on disinterested altruism. As in the business transactions observed among managers in the

Korean corporate world (Janelli with Yim 1993, 190–92),[15] the concept of *injŏng* is morally charged and strategically deployed in Cheju ritual practice. It is fundamentally a relational concept made explicit in the saying "*Injŏng* is also reciprocal*" (Injŏng to p'umasi ra).[16] The *injŏng*, sacrificial objects offered during rituals, have qualities of both bribes and gifts exchanged among humans—the latter in the sense that they "affirm and perpetuate a relationship . . . with different kinds of spirits" (Kendall 2009, 170). At the same time, however, *injŏng* differs from bribes and gifts in the secular sphere, a difference that is important in understanding the economy of Cheju shamanism.

The perception of the powerful as corrupt and amenable to bribes is prevalent in the Republic of Korea (ROK), where reciprocity underpins social relationships in everyday life and business.[17] Korean criminal law regarding bribery (articles 129, 130, 132) distinguishes gifts and bribes according to the following protocols: to whom things are given (whether they would be given even if the recipient were not in the same social or professional position), the purpose of giving (whether or not they are given in return for favors), and the closeness of the relationship between the giver and the receiver. Recognizing the difficulty of applying legal definitions to diverse situations, the Korean Chamber of Commerce and Industry attempted in 2007 to provide three criteria for a gift, as opposed to a bribe: one should be able to sleep well after receiving it, the gift should not provoke any scandals when known to the media, and, finally, one should be able to receive the gift even if one is in a position of influence (JTBC *Nyusŭrum*, 30 August 2016). These commonsense distinctions point out that bribery is a rather secretive and guilt-laden act.

From the perspective of these secular protocols, offerings—particularly to the gods—are indeed similar to bribes because they are given in anticipation of a favor and because of the perceived power asymmetry and existential distance between clients and the gods. In his book *Bribes*, legal scholar John T. Noonan Jr. speculates that bribes originated in religious teachings (Jewish, Christian, and pagan) and observes that religion "can be viewed as bribery on a grand scale, organized for the highest end, man's salvation, and practiced to persuade the Supreme authority" (1984, xx–xxi). Cognizant of the power difference that motivates such purposeful giving, *simbang* compare the offerings to bribes. Ironically, the term *injŏng* has also been used to refer to bribes offered to petty officials in the past, thus carrying with it the connotation of underhanded manipulation.

Despite the overtones of bribery inherent in *injŏng*, offering *injŏng*—like gifting—is not considered immoral, nor does it carry for the islanders the negative connotation attached to bribery. In other words, they do not feel guilty for sponsoring a ritual, although they may regret having done so when it does not bring the outcomes they desired. Some may of course feel embarrassed for resorting to such "superstitious" services (cf. Chongho Kim 2003, 219–20). The concept of *injŏng* emphasizes a sense of human-heartedness that softens the rigidity of propriety (*li*). Shamans and clients regard the idea of reward in accordance with deed—one gets what one deserves through one's actions—to be the general principle of life. However, "as a practical matter, to get along in this world," the laity does sometimes feel the need to utilize the services of a shaman (Sorensen 1988, 412) in the hope of gaining protection or finding a way to get beyond an impasse that they believe cannot be surmounted by any other means. Although bribery can also be dressed in the niceties of human interaction, as has been shown in the case of China, it does not require the degree of etiquette and propriety that ritual participants carefully cultivate (Mayfair Yang 1994, 123, 202). Neither shamans nor clients treat offerings as mere bargaining chips. Hoping that the favor will be returned, they acknowledge the superior power of the recipients by showing all due respect. Herein lies the reason for the existence of such rich verbal and nonverbal expressive forms in Cheju and more generally in Korean shamanism.

Whereas Confucian rituals are performed by kinsmen without professional clergy, shamanic rituals are presided over by ritual specialists who mediate between their clients and the invisible and are paid for their services. Therefore, the dyadic model focused on donor and recipient is inadequate for explaining the nature of the shamanic exchange (cf. LiPuma and Lee 2008). Cheju shamanic rituals are structured as an artistic form of exchange in which native shamans solicit the gods' aid by means of sacrificial offerings and competent performance (cf. Sandstrom 2008, 102). Though some dismiss the shamans' words out of hand, their verbal persuasion, along with their spiritual power, is vital. They infuse impersonal things with affective meanings and "activate" the social agency of the supernatural beings they engage.

The tactics and performance details to which a *simbang* attends firmly set the offering of sacrificial objects apart from both gifting and bribery in the secular realm. The overall atmosphere of making offerings is solemn, and there is little of the "playful extortion" that occurs at rituals performed by god-descended shamans on the Korean mainland (Kendall 2008, 156). For example, *simbang* appeal in ritual speech to the gods' moral sentiments by reciting in detail the desperate situations that prompted their clients to sponsor the rituals and by pointing out the relative generosity of their offerings:

> These [offerings] are not leftovers from what they have eaten.
> (Mŏktta namŭn pabi aniwoeda.)
> These [offerings] are not leftovers from what they have donned.
> (Iptta namŭn osi aniwoeda.)[18]

Simbang highlight the donors' sincerity by presenting the offerings as the fruits of their patrons' hard work rather than merely heartless *things*. In so doing, they attempt to evoke the gods' satisfaction with these sacrificial objects and generate sympathy for their patrons, thus obligating the gods to accept the offerings and exercise their power on behalf of the patrons (Bruno 2007a, 56–56; Hogarth 2009, 244). *Injŏng* differ from gifts, which should be given—according to Korean legal and popular protocols—without an overt expectation of reward. At the same time, bribes lack the degree of emotional affect and investment that *injŏng* connotes.

Precisely because of the indispensable role of shamans, even those who doubt them resort to their services. Patrons do believe that they must give up something valuable in order to encourage the deities to grant their wishes. They also know that abundant offerings (especially of real money, often prompted during rituals) please shamans as well—exactly to whom patrons offer the materials can be a rather slippery subject. When patrons believe that shamans collect "excessive" *injŏng*, they may view the behavior as extortion, and this becomes a reason for mistrust. Moreover, offerings do not guarantee automatic returns. Reciprocity is not a safe, mechanical give-and-take but involves risk that requires skill to circumvent.[19] However, because shamans are believed to have exclusive power in dealing with supernatural beings and because of the desire for ritual efficacy, even clients who are ambivalent toward shamanic power suspend their doubts and generally are willing to satisfy the shamans' demands. Fully aware that some clients have misgivings, *simbang* work to establish and maintain trust during rituals while tactfully employing their business skills and emphasizing the ritual significance of the offerings.

RITUAL ECONOMY

The relationship between religion and economy has been a central subject among social scientists since Max Weber maintained that the Protestant ethic encouraged the development of capitalism ([1946] 1958). In keeping with Clifford Geertz's insight into religion and society (1973), anthropologists have demonstrated the ways in which popular religions adapt in order to serve or subvert expanding capitalism. Michael Taussig argued that capitalist development brought about "devil fetishism" in South America (1980), and Aihwa Ong revealed how the frustration of Malay female factory workers coping with industrial production manifested itself in the form of "vengeful spirit attacks" (1987). Critiquing the long-standing dichotomist view of religion and economy, other anthropologists have demonstrated their intersection and compatibility. Daromir Rudnyckyj showed how contemporary Indonesian spiritual reformers deliberately employ Islamic virtues as they inculcate neoliberal economic values in the hope of enhancing profitability (2010). Pointing to an example of popular ritual practices in Wenzhou on the southeastern coast of China in the 1990s, Mayfair Yang argued that economy is a critical "part of the ritual and religious system" (2000, 480).

These insights drawn from fine-grained ethnographic research are fruitful given the prevailing and persistent attitude of resentment toward an attempt to associate religion and economy, one that sees the association as essentially blasphemous. For instance, religious studies scholar Martin E. Marty criticized the economic approach that sociologist Rodney Stark and Roger Finke took in examining the historical development of American Christian churches, characterizing their work as the reduction of the religious life to a "world [that] contains no God or religion or spirituality" (Marty 1993, 88, quoted in Stark 2006, 49). Employing an economic approach to religion is an illuminating undertaking. As Adam Yuet Chau argues in *Miraculous Response: Doing Popular Religion in Contemporary China*, acknowledging "the economic aspects of popular religion should not be seen as economic reductionism or as cheapening the religious experience" of people, and "not recognizing them and limiting our understanding of religious activities as purely 'religious' or 'spiritual' would risk another kind of reductionism" (2006, 9).

However, the view of the intersection of the two realms is still predicated on mutually exclusive categories in which each distinctive sphere becomes a component of the other or influences the other. I encountered this tenacious perspective particularly keenly when I presented an interpretation of the centrality of economic aspects in Cheju shamanic practice at a conference on the island. My discussant expressed his appreciation of my argument, which he found refreshing in light of previous scholarship that focused too heavily on indigenous spirituality, but then he asked, "How about the religious aspect of the practice then?" In his view, the economic and the religious were two separate elements that together constituted shamanism. My discussant's challenge gave me a strong push to sharpen my conceptualization and more clearly differentiate my thesis about the relationship between religion and the economy from those of other scholars.

Categories such as the economy, politics, and religion have been inherited from modern social science (Asad 1993) and mean little to shamans and their patrons on Cheju Island. Instead, they see ritual as a fundamentally economic activity in itself, one based on exchange and relationship management. Consider the processes involved in rituals: hiring shamans, negotiating ritual service fees, assessing the "proper" amount of each offering, and deciding the ownership of the offerings after a ritual is completed. This understanding of economy as micromanagement rather than a system or institution is close to the etymological meaning of the word "economy" as the "management (*nomos*) of the household (*oikos*)" that Michel Foucault traced in his examination of the history of the term (Rudnyckyj 2010, 138).

Additionally, as in many other parts of the world (e.g., Sandstrom 2008), every shamanic ritual in Korea requires an altar with offerings such as food, clothes, and money. The very process of ritual performance is predicated on the notion of exchanging negotiated gifts between humans and supernatural beings—that is, offerings are tendered and ideally the gods bestow rewards. This process is mediated by shamans, whose spiritual power and verbal skills are recognized (Harvey 1979, 45) as crucial to accomplishing satisfactory transactions and whose services are therefore sought by society. Thus, I part ways with the view that exchange in the realm of religion is less about money or price and more about the "*contents* of religion" such as doctrine and belief (Stark 2006, 48–49). In shamanic rituals on Cheju Island, as on the Korean mainland, the quantification represented by money and price is closely intertwined with belief; in fact, quantities of material goods and belief in ritual efficacy often cannot be separated. "Since the sponsors want wholehearted support from the spirits," Hyun-key Kim Hogarth pointed out, "it is imperative that the former offer the latter their whole heart" (2009, 243). Both quantity and quality of sacrifice are important in appeasing and pleasing the supernatural.

Thus, the term "ritual economy" emphasizes the entanglement of economy in rituals. It also highlights distinctive features of the transactions involved in shamanic rituals; for example, reciprocity, sincerity, and the expressive forms that practitioners use in authenticating ritual actions make exchange central to ritual practice while distinguishing ritual exchange from other forms of transactions. Ritual economy, predicated on generosity, has been described as an alternative to profit-driven capitalism (Mayfair Yang 2000), but just as we cannot develop an adequate understanding of ritual by relying purely on calculative logic, *ritual* economy cannot be fully explained by the concept of generosity alone in the case of shamanism, in which the practitioner's role is indispensable. If the perception that the only concern of ritual practitioners is self-serving is problematic, so too is the view that they are purely altruistic. They strike a delicate balance between generosity and calculation. This notion of ritual economy helps us not only appreciate that ritual transactions are filled with social and cultural significance but also understand why ritual consumption associated with Korean shamanism has been such a touchy issue and how it makes shamans vulnerable to the accusation of profiteering.

CHEJU AS A PLACE

A conversation about Cheju shamanism often turns into a discussion of local identity as the islanders define themselves through their own history vis-à-vis the mainland and the world as a whole. At the same time, Korean mainlanders have long considered Cheju part of a larger Korea, albeit another Korea. The island's location, near the southwestern tip of the Korean peninsula (see map 1), gives it a status somewhat analogous to that of Hawaii in the United States and Okinawa in Japan. Both the largest island and the smallest province in Korea,[20] Cheju is 39.8 miles wide and 45.4 miles long, with a total area of 713 square miles. Mount Halla, the highest mountain in South Korea, stands at the center. Due to the exotic landscape, flora, and dialect, the island itself is perceived as quite foreign by residents of the peninsula. In fact, because it is technically located across the southern sea, they half-jokingly and half-legitimately refer to it as "overseas" (*haeoe*).[21] Tangerines, a cherished winter fruit among mainlanders, flourish only in the island's mild climate and are a tangible and tasty reminder of the locale.[22] As a child growing up on the mainland, I felt a sense of difference and distance when looking at the island on the map of Korea during TV weather forecasts. Forecasters typically mentioned the province's weather last, an indication of its marginal importance, which left me with a lingering curiosity about this unfamiliar place.

Cheju has been called *sam-da-do*, meaning "an island with a plethora of three things": wind, stones, and women. More subject to typhoons than the

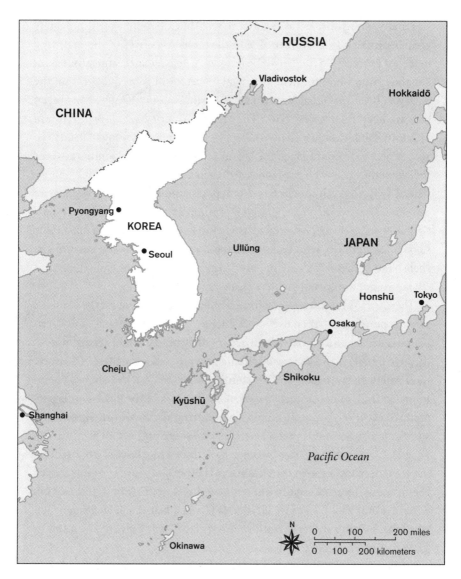

MAP I.1. Korea. Credit: Ben Pease

peninsula, Cheju, along with Ullŭng Island in Korea's east sea, is the wind-
iest region in South Korea (Kang Kyŏngsŏn 2003, 88). Created by volcanic
activity, the island is replete with black volcanic rock. One *simbang* called
people in her village who have to eke out a living from the poor, rocky, volcanic soil "pioneers of the [American] West" (*Sŏbu ŭi kaech'ŏkcha*). This
environment has rendered the islanders' lives extremely difficult, leaving
them subject to the mercy of indigenous deities.

Finally, many historical records report that Cheju has an appreciably greater proportion of women due to the dangerous lives of the seafaring men. For example, in his *Travel Writings on Cheju Island* (Namsarok), Kim Sanghŏn, who went to Cheju as a royal inspector in 1601, quoted from the local gazetteer (*chiji*) that "women are three times as numerous as men; even beggars keep mistresses" ([1601] 1992, 59). American diplomat William Franklin Sands, who was sent to Cheju by the emperor Kojong to pacify the 1901 rebellion, romanticized the island as "a real Amazon community, for the women were always ready to assert their power and uphold it by force" ([1904] 1931, 167). Although the current populations of men and women are roughly equal, women have played a prominent role in island life. In particular, women divers, referred to as *haenyŏ* by the mainlanders but locally known as *chamnyŏ*, who collect marine products such as sea cucumbers, shells, and seaweed for a living, are frequently cited as an embodiment of Cheju women's spiritual prowess (Hae-joang Cho 1983).

The *haenyŏ*'s lives are deeply rooted in shamanism. Because the women's work is dangerous—they use old-fashioned diving equipment, and occupational deaths unfortunately still occur—they need a shield against unpredictable dangers, and shamanic rituals provide solace for them. To ensure their safety in the ocean and an abundant harvest, *haenyŏ* sponsor communal rituals. When a *haenyŏ* dies, a *kut* to console the dead soul is performed. Most of the intellectuals I met during my fieldwork agreed that shamanic rituals were a pivotal element of *haenyŏ* and of Cheju culture in general. Unsurprisingly, these women have drawn much scholarly attention in recent decades (e.g., An 2008), and local newspapers have even introduced them as an "internationally known *brand* of Cheju" (e.g., Hong Sŏkjun 2004, my emphasis). In 2016, UNESCO (United Nations Educational, Scientific and Cultural Organization) recognized their culture as an intangible cultural heritage.

Cheju's exotic beauty has made the island an ideal tourist destination in postwar South Korea. The South Korean government focused on tourism as a major economic engine for the island beginning in the 1960s (Song Chaeho 2002, 119). When most popular honeymoon destinations were peninsular, a trip to the island was classed as overseas tourism and carried a connotation of distinction for those who could afford it. As more Koreans traveled abroad beginning in the early 1990s (Oppenheim 2011), this prestige began to lessen, but the island continues to attract domestic tourists and ever more foreigners, particularly Japanese and Chinese. In addition to several liberalizing factors, including the end of the Cold War and the rapid development of transportation, in recent years global recognition by international entities such as UNESCO and the New7Wonders Foundation has helped increase Cheju's popularity. While just one hundred thousand people visited in 1966 (Song Chaeho 2002, 115), nearly fifteen million tourists traveled to the island in 2017 (Jeju Special Self-Governing Provincial Tourism Association). This represents an increase by a factor of about 150 in half a century.

Most historical accounts by mainland elites are fraught with the colonial view in which the island is construed as Korea's internal other, a place lacking in civilization. In fact, Cheju was once an independent kingdom called T'amna,[23] before it was subjugated by the Koryŏ dynasty in the twelfth century. In the midst of power struggles between China's Yuan dynasty and the Koryŏ government in the thirteenth century, the island became a colony of both dynasties for nearly a century. In 1295, Koryŏ strategically replaced the national name T'amna with Cheju, derived from the word for a local administrative unit designation meaning "land across the sea," and began dispatching centrally appointed governors to the island (Yi Wŏnjin [1653] 2002, 16).[24] This quasi-colonization rendered the relationship between Cheju and the mainland extremely complex.

Confirming the degree of its perceived remoteness from the Center, Cheju was frequently chosen as a destination for exile beginning in the late Koryŏ, with the central government as well as the Yuan and subsequent Ming dynasties of China banishing political exiles to the island. The practice continued with increasing frequency from the middle to the end of the Chosŏn dynasty (1392–1910).[25] In contrast, many mainland criminals and slaves sought refuge on Cheju, to the extent that the central government sometimes sent officials to return them to the mainland.[26] It also happened that unable to meet the disproportionately heavy taxes and tribute imposed on them, a large number of distressed people ran away from the island or at least attempted to do so.[27] In 1629, in order to protect the island from the Japanese and to preserve the human resources necessary to continue to collect taxes and receive tribute, the government prohibited inhabitants from leaving; the emigration ban lasted about two hundred years (Kim Seong-nae 1989a, 62, 94; Kim Yŏngdon 2000, 81).

Cheju Island figures prominently in modern Korean history because of the April Third Events (Sasam Sakkŏn), the series of violent conflicts that ensued in 1948 between leftist insurgents and rightist counterinsurgents that led to a massive number of civilian deaths.[28] At least thirty thousand people, or one-tenth of the island's population at that time, were killed. This incident was triggered on 1 March 1947 by the police suppression of a demonstration protesting the policies of the United States Army Military Government. This led to a left-led armed uprising on 3 April the next year against police brutality and rejecting the upcoming general election that was to legitimize two Koreas. This revolt was followed by a brutal counterinsurgency supported by the ultra-rightist government of the Republic of Korea and the US Army Military Government. The ferocious conflict continued intermittently until 21 September 1954, when Mount Halla, which had been closed due to the uprising, was reopened to the public. The authoritarian South Korean government suppressed any discussion of the incident among civilians until close to the end of the twentieth century. However, the grievous history has been addressed in *kut* wherein tragic spirits return and speak to the living through *simbang* mediums.[29] These sorrowful spirits figured in many of the shamanic rituals I observed.

Recently, the island has been mired in new international power struggles in association with a naval base constructed in Gangjeong [Kangjŏng] Village (G. Kwon 2013; Yeo 2013). Local, national, and global activists for peace and the environment protested construction of the base on a site designated by the South Korean government as a "Peace Island" and recognized by UNESCO as a World Heritage site. Given their history of struggle, it is not surprising that native islanders have developed a strong sense of locality and even a degree of animosity toward mainlanders (Hun Joon Kim 2014, 29), whom they derogatorily call *yukchi-nom* (mainland bastards). While voicing demands for justice and more autonomy, the islanders (1.2 percent of the South Korean population)[30] nevertheless depend on the mainlanders, who view the place as a tourist mecca and own many local properties and businesses.

CHEJU SHAMANISM

Scholars have long noted the prevalence of shamanism on the island and its distinct features. Arriving on Cheju after having been demoted or exiled from the mainland, Confucian scholars of the Chosŏn dynasty observed the island's flourishing shamanic cult as a marker of cultural backwardness. One fervent governor, Yi Hyŏngsang, left a record of the purge of 129 shamanic shrines enacted in 1702 during his tenure. In contrast to this view, recent scholars have often romanticized the popularity of shamanism as an icon of the island's unsullied culture.[31] Regardless of their perspectives, more than 300 village shrines (*tang*) are maintained in present-day Cheju, testifying to the continued popularity of shamanism.

The indigenous vernacular religion of Cheju is not only more prevalent but also different from that of the mainland. As opposed to *mudang* or *mansin*, terms commonly used when referring to shamans on the mainland, native Cheju shamans are called *simbang*.[32] According to renowned scholars of Cheju shamanism, the word *simbang* comes from *sinbang*, a contraction of *sin ŭi hyŏngbang* (judicial officials of the gods) (Hyŏn Yongjun 1980a, 885; Mun 2001, 14), and *simbang* perceive themselves as attorneys working on behalf of their clients, whom they call *tan'gol*.[33] During rituals, *simbang* refer to themselves as *sin ŭi hyŏngbang* or as *sin ŭi ai* (servant children of the gods).

Cheju *simbang* typically are categorized as hereditary shamans (*sesŭp mu*), as opposed to god-descended shamans (*kangsin mu*). According to Korean shaman typology and terminology based on ecstasy, origin, and region,[34] hereditary shamans, predominant in the southern regions below the Han River, are born into shaman families and trained by their family members, while god-descended shamans of the central and northern regions are called by spirits and trained by their spirit mothers and fathers. Unlike god-descended shamans, who enact physiological features of the dead (Janelli and Janelli 1982, 160), *simbang* try to neither sound nor look like those for whom they are speaking during a séance.[35] They do not hang portraits of deities (*t'aenghwa*) on ropes strung along the walls before rituals or change costumes in order to manifest different gods during rituals.

The ecstatic experiences of god-descended shamans have been perceived as a true mark of shamanism by many Korean scholars since Ch'oe Nam-sŏn, who, using Siberian shamans as a model, claimed in 1927 that Korean shamanism was a unitary phenomenon diffused from Siberia. Considering Eliadian ecstasy as the core of authentic shamanism as it is practiced in Siberia, Ch'oe Kil-sŏng argued that hereditary practitioners should be called "priests" (*sajeja*) as opposed to "shamans" (*shyamŏn*), a term appropriate only for god-descended shamans in the northern regions (1978, 18–30; 1981, 83, 92).[36] According to Kim Tae-Gon (T'aegon), an internationally known scholar of Korean shamanism, these shamans "constitute the main body" of Korean shamans (1972, 18). Indeed, most studies of Korean shamanism have concentrated on them, and only a handful of scholars have paid attention to hereditary shamans.[37]

However, one should not blindly accept this polarized classification based on untraceable speculations with little documentary evidence or on-the-ground experience. It would be more productive to look at shamanic power and its role in concrete social contexts rather than focus on typology, which cannot explain complex reality (Cho Hung-youn 1983; Kim Seong-nae 1998, 41). Belying the categorization, *simbang* do not automatically succeed to the profession through family descent (Tangherlini and Park 1988, 24; Kyoim Yun 2016), and god-descended shamans are not only called by spirits but also born into shaman families (e.g., Chongho Kim 2003, 200). As with god-descended shamans, *simbang* also experience spirit illness (Kim Seong-nae 1989a, 431; Mun 1998; 2005, 280–99) and possess spiritual power, albeit of a different type from that of god-descended shamans. Moreover, rigid typology is inadequate to explain the radical changes taking place on the island. During the past several decades, migrant god-descended shamans have come to dominate the vernacular religious market (Cho Sung-Youn 2003), challenging the understanding of Cheju shamanism as pristine. Influenced by the idealized native shaman group in academic literature, I once took the term "Cheju shamans" to mean exclusively *simbang*. Thus, I was more than a little disappointed when told, on arriving in Cheju to begin my research, that there were few "genuine" *simbang* able to perform "genuine" Cheju rituals. In fact, my fieldwork led me to a few god-descended shamans, known locally as *posal*.[38] One *posal* lived in a village where an elderly male *simbang* lived. Whereas her services were very much in demand, his were not, which, he explained, was a result of the poor economy. However, I worked mostly with *simbang*, not because I saw *simbang* as the only "authentic" Cheju shamans, but because I was determined to learn about the island's indigenous shamanic tradition and found it difficult to maintain good relations with both *simbang* and *posal* due to the rivalry between them (Kyoim Yun 2016).

Born and raised on the island, *simbang* perform traditional Cheju-style rituals heavily based on an indigenous oral tradition composed in the local dialect and including liberal use of archaic phrases.[39] In particular, the extensive *ponp'uri*, which *simbang* chant accompanied by a bell or an hourglass-shaped drum for rhythm during rituals, have received an enormous amount of scholarly attention, initially from a few Japanese scholars (Akamatsu and Akiba [1937–38] 1991, 211–336; Murayama [1932] 2014, 379–89) during the colonial period (1910–45) and then many South Korean folklorists after the Korean War (1950–53).[40] The *simbang*'s knowledge of and competence in reciting prodigious amounts of ritual lore are pivotal to their trade and a source of pride for them—they set themselves apart from *posal* and a variety of fortune-tellers. Only those *simbang* who can perform large-scale rituals that are elaborate and symbolically complicated earn the honor of being named *k'ŭn* (great) *simbang*.

While conducting rituals for individual households, usually in a domestic space, select *simbang* also perform communal rituals at village shrines, alone or with a few assistants. Those in charge of the shrine are called *tang maein simbang* and are appointed by villagers. Customarily, the *simbang* are well versed in a community's specific pantheon, ritual history, and customs, including the *ponp'uri* of shrine deities and deified family ancestors.[41] For the most part, these village *simbang* also possess a broader and more thorough knowledge of the community members' general concerns and interests than do *simbang* from other locales. Therefore, they can best reflect the community's wishes in their rituals and in turn are thought to bring about more fortunate outcomes. However, not every village has such *simbang*, and some must hire a shaman from another village who may even perform a mainland-style ritual (Hae-joang Cho 1988, 304–5; Kang So-Jeon 2005, 69–70).

The task of performing the communal rituals also represents an important contract between the *simbang* and the community members. The diving women, customary sponsors of large-scale village rituals, harvest marine products and prepare food together before the ritual and pay the service fee from their association's budget.[42] Because lead *simbang* deal with the villagers, they have less leverage with fee negotiations than when they are contracting for household rituals. Villagers who are dissatisfied with the local *simbang* will hire a shaman from outside the neighborhood for their private rituals, although these same individuals will still participate in the communal ceremonies conducted by the village *simbang*. Although the position of *tang maein simbang* is not associated with government offices, it carries with it considerable priestly prestige in its own region. Moreover, the rice and cash that people offer at community rituals represent a significant portion of a *simbang*'s income. As a result, conflicts sometimes arise among *simbang* competing for the title of *tang maein simbang* (Kim Seong-nae 1989a, 187–88, 202–4).

Unlike rituals sponsored by individual clients, which remain popular, community rituals are in decline on Cheju Island and in South Korea at large (Hwang Ru-shi 1988, 15–16, 21; 2000, 230). Nowadays only a few villages continue to hold community rituals because many divers, the customary sponsors, have given up their traditional professions due to property development or other job opportunities. This decline explains in part the central and local efforts to have UNESCO recognize an annual community ritual on Cheju as an intangible cultural heritage, in an attempt to keep it alive and justify its use in commercializing the region.

Given the preponderance of female shamans on the Korean peninsula, it is not surprising that since the time of Japanese ethnologist Akiba Takashi, who emphasized the feminine essence of Korean shamanism ([1950] 1987), many scholars have explored gender issues associated with the popular religion.[43] It is noteworthy that, historically, a larger proportion of Cheju shamans were men. Kim Chŏng (1486–1521), who was exiled to the island in the early sixteenth century, wrote that "there are many male shamans" (Cheju Munhwawŏn 2007, 16), and about two centuries later, Yi Hyŏngsang, the governor of Cheju, related his encounter with "several hundred male shamans" ([1704] 2009, 119). According to a survey by the Cheju police office conducted by order of the Government General of Korea (GGK) in September 1930, there were 119 male and 110 female shamans on the island (Akiba [1950] 1987, 51). Although the gender ratio changed to 99 male and 128 female in 1959 (Chang 2001, 20), the percentage of male shamans is still higher on Cheju than it is on the peninsula. German anthropologist Eno Beuchelt, who lived on the island in the early 1960s, commented on the higher proportion of male shamans.[44] One of his informants offered an interpretation: "Women dive [in the ocean] and work in the fields, while men have little to do and so have time for what is actually an unmanly occupation." Beuchelt felt that the description of the division of labor was accurate, but the explanation was probably a popular rationalization and speculated that it might be left over from earlier times on the island when, at the height of mainland court shamanism (before Confucianization), many men occupied the influential role of shaman (1975a, 148). This view is congruent with that of Boudewijn Walraven, who observed that on Cheju "the Confucianization of society came quite late and never was as thorough as in other regions" (2007b, 285). However, female shamans outnumber their male counterparts in present-day Cheju, and I worked with both male and female *simbang*, albeit more closely with the latter.

RESEARCH METHODS

This study uses interdisciplinary methods to mediate between past and present, between lay and expert knowledge, and between theory and on-the-ground experience. I conducted ethnographic fieldwork on Cheju Island from 2001 to 2002 and made several follow-up research visits to the island

(2003, 2005, 2007, 2010, 2015). My ethnographic study was enhanced by historical research at Cheju National University, Korea University, and Seoul National University. On the one hand, an ethnographic study not only addresses a particular moment in history but can also shed new light on past views and events; on the other hand, historical research can provide insight into current affairs and thereby facilitate in-depth analysis.

Kut were not performed frequently, and I was interested in a variety of performances, so I ventured farther afield to find several *simbang*. Staying on good terms with all of them was not particularly easy. A few male *simbang* tried to discourage me from attending certain rituals, and I had to maneuver carefully in order to remain in everyone's good graces. Nevertheless, I did not attempt to hide my broad interests or deny that I was working with other practitioners. Shamans perform not only in homes and at shrines but also onstage on the island and the mainland. Several also travel to Japan to perform for Cheju natives living there; however, I did not have an opportunity to observe a performance in Japan.

A scholar's special interest might be considered indicative of a shaman's fame and could boost his or her reputation, thus many Korean shamans have welcomed and even solicited scholarly attention (e.g., Chungmoo Choi 1991; Sarfati 2009; cf. Romberg 2003, 134). However, taking a stranger along to a ritual event could also be problematic, especially if the shaman has not yet established rapport with the client. A patron family would need to host and feed the researcher along with the lead *simbang*'s entire entourage. For large-scale rituals, I donated a modest sum as *pujo* (allowance aid) in order to provide at least partial recompense for my accommodations. More crucially, because shamanic rituals expose a patron family's often tragic and most private history, a researcher risks upsetting patrons, especially when he or she intends to document such intimate moments. As Maureen Pritchard observed in her study on *koshok*, a "ritualized expression of grief" performed in Kyrgyzstan, documenting ritual is "extraneous to the event" and can even be seen, from the standpoint of the host family, as "disrespectful of the grief of the living and irreverent to the dead" (2011, 167, 168, 181). At the same time, patrons would not want to offend shamans who have come to work for them by objecting to a member of their company. Aware of this delicate situation, some *simbang* discouraged videotaping and recommended the use of less conspicuous audio recordings instead. One lead shaman declined my request to record her ritual, asserting rightly that she was not performing for someone's research, although another *simbang* opined that the lead *simbang* had not consented to my documenting the ritual because she lacked competence and confidence. I appreciate all the shamans and patrons who did allow me to attend and record their performances. Watching the visual materials again and again and examining transcribed ritual speech genres were essential to understanding the complex Cheju rituals. A few *simbang* were particularly sympathetic to my situation as an outsider and made an extra effort to assist me.

When I accompanied the *simbang*, patrons treated me in some respects as though I were a *simbang* even after learning that I was a researcher. In fact, I often played the role of assistant *simbang*, for example, playing a metal percussion instrument (*sŏlsoe*) and folding and cutting stacks of thin paper to make imitation money. One of the most difficult customs to follow was to leave the patron family without saying farewell. During the early stages of my fieldwork, *simbang* scolded me for not following their instructions. When I asked one *simbang* for the reason, she explained the custom from a client's perspective. Patrons believe that *simbang* take with them any lingering spirits of misfortune, and after investing so much effort and a considerable sum, people do not want to take even the slightest chance. What if making eye contact with *simbang* caused the spirits to turn around and remain? This scenario made it abundantly clear that patrons perceive *simbang* as those who bring both protection and danger; thus, they both desire and fear the practitioners (cf. Geschiere 2013; Chongho Kim 2003).

Given the sensitivity of the monetary issue, I "let the knowledge 'happen' to me," rather than asking about it directly (Chau 2006, 110), and satisfied my curiosity mostly through conversations between *simbang* and patrons, as at Mr. Cho's. Sometimes, however, shamans offered the information while discussing another subject. Interacting with ritual sponsors and other Cheju residents outside ritual contexts was helpful in rounding out the shaman-centered research by providing insight into diverse and often ambivalent views on ritual consumption and shamanism in general (Chongho Kim 2003, 8).

Situated ritual contexts alone do not adequately explain the various and contradictory views on Cheju shamanism, which are embedded in and related to broader political and historical contexts. Some scholars have argued that economic concerns have become more salient in contemporary shamanic practice, a new phenomenon that either has emerged largely in response to the commodification of life during the past few decades or is a corrupted by-product of the exposure of a supposedly purer, more "authentic" indigenous religion to Western influence.[45] Although the extent and character of ritual materialism may look novel, the very economic nature of rituals cautions against blindly assuming that the laity had no ambivalence toward ritual transactions and practitioners in the past. In contrast to post-socialist Mongolia, where recent suspicion of shamans' motivations arose in the midst of the revival of shamanism after it had been harshly suppressed (Pederson 2011; Buyandelger 2013, 30–31), distrust of shamans, who, as self-employed entrepreneurs, have long sold their services, is by no means new in Korea.

A historical perspective helps us understand why ritual consumption has been controversial and why advocates of shamanism have eschewed the issue. Embroiled in the politics of civilization (Confucian and Christian), nationalism, and colonialism, both critics and advocates of shamanism have denigrated ritual consumption and the practitioners' economic interests while seeing them as something that should be external to a "religious" practice. Ironically, a select Cheju ritual has recently been used as heritage goods, supposedly to boost the local economy. Although the interpenetration of politics and religion is not unique to shamanism in Korea,[46] it manifests more saliently in the popular religion.[47] The folk religion is not an organized religion based on doctrines and hierarchy, such as Buddhism and Christianity, and its practitioners lack elite channels of power and communication. Consequently, groups of different political stripes could speak for shamans about the nature and purpose of Korean shamanism with little scrutiny or protest by shamans, who needed the social elite to maintain or advance their position. Cheju shamanism cannot be fully understood in isolation from broader political and historical transformations in Korea, yet it should be considered in its own right because of the distinct features of Cheju shamanism.

1 A NEO-CONFUCIAN REFORMER'S 1702 PURGE

A PAINTING FROM *ILLUSTRATED RECORDS OF THE T'AMNA INSPEC-tions* (T'amna sullyŏkto) (fig. 1.1) depicts burning buildings with Mount Halla and small volcanic craters (*orŭm*) in the background. The term "shamanic shrine" (*sindang*) is written under each flaming building (see enlarged image in top left of fig. 1.1), leaving no doubt what the scene depicts: the oft-cited torching of 129 island shrines in 1702, for which Governor Yi Hyŏngsang (1653–1733) is infamous among the locals to this day.

While like-minded Confucian scholars complimented Yi for his deed,[1] *simbang* themselves manifest quite a different take on his act when reciting Cheju's history during the performance of large-scale rituals: "This is an island where five hundred shrines were burned, and five hundred temples destroyed during the time of Governor Yi from Yŏngch'ŏn [in Kyŏngsang Province]" (Hyŏn Yongjun 1980a, 44). The exaggerated number of shrines and temples destroyed demonstrates how large the incident looms in the memories of the practitioners. Though it is difficult to know how the populace actually reacted to Yi's measures at the time, his actions quite likely caused much resentment among them, as mirrored in oral narratives that recount how Yi returned to the mainland only to discover that his sons had died, victims of vengeance exacted by the local deities he had offended (Hyŏn Yongjun and Kim Yŏngdon 1983, 100–110, 734–42; *P'ungsok muŭm* 1994, 2:417–29).[2]

Based on this story and in light of Confucian principles, most studies have interpreted the purge as the manifestation of a confrontation between a centrally appointed magistrate (*suryŏng*) armed with Neo-Confucian ideology and the subaltern local people on the periphery who were dependent on the "unorthodox" beliefs.[3] While the confrontational nature of the event is undeniable, such a dichotomous interpretation blinds us to Yi's extremely pragmatic approach to the management of resources involved in the popular religion and to his critical stance on Confucian officialdom's double standard toward the vernacular religious practice—they condemned shamanic

FIG. 1.1. Burning shrines, detail from *Kŏnp'o paeŭn* (Obeisance to the royal court), *Illustrated Records of the T'amna Inspections.* Courtesy of the National Museum of Jeju

rituals as illegal but benefited from the shamanic tax (*muse*) purportedly enacted to discourage them.

The dominant interpretations of the incident predicated on an ideological and geopolitical dichotomy are plausible. But Yi's accounts of the purge demonstrate the way in which state policy on rituals led reformists faithful to Neo-Confucian principles, such as Governor Yi, to appraise ritual consumption. In his disapproving view of the popular religion, sacrificial objects dedicated to rituals were devoid of any symbolic meaning and the laity was being exploited by shamans. He could not conceive of the possibility that people would willingly give up goods in the hope of achieving desired outcomes and that shamans were providing the laity with something valuable in exchange for what they were given. However, unlike other governors appointed to Cheju, he attempted to liberate the laity from the "waste" of resources expended on "wrongful" practice and practitioners from their profession by abolishing shamanic taxes. Moreover, he criticized officialdom and the government for tacitly supporting the very practice they insisted should be abolished in order to reap the economic benefits it generated.

CHEJU, CHOSŎN'S PERIPHERY

In the minds of the metropolitan elites of the Chosŏn dynasty, Cheju was at both the geographical and the cultural periphery. An island "as small as a bullet," it was "the farthest place from the central government" (*Chŏngjo sillok*, 17 June 1781). According to Confucian cultural discourse that was prevalent during the dynasty, "any land far from the center," to say nothing of remote areas like the island, "was deemed to be less civilized than the center itself" (Sun Joo Kim 2010, 10). However, the central elites' discriminatory view that outlying regions were "culturally defective" (Sun Joo Kim 2008, 161) was particularly pronounced with regard to the island that had once been an independent kingdom. Cheju was at the same time strategically significant for national defense and a valuable source of tax revenue and local tribute (e.g., horses, tangerines, and sea products). The new dynasty made an effort to establish a strong governing presence in the countryside, which the previous Koryŏ dynasty had lacked (Duncan 2000; Pettid 2001, 174; Yi Yŏnggwŏn 2005, 164). For administrative purposes, the central government assigned Cheju to Chŏlla Province, located in the southwestern part of the Korean peninsula, and divided it into three parts: one special county (*mok*) and two lesser counties (*hyŏn*). As shown in figure 1.2 (note the inverted compass directions), north of Mount Halla was designated Cheju Mok, the seat of the governor (*moksa*); the southwest sector was named Taejŏng Hyŏn; and the southeast sector was Chŏngŭi Hyŏn (see the enlarged images in fig. 1.2).

Due to the great distance and the difficulty associated with travel, an appointment to Cheju usually signified a demotion or sinecure for civil servants, regardless of the bureaucratic rank of the position. Reluctant to accept their appointments to Cheju, some officials declined their posts, and others left Cheju without permission before the end of their tenure (Yi Yŏnggwŏn 2005, 160).[4] In the eyes of metropolitan administrators, Cheju was a hinterland that lacked Confucian civilization and thus a place where the people and mores were "still in chaos" (158). On this unfamiliar ground, centrally appointed officials desperately needed help from local elites in order to govern a populace that was culturally quite different from that of the mainland, but they found it difficult to obtain such support especially during the early years of the dynasty.

The island's indigenous power holders (*t'oho*), mostly from the families of Ko, Yang, and Pu, construed magistrates as metropolitan intruders and initially resisted centralization. Well established in the region, few of these hereditary local strongmen with military, economic, and political power would have wanted to leave home and undertake the risk of traveling to Seoul in order to advance their social position with the central government (Cho and Pak 1998, 200). They maintained a symbiotic relationship with

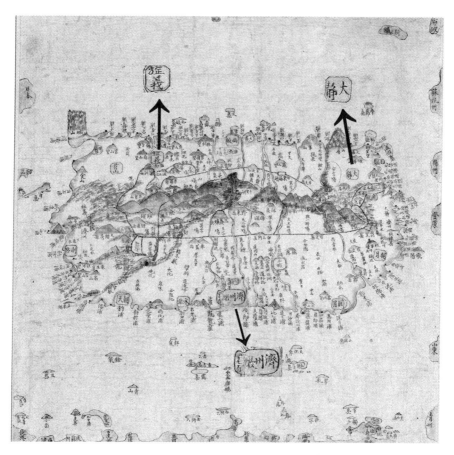

FIG. 1.2. Detail from *Halla changch'ok* (A panorama of Cheju Island), *Illustrated Records of the T'amna Inspections*. Courtesy of the National Museum of Jeju. Arrows point to enlarged labels: (top left) Chŏngǔi, (top right) Taejŏng, (bottom) Cheju.

the central government after its subjugation to the Koryŏ in the twelfth century—the latter depended on them in practical matters, such as defending the territories and levying taxes and tribute from the populace; in return, the dynasty granted the local leaders a certain amount of autonomy and protection. Despite the change from Koryŏ to Chosŏn, the native officials (*t'ogwan*) still participated, in parallel with centrally appointed officials, in the local administration, each having his own official seal and military power (*Sejong sillok*, 10 June 1427). Moreover, qualified candidates for *hyangni*, the hereditary "clerks who ran day-to-day operations in the local administrative districts" and whose multifaceted role was indispensable to the Chosŏn government's efforts at centralization (Kyung Moon

Hwang, 2004, 2), were not readily available on Cheju due to the lack of formal education (Kim Dong Jeon 1991, 63–64; *T'aejo sillok*, 27 March 1394).[5]

However, local authorities eventually had to cooperate with appointed officials in order to maintain and enhance their privileges in the face of the central government's deepening control of the countryside, which systematized and intensified tax collection. For their part, thrown into a strange place,[6] magistrates had to negotiate local allegiances for effective governance and for dealing with practical affairs (Palais [1975] 1991, 13), and they often turned a blind eye to corruption and the illegal activities of their local standing staff. The Confucian ideal of administering the state in a way that relieves the suffering of the people (*kyŏngse chemin*) was much compromised, and many governors were infamous for abusing their power and exploiting the local people.[7] By making this practical compromise, the central government finally brought the power of the island's hereditary local leaders under control by the beginning of the seventeenth century.

Nevertheless, the mainland elites' condescending view of Cheju lasted throughout the dynasty. *Augmented Survey of the Geography of Korea* (Sinjŭng Tongguk yŏji sŭngnam) (hereafter *Geography of Korea*) characterizes Cheju as a place where "customs are peculiar, the military is fierce, and the people are ignorant." It cites an excerpt from a letter written by Kwŏn Kŭn (1352–1409), a major figure in Neo-Confucianism, to Yi Wŏnhang, who had just been appointed governor of Cheju: "The foolish islanders are human only when they are happy, but when angry they become beasts" ([1530] 1969, 5:96–97).[8] While exiled in Cheju, Kim Chŏng (1486–1521) observed, "Only a few are literate," "their minds are vulgar," and "they have no sense of honor or justice" (Cheju Munhwawŏn 2007, 17). Another exile, Kim Chŏnghŭi (1786–1856), a scholar renowned for his original style in calligraphic art, reveals one more humiliating perception of Cheju residents: "Their obtuseness and ignorance are like those of the barbarians in Hokkaido of Japan."[9] In a fashion little different from what cultural historian Taylor E. Atkins refers to as "dyads for articulating difference" between colonizers and the colonized, such as "literate/nonliterate" and "civilized/barbaric," the elites depicted the islanders as "primitives," thereby asserting their own superiority (2010, 55).

The Dutchman Hendrick Hamel, a bookkeeper on the *Sperwer* (Sparrow Hawk), which was shipwrecked in 1653 on Cheju, known to him as Quelpaert, also observed the mainland intellectuals' opinion of the islanders.[10] After being held captive with his fellow shipmates for more than nine months before being transferred to the mainland, he wrote in his journal that the inhabitants were "held in low esteem by people from the mainland" (2011, 12). Although he was perhaps unaware of it, the islanders' devotion to shamanic practices on a greater scale than elsewhere in Korea added to the metropolitan elites' perception of Cheju as the least civilized part of Chosŏn Korea.

IMPROPER LOCAL CULT

The volume of the *Geography of Korea* that deals with Cheju mentions several distinctive local characteristics in the section on customs (*p'ungsok*), among which an entry on shamanic rituals receives the most extended attention. This entry provides the most detailed information available at the time concerning popular beliefs and rituals: kinds of deities worshipped, seasonal communal rituals (dates and participants, as well as musical instruments used in ritual processions), representative shrines, and beliefs about snakes:

> Respecting licentious rituals (*sang ŭmsa*). The islanders take *ŭmsa* so seriously that they sacrifice to the mountains, forests, streams, ponds, high and low hillocks, trees, and stones. Female and male shamans hold up ritual banners and perform the *nahŭi* every year from January first until January fifteenth.[11] The group, led by gong and drum players, visits each household, and the host willingly donates goods and grain. On the first day of February, people in Kwidŏk, Kimnyŏng, and so on, set up twelve wooden poles to welcome the deity [of the wind] and make sacrifices to her. People in Aewŏl make rafts [whose floating platforms are] shaped like a horse's head, decorate them with colorful fabric, and entertain the deity by performing the Yangmahŭi.[12] This ceremony is called Yŏndŭng[13] and ends on the fifteenth [of February]. Sailing on a ship is prohibited during the month [of February]. Groups of people, both men and women, gather to conduct rituals, offering wine and meat at the shrines of Kwangyang and Ch'agwi in spring and fall. Snakes, large and small, and centipedes are abundant in the earth. When people see a gray snake, they call it the god of Ch'agwi and avoid killing it. ([1530] 1969, 5:95–96)

Although the *Geography of Korea* discusses these beliefs and practices in a few other regions, the level of detail is lower, indicating its prominence in the locale.

The seemingly neutral portrayal notwithstanding, the entry characterizes shamanism as improper. Originally from the *Record of Rites* (Liji), the
word *ŭmsa* (C. *yinsi*) means illicit or licentious rituals conducted without
regard for the hierarchical status of ritual performers and sponsors (Choi
Jong Seong 2002, 52; Lee Wook 2009, 44).[14] Even Confucian rituals could
be relegated to this category if not performed properly, and not all rituals
that shamans performed were *ŭmsa*. As the Chosŏn dynasty adopted Confucianism as the state ideology, ritual received special attention from officials as a key area for reform (Deuchler 1992; Haboush 1991). Administrators
prescribed Confucian-based ceremonial protocols and gradually institutionalized the system,[15] allowing only officials to officiate at state-sponsored
rituals and excluding religious clergies such as Buddhist monks and shamans (Lee Wook 2009, 50–59). As with the excerpt above, shamanic rituals were addressed in local gazetteers, while state-sponsored rituals were
treated in the official manual prescribing the mode of conduct for state
ceremonies.[16]

At the same time, Confucian critics highlighted the supposed defects of
other religions such as Buddhism, Daoism, and shamanism, constructing
these as foils for Confucianism. Efforts to stamp out these traditions, which
were in and of themselves a means of Confucianizing the society, were far
more severe and systematic during the Chosŏn era than during the Koryŏ
dynasty, whose administrators had tolerated multiple religious traditions
(Duncan 2000; Walraven 1999a, 160). Neo-Confucian scholars came to use
the word *ŭmsa* specifically to refer to non-Confucian ceremonies (Choi Jong
Seong 2002, 53, citing *Sejong Sillok*, 9 December 1441), among which shamanic rituals were considered to be of the lowest order. They officially
derided shamanic rituals and gradually branded all shamanic rituals and
shrines as *ŭmsa* (淫祀 and 淫祠 respectively), regardless of whether or not
they were personally sympathetic toward shamanism. Moreover, by virtue
of their status, power, and established credibility, they suppressed shamanism through laws, taxation, punishment, and expulsion (Yi Nŭnghwa [1927]
2008, 161–217).

Scholar-officials from the mainland often noted the prevalence of shamanism in Cheju and pointed to it as a marker of the region's backwardness.
In his *Cheju Topography* (Cheju p'ungt'orok), the fervent Neo-Confucian
scholar Kim Chŏng worried about the increasing popularity of shamanism
on the island: "Though over three hundred shamanic shrines already dot the
island, more are being constructed each year" (Cheju Munhwawŏn 2007,
11–12).[17] The infamous Governor Yi Hyŏngsang noted that shamanic practice

in Cheju was one hundred times more popular than it was on the main-land and he was determined to abolish it.

GOVERNOR YI'S CIVILIZING CAMPAIGN

Yi was appointed governor of Cheju in March 1702 at the age of forty-nine and was dismissed only a year later, well before the end of his term of office.[18] It was one of the eight local government posts that he held during his life-time in addition to four in the capital. Although it is difficult to pinpoint his political alignment (*tangp'a*), Yi is acknowledged as an important fig-ure who contributed to the development of Practical Learning (Sirhak), a Confucian social reform movement active between the late seventeenth and early nineteenth centuries. Unlike the more speculative and doctrinaire Neo-Confucianism, Practical Learning emphasized improving constitu-ents' quality of life. Soon after Yi arrived on Cheju, he swiftly made a great effort to improve the lives of Cheju natives. In 1796, the government posthumously honored him as a clean-handed official (*ch'ŏngbaengni*). He is known to have neither actively pursued nor succeeded in advancing a bureaucratic career in a political system rife with clique politics (Yi Sang-gyu 2009, 8). Indeed, Yi's period of administrative service, spanning only twelve years, seems of short duration given his eighty-year life span.

After Yi departed from Cheju, he dedicated the rest of his life primarily to writing and produced more than three hundred titles on a variety of top-ics including geography, astronomy, Daoism, Neo-Confucianism, ritual and music (*yeak*), and folkloric subjects.[19] He left detailed records of his observations and deeds on the island in two of the pivotal extant records concerning Cheju during the dynasty: *Illustrated Records of the T'amna Inspections* (hereafter *T'amna Inspections*) and *Various Things Observed in the South* (Namhwan pangmul) (hereafter *Various Things*). *T'amna Inspec-tions* is an illustrated book documenting a variety of events that occurred during Yi's expeditions to different locations on the island.[20] *Various Things* is one of the most detailed sources of information about the region, includ-ing history, geography, products, and natural ecology.[21]

The Cheju that this paragon of Confucian virtue saw upon his arrival was an uncivilized territory where Confucian schools had been allowed to deteriorate, men and women bathed together, those with the same surname married, and people sought the aid of shamans, instead of medicine, to cure disease.[22] In his records, Yi dramatized the cultural differences between the mainland and the island, a useful tactic that served to justify his urge to civilize the backward inhabitants. Given his rather pretentious comments, it is not difficult to conjure up a "colonial image" in Yi's presentation of the island's inhabitants (Walraven 1993, 7). Further, his inspection tour and writings on Cheju afforded him a power similar to that of on-site imperial ethnographers, who were, in the words of Atkins, privileged "to gaze, to gather, to survey, to define, to quantify, [and] to judge" (2010, 52).

Unlike officials who merely bemoaned the islanders' backwardness, Yi wasted no time in enforcing Confucian values. He repaired dilapidated Confucian shrines, strengthened Confucian education, and reformed public rituals in accordance with Confucian protocol, a condition necessary for institutionalizing Confucianism. Until his arrival, Cheju had continued in its own fashion the *p'ung-un-noe-u-je* (a ritual devoted to the gods of wind, clouds, thunder, and rain), although only the court, not regional governments, was allowed to perform the ceremony. In contrast, Cheju Island ignored the obligation to conduct a cardinal ceremony for the god of Mount Halla and instead performed shamanic rituals at Kwangyang and Ch'agwi Shrines (Yi Hyŏngsang 1990, 191–95). Given that Confucian rites, along with wars, were considered the most significant affairs of state and that officiating rituals in accordance with the ritual protocols was an official's duty, governors before Yi would surely have known of the regional violations but chose to tolerate them.[23] Unlike his predecessors, who went along with prevailing religious practices, the radical reformer Yi Hyŏngsang abolished the *p'ung-un-noe-u-je* and eliminated places of improper propitiation, even taking the trouble to request the king's permission a second time after his first petition had been rejected (*Sukchong sillok*, 29 July 1703). The practical governor saw to it that resources such as grain and prebendal land previously used for the "impure" rituals were instead used for Confucian schools and the local government.

The local inhabitants subsequently interpreted years of bad harvests and contagious illnesses to be a direct result of Yi's abolishment of the ritual. In response to their pleas, Governor Chŏng Tonghu requested in 1719 that the *p'ung-un-noe-u-je* be revived, which the court duly allowed (*Sukchong sillok*, 4 November 1719). Other governors after Chŏng also tolerated "improper" ritual practices. For example, Governor Yi Wŏnjo recorded a performance of the Ipch'un Kut (a communal *kut* celebrating the onset of spring) conducted by *simbang* and the chief clerk of the magistrate's office in the yamen in his 1841 *Records of T'amna* (T'amnarok) (Cho Sung-Youn and Pak Chan-Sik 1998, 216), which the staunch governor Yi Hyŏngsang would never have allowed. These actions suggest that Yi Hyŏngsang, a man of Confucian principles, took quite a different approach to the popular religious practices in the region and that, although Confucianism operated with a great deal of central direction, it did not always insist on the imposition of state policy from above.

PURGE

Among Yi's civilizing efforts on the island, his destruction of 129 shamanic shrines, where village tutelary spirits were worshipped, has gained the most notoriety. Although Yi was not the only governor who attempted to suppress local shamanic practice,[24] no other governor conducted such an aggressive campaign against it or left such a substantial record of tightening control over Cheju residents' religious mores during the five hundred years of the dynasty. One can piece together a picture of the 1702 purge through Yi's own records, particularly a page from *T'amna Inspections* and an entry in *Various Things*. In the section on customs in the latter book, Yi introduced nineteen local customs, and the longest entry is devoted to the shamanic tradition, a clear indication of his deep investment in the matter.

Before examining the purge, an explanation of the structure of the entry in *Various Things*, a book completed a year after Yi returned from Cheju, is helpful for a better understanding of its contents. Following the literary convention of writing human-geographic books during the period, he quoted a few earlier records on the topic,[25] then added his own observations and opinions, noting that local shamans' high-handed manners had worsened considerably by the time he arrived compared to the situation depicted in earlier records. He then copied his own lengthy message to King Sukchong (r. 1674–1720), originally written while he was on Cheju in the form of *changgye*, a letter genre in which officials report crucial local affairs to the king and request policy changes. The message was unsent, however, owing to his early dismissal.[26] In this *changgye*, he reported in great detail the shamanic tyranny, the purge, and its aftermath and requested a more qualified medical official (*simyak*) on the islanders' behalf. This *changgye* is of paramount importance because it reveals his view of local shamanic practices, his motivation and goals for the purge, and the way that he presented the process of the campaign. He closed the entry on the local vernacular religious practice with a report on what he had heard about the state of shamanic practice on Cheju after his return to the mainland. Despite Yi's undoubtedly disparaging view of shamans, his self-consciously crafted writings vividly illustrate the complexity of the political economy that revolved around the popular religious practice.

What would have motivated the governor to undertake such a radical measure against shamans, who were not deliberately challenging Confucian ideology? Yi's motivation can be better understood in the context of the sociocultural structure and government policies on the vernacular religious practice. The elites protested against shamanism ostensibly for the sake of the people, but, as many scholars argue, in reality for themselves: it was actually a power grab—an attempt to monopolize rule of an unruly people through the Confucian way.[27] The administrators of the Chosŏn dynasty thought of shamanic deities as supernatural counterparts of themselves (Walraven 2007b, 286) and considered shamans dealing with the deities to be their rivals for influence over the populace (though they would have been reluctant to admit it). The social influence of shamans, which undermined the political authority of officials, constituted a challenge to their governance of the people. According to Yi's *changgye* to the king, the practitioners' influence over the islanders was so immense that it beggared description. He lamented that when traveling by boat, concerned only about the calamities believed to be caused by ghosts, the populace turned a deaf ear to official orders.

However, the minister worried more about the practitioners' material exploitation of gullible people. Because rituals relegated to the category of *ŭmsa* were to be prevented, the upper class frowned on the financial profligacy involved.[28] Moreover, the elite denigrated shamans and their patrons for focusing on self-interest, which in their eyes indicated a deficient sense of honor because people should earn blessings through virtuous acts rather than by patronizing shamans (Walraven 1999a, 168). They often expressed their utter disdain for shamans by characterizing them as wicked, avaricious, and greedy (Kendall 1985a, 31), a view held by Confucian scholars since the thirteenth century.[29] Kim Chŏng observed during his exile on Cheju: "Shamans *threaten* people with misfortune (*chaehwa*) and amass a [material] *fortune* as [easily as they gather] earth" and "shamans who serve ghosts *scare* people into offering rice cakes and alcohol. They are interested only in *gain*" (Cheju Munhwawŏn 2007, 16, 18; my emphasis). He perceived shamans as goading innocent people into squandering their resources on vulgar rituals by skillfully playing on "wrong" beliefs with the promise to ward off misfortune and bring blessings. However, as Kim himself admitted, that he lived under surveillance in a remote temple area with no neighbors and went out only rarely to stroll in the vicinity rather undermines the validity of his observations on Cheju shamans. Despite the question-able veracity of his descriptions, his statements clearly demonstrate his neg-ative view of shamans.

Governor Yi's descriptions of the alleged crimes of Cheju shamans are more specific than those of the exile Kim, but still do not seem to be based on firsthand observations. Yi had complete freedom to observe shamanic activities but probably would have felt that doing so would be unworthy of him, given his views on un-Confucian practices. His *changgye* to the king does not allude to scenes of a specific ritual but instead exaggerates the social ills generated by shamans, which served to justify the urgent necessity of bringing the practice under control.

> So-called male and female shamans (*namgyŏk yŏmu*) shamelessly manipulate the people. These hooligans call themselves *tanghan* and organize *kye* (financial associations); they [shamans] number more than one thousand. They not only take people's food but slaughter cattle and eat them in shrines. They make people give of their stock of cotton and silk cloths by threatening them with misfortune caused by ghosts. If people still do not give, they send *tanghan*, referring to them as messengers of ghosts (*kwi*), who tie up the laity and rob them. They even go so far as to rob them of their cattle and horses, nearly one hundred in number. In addition, they take the paddies and fields, calling them prebendal land or almsgiving, and share the spoils among themselves. The land taken extends to the embankment around the periphery of the fields. They heap up plundered jewelry in the shrines. (Yi Hyŏngsang 2009, 117)

The governor describes shamans as little better than bandits who, through threat and coercion backed by their organizational power, took virtually anything the laity could possibly own. In his commentary, the extent to which shamans extorted the property of the poverty-stricken populace is so extreme as to suggest that it reflects personal prejudice rather than por-trays reality. This seems especially so given his own *changgye* requesting relief from the heavy burden of tributes for the islanders (Yi Hyŏngsang 1990, 181–91).[30] Note the grand round numbers of the confiscated livestock and shamans. If, as he reported, there were one thousand shamans on an island with 9,552 households, the ratio of shaman to layperson was extremely high—about one for every nine to ten households. From Yi's perspective, rituals were performed only for the sake of shamans' gain, the laypeople were simply exploited by practitioners, and material resources expended in rituals lacked any symbolic meaning. His premise did not consider why people would sponsor rituals and sacrifice their valuables in spite of their abject poverty. Yi intervened to control the shamans' social and economic power on behalf of a populace he was certain did not possess the moral competence to manage its own finances.

The image titled *Kŏnp'o paeŭn* (fig. 1.3), literally, "bowing to the king's grace at Port Kŏnp'o,"[31] from *T'amna Inspections*, illustrates the way in which the purge proceeded. At the center of the frame, a host of people both inside and outside the wall are on their knees, bowing while the shrines burn. As the title indicates, the people are expressing their gratitude for the sovereign's grace and are kowtowing toward the north, in the direction of the king's throne. The costumes of the people (fig. 1.4) and the five-line text at the bottom right (fig. 1.5) indicate who the bowing people are.

> On 20 December 1702,
> altogether around three hundred people of official rank—civil and
>   military, high and low—
>   living in the countryside
> burned 129 shrines,
> destroyed five Buddhist temples.
> Two hundred eighty-five shamans returned to farming.

The caption itself provides few clues to the royal favor that local officials are acknowledging or to a diachronic connection among the three events—their salute to the ruler, the destruction of the shrines and Buddhist temples, and the shamans ceasing their trade. One can make better sense of the scene by attending to intertextual links between the captioned illustration and other sources.

Much can be inferred from Yi's *changgye* to the throne that he copied into the entry on local shamanic practice in *Various Things*. On 20 December 1702, the allegedly appreciative local representatives—including Confucian scholars, military officials, civil functionaries, petty officials, and village heads—bowed first to his highness at Port Kŏnp'o and then to the governor in the courtyard, where they enumerated the specific benefits that the governor had swiftly brought to their lives. He had earlier proposed six amendments to the king on behalf of the local residents, and these were all approved, inter alia, the heavy tax burden on commoners was reduced, and local military officials and gentry were able to fulfill some of their more practical wishes (Yi Hyŏngsang 1990, 181–91, 202–4; *Sukchong sillok*,

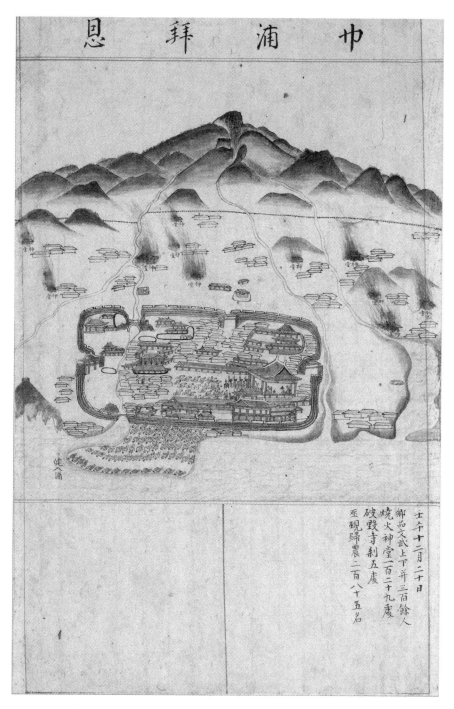

FIG.1.3. *Kŏnp'o paeŭn* (Obeisance to the royal court), *Illustrated Records of the T'amna Inspections*. Courtesy of the National Museum of Jeju

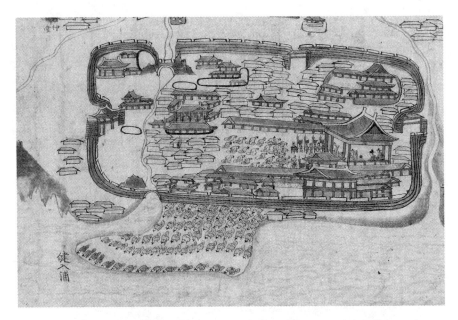

FIG.1.4. Bowing, detail from *Kŏnp'o paeŭn* (Obeisance to the royal court), *Illustrated Records of the T'amna Inspections.* Courtesy of the National Museum of Jeju

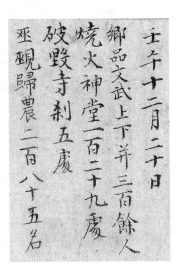

FIG.1.5. Text, detail from *Kŏnp'o paeŭn* (Obeisance to the royal court), *Illustrated Records of the T'amna Inspections.* Courtesy of the National Museum of Jeju

12 July 1702). By way of reporting their words, Yi implicitly expressed his own gratitude to the throne for approving his requests and presented himself as a caring steward for the people on the distant island. As a way of showing their appreciation to the king, whose grace (*ŭnhye*) enhanced the quality of their lives and touched their hearts, local authorities pledged to forbid

some of the "vulgar" customs that violated Confucian norms (e.g., marriages between close kin and excessive nudity of women) and to abolish shamanic shrines. On the following day, they allegedly burned 129 shamanic shrines, the most tangible and immediate action that Yi proudly reported to the king as a demonstration of the local elites' efforts at reform. More impressively, according to Yi, several hundred male shamans expressed their willingness to permanently end their profession and become ordinary people.

Yi's *changgye* to the king portrayed Cheju only six months after the purge as a haven free from shamanic menace—a state that he described as remarkable given that the changes were made voluntarily by the people. According to Yi, the laity realized that they had been deceived by shamans, felt embarrassed about their involvement with the practice, and had come to see shamans as their foes. They also took medicine to treat smallpox rather than depending on shamans and wished to have better-qualified medical personnel sent to the island, a request Yi made on their behalf in his *changgye*. These changes are in stark contrast to the prevailing "vulgar" practices that he described upon his arrival on the island and thus emphasized his own achievements.

FACILE REFORM AND SELF-PROMOTION

In his *changgye* to the king, the governor portrays himself as a responsible shepherd who has liberated the populace from shamanic tyranny, a tactic used by social elites in promoting their moral authority during a time when Confucian values reigned supreme and the stance on ritual practices was highly politicized (Haboush 1991; Walraven 2001, 169). Despite the impressive radical changes that the governor purportedly brought to Cheju, his reform of the popular religious practice was a facile one implementing only superficial changes and achieving little that lasted beyond his term. Moreover, although Yi reports to the throne that the reformative actions of the local residents were volitional, critical scrutiny of available records related to the purge contradicts his claim and calls for a more circumstantial understanding.

The governor's initial reform policy was oriented toward local welfare and dissemination of Confucianism and might have earned the respect of a growing number of local Confucians, who until then had not experienced such a "benevolent" and "practical" administrator. The process of Confucianization proceeded much more slowly than on the mainland (Walraven 2007b, 284–85), but Cheju did not escape it. For example, several years before

Yi's appointment, the distinguished scholar Song Siyŏl, who had once been exiled to Cheju, was posthumously inducted into the Kyullim Academy, which elevated the academy's stature and would have boosted the pride of local Confucians (Ha 2000, 348).[32] Animated by Yi's authority and by the increasing attention given to Confucian values, some local scholars and officials might well have felt obliged to comply with his wishes.

However, it is not difficult to gauge the level of the local leaders' commitment to the allegedly voluntary reform by which they intended to express their appreciation of the king's and governor's virtues. The scale of the repression aside, their actions seem subservient enough to suggest other possible interests and motivations. They were effusive in their thanks for the king's grace, expressed through verbal and nonverbal means, and willingly swore to eliminate "embarrassing" local customs. Oddly, they also handed over deeds to people's land (*minjŏn*) that they had extorted, thus revealing the degree of their corruption that Yi, known for his incorruptibility, may well have been unwilling to overlook. Faced with such an unprecedentedly strong-willed figure who promptly and vigorously carried out reforms, these guilty parties might have felt an urgent need to avert potential trouble. At this juncture, destroying shamanic shrines in compliance with the governor's policies was undoubtedly a way of currying favor with the new administrator and ensuring their social survival.

Moreover, his biographical details suggest that Yi had a more direct influence on the local elites in annihilating the "unorthodox" practice. As a Confucian activist, Yi had already destroyed two shamanic shrines in a government office and thirty-six others in various districts of Kyŏngju shortly before his appointment to Cheju (Cho and Pak 1998, 209; Kwŏn Yŏngch'ŏl 1978, 12–13), which may well have been known to some local officials. Yi's *haengjang* (account of conduct), written by his son, indicates that the governor was directly involved in the purge (Cho and Pak 1998, 209; Walraven 1993, 6–7). Even if the burning of the shrines had been instigated by local elites, they would not have chosen that particular means of expressing their gratitude to the king without first witnessing the governor's fierce efforts to establish Confucian principles on the island. Evidently, both Confucian scholars and the general public recognized the governor as the one responsible for the destruction, although their appraisals of the incident were completely different.

Yi's reports on the purge sound altogether too grand to be accepted at face value. The number of shrines burned is exactly the same as the number of *li* (the smallest administrative unit) on the entire island at the time of his tenure.[33] Despite the statistical soundness, this bureaucratically convenient coincidence renders Yi's claims about a general eradication of shamanism somewhat suspect. In his narratives, shamans and locally dominant groups always act uniformly and speak with a unified voice. Belonging to the lowest social stratum of the rigidly hierarchical Chosŏn society (Deuchler 1992, 13), the male shamans seem unusually bold in mobilizing and interacting directly with the governor. Given that practitioners cannot easily give up their vocation due to the admonitions of the deities, discarding their faith in the power of supernatural beings would perhaps have been a difficult option for them. Therefore, their collective vow, had it happened as Yi described, might have been a tactic for preempting the punishment they feared would fall on them after witnessing the massive destruction of shrines. In fact, as soon as Yi's replacement took office, the shamans broke their promise and revived the shamanic shrines.

By deferring credit for the social changes to the king, a rather conventional gesture among the literati during the Chosŏn dynasty, Yi indirectly communicated his own accomplishments to the addressee of the *changgye* and potential readers of his book. Voicing his own political view through reformative actions and the act of writing, he promoted himself as a guardian of Confucian orthodoxy, regardless of whether or not his efforts proved successful in the long run.

CRITIQUE OF GOVERNMENT POLICY ON THE SHAMANIC TAX

Yi's records reveal much about his critical view, not only of shamanic exploitation, but also of government policies on the shamanic tax, a topic that has been little discussed in the English-language literature on Korean shamanism.[34] In general, government policies on shamanism were inconsistent, hypocritical, and even contradictory throughout the dynasty (Choi Jong Seong 2002). While the administration made shamanic rituals illegal and punished shamans for performing them—in one extreme case in 1398, a shaman was decapitated (*T'aejo sillok*, 14 April 1398)—it also took advantage of the multiple functions shamans performed as healers, priests, and seers. In the face of national calamities such as drought, famine, and epidemics, the government itself resorted to shamans (Choi Jong Seong 2002; Lee Wook 2009). For example, as late as the seventeenth century, it employed them to pray for rain and assigned them to the government's medical agencies for the sick (Choi Jong Seong 2002, 124–25, 142; Walraven 1999a, 173).

The most hypocritical act of all was the institution of the shamanic tax collected until the 1895 Kabo reforms, when legal class distinctions were abolished.[35] The central and local governments kept rosters of shamans (*muan*) and collected taxes from them for performing rituals (*muŏpse*), for property associated with shrines (*sindangse*), and for the ceremonial goods left over after rituals (*sindang t'oemulse*).[36] In principle, the tax was collected in the form of cotton cloth that was commonly used as currency, although money equivalent to the value of in-kind taxes was also accepted.[37] The ostensible purpose was to discourage rituals at which people frequently offered more than they could reasonably spare. In reality, the tax went into the government coffers and was used for a variety of important activities such as publishing books, running government medical facilities, building Confucian schools, and purchasing hides, horses, and cattle (Min 2000, 41).

Aware of the contradictions involved in taking taxes while suppressing the practice, several kings and their officials discussed whether or not the tax was warranted (Min 2000, 40; Rim 1993, 95; Yi Nŭnghwa [1927] 2008, 161–78). However, once it had become an indispensable source of national and local revenue, it was not easy for the administration to give it up entirely. The governor's contemporary Yi Ik (1681–1763) pointed out unequivocally the double standard of the government policy:

> The law cannot prevent shamanic practice. It is not that the government cannot prohibit shamanic practice by law but that there is actually a reason for encouraging the practice. All shamans pay tax, and the government has the gain.
>
> What is the source of shamans' income? Ritual practice. This is what makes it difficult to prohibit. . . . The government already benefits by collecting shamanic taxes, but it makes further profit by fining those who participate in the practice. The government's intention was not really to stop the practice but rather to obtain money and cloth from shamans. (1978, 3:24)

According to the author, the government was purposefully lax about regulating illegal cults in order to protect its interests.

Apart from its inherent hypocrisy, the confiscatory taxation caused much harm, due largely to the greed and corruption of local officials and the lack of an effective system for regulating the collection process. Reportedly, magistrates listed citizens who were not actually shamans in the rosters (*Chungjong sillok*, 23 September 1517). Although the centrally appointed officials had nominal responsibility for collecting taxes, in practice it was the *hyangni* who collected taxes from ordinary people. Since these local clerks did not receive stipends, they kept a portion of the taxes they collected as their salaries. In effect, their livelihood relied on tax collection, which earned them the reputation of "unwelcome enforcers of state exploitation" (Kyung Moon Hwang 2004, 171). The sixteenth-century scholar Ŏ Sukkwŏn describes an apparently prevalent situation of his time.[38] Confronted with petty officials storming into their houses, shamans who had been unable to pay the burdensome tax on time would attempt to gain an extension of the deadline by offering the officials food and wine. Other functionaries got kickbacks for releasing shamans accused of illegal practice. It is not surprising then that the relationship between humans and the spirits has traditionally been very similar to that between humans and the powerful officials of Korea's past who had to be placated and swayed by bribery (Kendall 1985b). The revenues from locally collected taxes were supposed to be fairly distributed among the central government, provincial governors, prefectures, and counties, but this was not always the case in practice. The Office of the Inspector General (Sahŏnbu) complained that the magistrates and inspectors kept too much of the tax proceeds for themselves without remitting a fair amount to the national revenue (*Munjong sillok*, 12 April 1451).

Yi Hyŏngsang shared Yi Ik's critical view of the shamanic tax, though he expressed it more indirectly. Reporting what the shamans purportedly told him, he diplomatically addressed the contradictions of the controversial institution:

> It is not that we perform rituals because we like to. Since the burden of supplying all the cloth for governmental use is imposed entirely on the shamans, we have become involved in ritual practices in order to provide the goods that we would not be able to supply otherwise, given our empty hands and naked fists (*chŏksu konggwŏn*). Since we have already discontinued it, the evil practice will disappear forever. If you remove our names from the tax register of shamans, we will prohibit the practice from generation to generation and encourage one another to abolish the title of shaman (*mu*); we thus desire to become ordinary people.
> (Yi Hyŏngsang [1704] 2009, 119)

The governor presents the shamans' point of view as a matter of fact, without sarcasm and with sympathy for the taxpayers who had to meet the demand for cloth, highly valued especially on Cheju because its importation from the mainland involved risky sea trips. Despite his attempt to undermine the practitioners' spiritual and economic base by destroying the shrines, his purge did not seem to have involved the punishment of individual shamans by arrest or flogging, as occurred on the mainland in Chosŏn Korea. Shamans in his account countered the charge of exploitation made against them by Confucian critics: they practiced not for personal gain but because of the punitive tax imposed on them. Thus, they laid bare the reality in which their profession was fundamentally intertwined with the government's interest in revenue. Note also that their promise to abandon the practice was made on a quid pro quo basis: "If you remove our names from the tax register of shamans . . ." How faithfully the governor was quoting the shamans is uncertain, but he certainly focused on the structural problem associated with perpetuation of the practice—tax collection. By borrowing the shamans' voices, he was in effect declaring himself a true shepherd who cared about them and acted on their behalf, a rhetorical strategy conducive to avoiding a confrontation with the king over a topic as controversial as the shamanic tax and to making his request for sending a medical official more palatable. However, in both denigrating and redeeming the practitioners, he reduced their trade to a purely utilitarian act without considering their devotion to the profession and their commitment to clients.

This righteous paternal leader clearly hoped to establish an island of Confucianism, keeping shamans at bay, and according to his *changgye* to the king, this goal seemed to have been realized before his departure. However, he did not succeed in expunging the popular religious practice at a single stroke. His successor Yi Hŭit'ae did not pursue the matter further; rather, the new governor immediately reverted to the laxity that had prevailed before his predecessor's tenure. Yi Hyŏngsang closes his entry by bemoaning the changes that nullified his efforts to eradicate the practice: "I heard it said that a big *kut* was conducted on the day after my successor took office. He permitted shamans to restore shamanic shrines and dismissed [medical] doctors. The populace, disappointed with these measures, petitioned him to stop, but he refused to hear them. In addition, he returned to the practice of keeping the tax register of shamans and collecting cloth. As a result, shamans have begun to jointly finance the rebuilding of the demolished shrines. This is a truly disappointing state of affairs" ([1704] 2009, 117–18).

This practical-minded governor makes it clear that the fundamental problem with perpetuating the "uncivil" practice lay in the taxation supported by officials. He faults neither the shamans nor the laity but his fellow officials for the revival of the practice. His successor received a welcome ritual and facilitated shamans' return to practice even against the wishes of the now "enlightened" populace. The shamans then had to rebuild the shrines in which rituals were performed in order to pay their taxes. As reported in his *changgye*, Yi characterizes the shamans' reason for resuming the practice as solely a matter of dealing with their tax burden. He renders the islanders blameless for the "unorthodox" practice while completely and conveniently ignoring any value that they themselves might ascribe to the practice.

CONCLUSION

Yi's records pertaining to the 1702 purge, one example of the harsh regulation of the popular religion in Chosŏn Korea, ironically reveals much about his critical view of the system that he believed facilitated the perpetuation of the uncivilized cult. Many scholars have linked the tenacity of the popular religion with the needs that more formalized and restrained Confucian rites failed to provide, such as comfort and emotional support.[39] Without denying this thesis, but taking a more pragmatic view, Walraven adds that the cultural distance between the Confucian elite and the lower echelons of society represented by the bifurcation of rituals—orthodox versus unorthodox—helped the privileged maintain their social identity and preserve class distinctions (1999a, 169–70). Indeed, shamanic rituals—based on an oral tradition, involving wild dance and music, and performed and consumed on the mainland primarily by women—disturbed male literati (culturati), who conducted more sober and orderly Confucian rites (Kendall 1985a). The elite men cast off the supposedly vulgar rituals for themselves but tolerated them for the rest of the population (Walraven 1999a, 181). However, Yi's account shows that their practical considerations went beyond the realm of symbolic capital. Both local and central officials reaped fiscal benefits from the popularity of "illegitimate" rituals through taxation, a measure supposedly enacted to discourage the practice.

Analyzing Yi's purge in relation to central-local politics helps us understand why such a severe repression of shamanism was far from the norm in regions outside the capital, most especially on Cheju. Longing to return to the mainland, Cheju governors were not particularly ambitious when it came to edifying the residents at the expense of the social, economic, and political benefits that accrued from engaging with the local population.

Moreover, as Yi stated in one of his earlier *changgye*, because the court had little regard for Cheju, official requests to the king on the islanders' behalf were frequently rejected, which discouraged reform efforts (Yi Hyŏngsang 1990, 182).[40] Knowing that shamanism was deeply rooted in local life, most governors apparently dared not aggressively undertake its suppression on an island saturated with "heretical" beliefs and practices. Teaming up with local officials, they took advantage of the prevalence of the long-standing practice. Indifferent to the Confucianization of regions outside the capital, but keen on enjoying the tax revenues collected from shamans, the central government quietly allowed the practice to continue undisturbed until the end of the dynasty.

Unlike many other governors, the zealous governor Yi worked to reduce the financial burden of commoners who eked out a meager living from the ocean while being subjected to demands for heavy tribute by writing a persuasive *changgye* early in his tenure (Yi Hyŏngsang 1990, 181–91). This suggests that he genuinely cared about the islanders and therefore aimed to spare them the "useless" consumption involved in the "unorthodox" practice, even though forcing shamans to cease their practice would result in reduced tax revenue. However, because they were his social inferiors whom he deemed in need of edification, he did not consider their perspective on ritual affairs, namely, why they would invest their valuable resources and what they believed they stood to gain from rituals. In his view, the goods expended for improper rituals would be better used more prudently. His vigorous efforts to eliminate the practice for the benefit of the people were executed without consideration for their beliefs, which explains why his apparent success evaporated so quickly after his departure.

2 CULTURAL POLITICS OF CHEJU SHAMANISM IN THE TWENTIETH CENTURY

DURING MOST OF THE CHOSŎN DYNASTY (1392–1910), SHAMAN-ism was derided in the administrative discourse of Confucian scholars as heterodox and shamans were characterized as exploiters of innocent people. As the influence of Confucian ideology waned with the influx of new ideas at the end of the nineteenth century, the popular religion began to be censured within broader worldviews by diverse groups, both Korean and non-Korean. Reformers, mostly from the outside, such as Catholic missionaries, the Japanese colonial regime, and the central government of the Republic of Korea, dismissed the moral-economic value of the practice. At the same time, embroiled in the politics of ethnic representations during the Japanese colonial period, shamanism also came to be extolled as the touchstone of Korean thought, an idea that buttressed a range of elite validations and appropriations of the tradition in the Republic of Korea. New debates about the old folk religion could not have been more sharply contradictory than in the case of Cheju shamanism, due to its popularity and distinctive features and to the island's position in Korea as the internal other.

Why then did scholars, cultural activists, and even the government that had once suppressed shamanism elevate it despite the prevailing criticism of its economic harm, and how did they deal with these allegations? Divergent ideological claims about Cheju shamanism arose from historical conditions during the twilight years of the Chosŏn Kingdom, through the colonial period, to the end of the twentieth century. During each of these phases, ritual consumption, the very key to the practice, was avoided or, worse, condemned in the discourse on Cheju shamanism, and this polarization inadvertently led to the lack of appreciation for ritual economy. Mired in the elite politics of culture, proponents of Cheju shamanism have valorized their own idealized version of it while diverting their attention not only from the fabric of contemporary practitioners' lives but also from the social current of anti-superstition sentiment. By shunning the criticism of ritual expenditure rather than explicitly dealing with it, the defenders perpetuated the idea that economic matters are peripheral to the practice and tacitly gave support to opponents who denounced the practice for the purported financial damage it caused to the home and national economies.

CATHOLIC MISSIONARIES IN CHEJU AROUND 1900

Western missionaries appeared on the peninsula in greater numbers during the last quarter of the nineteenth century and played an important role in shaping the discourse on shamanism. Loyal to their own one true God, they rejected the country's long-revered local gods and goddesses. Given that Confucians embraced the spirit world in which both shamans and commoners believed and accepted the intervention of spirits in human affairs (Deuchler 1992, 175; Walraven 1991, 38–39; 1999a, 163–67), this denial of supernatural phenomena may be seen as a dramatic rupture with the Confucian worldview (Kendall 2009, 3–4). Indeed, the Cheju local elite were perturbed by the fact that Catholics did not serve the spirits (*sin*) or conduct *chesa* (Confucian ancestor rites) (Park Chan-Sik 2013, 102). Despite fundamental differences between Confucian and Christian worldviews, however, both denounced shamanic rituals as improper and transgressive, criticized shamans for exploiting the laity, and construed ritual consumption as pure waste.

Catholic priests who arrived on the island at the turn of the century presented far greater challenges to shamans and lay residents than the centrally appointed Confucian governors, who, except for a few radical reformers, notably Yi Hyŏngsang, allowed the local practice to continue. A Korean priest's confrontational evangelical approach, coupled with the abuses wrought by native converts and the ruthless taxation of a royal tax commissioner, resulted in a fierce backlash from the islanders, leading to the Rebellion of 1901, in which furious rebels slaughtered several hundred native Catholics, far more casualties than in any other Korean religious conflict.[1] A detailed discussion of this complex event is beyond the scope of this book, but the accounts of Catholic missionaries, which are consistent with Confucian records on the subject and had an impact on the anti-superstition campaign in succeeding generations, illuminate the missionaries' view of the island, its popular religion, and ritual consumption.

The French priest Jean-Charles Peynet and the Korean priest Kim Wŏnyŏng reached Cheju Island in late May 1899, much later than the

Roman Catholic and American Protestant missionaries who had already made widespread evangelical inroads on the mainland. Influenced by common assumptions about the islanders long held by mainland Korean intellectuals, they described the islanders as rude, overbearing, and murderous savages.[2] If racial prejudices were common in the turn-of-the-century Anglo-Saxon world (Ryu 2003, 187), the islanders were doubly racialized in these accounts.

The missionaries unequivocally expressed an extreme degree of animosity toward local practitioners. Bishop Mutel in Seoul believed them to be the embodiment of Satan and viewed proselytizing on the island as a way of snatching those souls from "the claws of Satan" (*Charyojip* 2:237). Informed by letters from Kim and Peynet, he emphasized the prominence of the practice and the power of shamans in the region in his 1901 annual report to the Société des Missions-étrangères de Paris, France's high-profile foreign missionary society: "Sorcerers (*sorciers*), forming among themselves an association, are very powerful, and they are spread throughout the island. Seeing a number of their former clients converting to Catholicism, they use every means to spread fear among the people. They spread the rumor that we gouge out the eyes of children and suck the marrow from the bones of the dead: absurdities that one hears in all parts of the world, thus clearly demonstrating their satanic origin" (*Charyojip* 4:236–41).

Mutel seethes at the very thought that the practitioners could accuse missionaries of being demonic cannibals.[3] Regardless of the actual perceptions of Cheju shamans, it is not difficult to imagine their resentment of the black-gowned priests who dared to introduce a foreign god and undermine the deities on which they relied. Indeed, the two parties were rivals competing for followers from the same pool.

In contrast to the rather apathetic Peynet, who, having had little success in proselytizing, left less than a year after his appointment, the Korean priest Kim was far more aggressive in his efforts to convert his own countrymen. Armed with his Christian ideology, the fervent priest worked fiercely for the spiritual salvation of the "ignorant and backward" people to whom "the benefits of Christianity were unknown" (Martel 1901, 539–40). In company with Mutel, he asserted, "All those who conduct shamanic rituals are servants of Satan and will become the enemy of God" (Kim Wŏnyŏng 1900, 68). The pious young Kim saw his missionary work as a battle with the devil.[4]

Kim called the local religious practice *idan* or *misin*, the Korean equivalents of heresy and superstition, respectively. His view echoes that of Western missionaries who began to arrive on the peninsula in greater numbers during the last quarter of the nineteenth century and played an important role in shaping the dominant anti-shaman discourse.[5] They replaced the Confucian-based term *ŭmsa*, referring to illicit or licentious rituals, with the Christian-centered *misin*, which remains in use today. The Sino-Korean compound *misin*—the first ideogram means "misguided" and the latter "belief" (C. *mixin*; J. *meishin*)—was a neologism of the late nineteenth century, although each of its ideograms had long been used in East Asia (Mayfair Yang 2008, 12). Influenced by Kim's disparaging view of shamanism, native Catholic converts, mostly the poor, committed numerous crimes against shamans and their followers. They set fire to shamanic shrines, demolished some of them, and used the lots for farming. They also cut down sacred trees and sold them or used the wood for building houses. In one instance, a posse of Catholics marched to a house where a ritual was being held, tied up the head of the household, and beat the shamans (*Charyojip* 2:51–77). These misdeeds surely offended deeply ingrained Cheju sensibilities. As a result, unlike urban cosmopolitans, who were attracted to the idea of Christianity as a bringer of modernization to Korea,[6] Cheju provincial elites were infuriated by the "uncivil" nature of Christianization and joined the anti-Catholic rebellion.

The church flatly denied that its converts had committed offenses,[7] emphasizing instead that the practitioners' long-lasting tyranny on the island needed to be eliminated. The church's accounts essentially resonate with Confucian scholars' view of shamans in that both spurned shamans for manipulating clients for gain and assumed the role of protector of the laity.

> Cheju has long been subject to many abuses by shamans, and they are especially serious in T'osan.[8] One head shaman leads many shamans in three counties and a financial association, from which he collects an enormous amount of profit. He distributes this profit to the shamans [in his association] and lets them go around each village and deceive gullible people.
>
> The so-called *sindang* are places that wicked shamans have designated and call *tangchip* [lit., "shrine house"]. . . . Unable to distinguish gods from evil spirits and without knowing that fortune and misfortune are of one's own making, ignorant women believe the perverted words. Many of them waste their assets in the worship of snakes and the shrine deities, neglect their livelihoods, and become lost.
>
> . . . Those family members who have not converted are carried away by shamans' infatuating words and waste a lot of money. The converted

members of the family work in vain to prevent this waste, leading to family disputes. Enraged, some converted members might even burn shrines and cut down [sacred] trees, but this is not intended to harm shamans. (*Charyojip* 2:50–51)

Local representatives of the church, who might not have directly observed the "satanic" rituals, relied on Confucian scholars' previous denunciations of shamanism to accuse contemporary shamans of being exploiters. In fact, except for the Christian notion of "distinguish[ing] gods from evil spirits," the first two paragraphs of this passage echo the Confucian descriptions of "respecting licentious rituals" (*sang ŭmsa*) from *Geography of Korea*. The church diverts attention from the primary cause of the problem, native Catholics' abuses, to the practitioners' purported financial tyranny. From its perspective, the guilty were not converted Catholic natives but wicked shamans, who were interested only in making a profit and deceiving the people, especially "ignorant women," with their "infatuating" words.[9]

Confident in the superiority of their own worldview, as were Confucian scholar-officials, Christian missionaries overlooked both the value of shamanic services to the laity and the ritual sponsors' notion of offerings. Ignoring the fact that, in contrast to Christian services, feeding the deities and spirits is essential to shamanic rituals, Robert Moose expressed his sadness on witnessing the "idiotic performance" that involved "a spread of the greatest array of Korean foods and fruits that [he and his wife] had ever seen" (1911, 195–96). Although the Catholic Church rather damaged the contemporary image of Christianity on the island due to its negative proselytizing, the new religion set a precedent for the way that Christians and other modernizers framed shamanic practice as a *superstition*, a term that quickly gained enormous currency during the colonial period and is even deployed today with discursive potency.

COLONIAL PERCEPTIONS: SUPERSTITION OR INDIGENOUS SPIRITUAL TOUCHSTONE?

Mired in the elite politics of the ethnic nation and culture, discourse on shamanism in colonial-era Korea became truly contested terrain. After Japan annexed Korea in 1910, the political power to regulate society officially shifted to the Government General of Korea (GGK), which intermittently attempted to eradicate the "superstition," purportedly for the sake of Korean civilization. In its eyes, the flourishing shamanism on Cheju was indicative of the island's backwardness, and its economic harm to the populace had to be eliminated. Desperate to regain their country's sovereignty, Korean reformers castigated the practice, particularly for its wastefulness and irrationality, a view not at odds with that of the colonial regime and thus inadvertently justifying Japan's colonial intervention.

In the midst of this anti-superstition sentiment, the unprecedented theory of shamanism as Korea's national spiritual repository emerged, making the vernacular religion an object worthy of study (Kim Seong-nae 1990). This conceptual frame of Korean shamanism persisted in the discussion and appropriation of the local popular religion during the postcolonial period. The grandiose elevation of shamanism would appear to be diametrically opposed to its long-standing vilification, creating an acute contradiction, but that does not hold when it comes to the subject of ritual economy. Entrenched in the idea of an uncorrupted primordialism, scholars, both nationalist and colonial, eschewed or dismissed the practical matters of practitioners and laity, such as the centrality of financial negotiations in ritual practice. Because they perceived Korean shamanism as an entity representing Korea, they viewed Cheju shamanism simply as a part of the whole rather than in its own right. However, the island's indigenous myths, recited during live performances, did draw the attention of Japanese scholars because of their "primitive" beauty.

ANTI-SUPERSTITION CAMPAIGN

The Meiji Government (1868–1912), which saw "irrational" folk religions as a challenge to the invention of state-centered Shintoism and a hindrance to civilization and enlightenment, termed them "pseudo-religions" (ruiji shūkyō) and made them subject to criminal law (Aono 1992; Choi Seok-Yeong 1999). The GGK applied this home policy to Korea, characterizing the prevalence of shamanism in its colony as a sign of the underdevelopment of Korean civilization. When legal class distinctions were abolished in 1894 as part of the Kabo reforms enacted under the auspices of the Japanese, shamans were emancipated from their lowborn status and ostensibly acquired the same status as the aristocratic elite class. However, once their activities became illegal, shaman organizations were forcibly disbanded, and first the Korean police and then, beginning in 1907, the Japanese military police pursued practitioners (Choi Seok-Yeong 1999, 87–90; Oppenheim 2005, 696; Walraven 1995, 110, 121). Lacking an elite conduit for communication and information, shamans had few official means of countering such indictments or the ever-increasing oppression from both the Japanese colonial power and their own countrymen.[10]

For more effective control of a poverty-stricken countryside roiled with discontent, where more than three-quarters of the population lived, the colonial regime launched the Rural Revitalization Campaign (Nongch'on Chinhŭng Undong) in 1932 (Shin and Han 1999). In 1936, a year before the Second Sino-Japanese War (1937–45), it also began the Mind Cultivation Movement (Simsin Chakhŭng Undong), intended to speedily turn Koreans into "subordinate citizens of the empire" (*hwangguk sinmin*) by teaching them "how to see the world through the prism of hope and spiritual wealth" (Kwang-Ok Kim 2013, 281). One of the chief tasks of these movements was the eradication of shamanism because the regime perceived it to be deleterious to Koreans' economic, medical, and spiritual or moral well-being (Murayama [1932] 2014, 389–403). The situation on Cheju was determined to be even worse than that on the mainland. Echoing the negative perceptions of Korean mainland elites, Zenshō Eisuke, a GGK-employed scholar, reported in 1929 that because the islanders had long been ignorant and benighted, many of them relied on practitioners of superstition (154).

Maeil sinbo, the GGK mouthpiece, often reported on the total campaign mounted by government authorities against a "cancer of the Korean mind" (*Chosŏn minjung ŭi chŏngsinjŏk am*) on Cheju, "known for the deeply rooted *misin* since a long time ago" (12 November 1937). It criticized shamanic activities for being anticultural and antiscientific, shamanic healing for going against a religion's primary purpose, and shamans for swindling gullible people (17 March 1938, 18 September 1938). One editorial lamented that "despite Governor Yi Hyŏnsang having destroyed shamanic shrines three hundred years ago, *misin* going against the current of the time" is still prevalent (12 November 1937). Staff members of the village office of P'yosŏn destroyed the T'osan Shrine, the oldest shrine on the island, purportedly in collaboration with residents during the autumn cleansing period (18 September 1938). According to the Japanese scholar Izumi Seiichi (1915–1970), who observed Cheju villages from 1936 to 1937, only smaller islands such as U-do and Kap'a-do near the main island were excepted from the purge (2014, 227, 229).

As did Japanese colonial officials, Korean elites used shamanism to define modernity and to assert themselves as modern subjects. To Korean intellectuals, shamanism represented an impediment not only to modernization but also to Korea's independence from Japan, making its eradication all the more urgent. Therefore, they were far more adamant about suppressing the practice than were the Japanese colonizers (Yi Yong-Bhum 2005, 169). Influenced by the proliferating anti-shamanism sentiment and campaign, the youth organization on Ojo-ri, located in southern Cheju, discussed the harm caused by the Spirit Worshippers' Association (Sungsin-in Chohap), a nationwide shamans' organization, and decided unanimously to prevent *kut* from taking place in their village (*Tonga ilbo* 1922, 4).

Korean newspapers, the voices of progress and modernization, frequently led the call for the "eradication of superstition" (*misin t'ap'a*).[11] Although newspapers are not always reliable "as a record of events," they are nonetheless "invaluable as witnesses to tastes, interests, and popular values" and as instruments of "a political program" (Noonan 1984, xiv). The word *misin* gained currency through print media, replacing the Confucian term *ŭmsa* and facilitating an active and purposeful suppression of the practice.[12] Following in the footsteps of Chosŏn dynasty Confucian scholars and turn-of-the-century urban elites influenced by Christianity, Korean newspaper writers bemoaned the unwholesome effects of the practitioners and asserted their fraudulence.[13] They portrayed shamans as stock villains who extorted fees through verbal sleight-of-hand, even comparing them to "stomach parasites" (*Tonga ilbo* 1932, 3). As a means of disparaging the practice, they often emphasized the significant national and personal expense incurred in sponsoring *kut*.

The anti-superstition rhetoric in Korean newspapers also had much in common with that of Japanese colonial authorities and their newspapers. Moreover, whereas the Japanese colonial scholar and policy maker Murayama Chijun (1891–1968) recognized both the benefits and the harm of shamanism and never recommended its total eradication ([1932] 2014, 371–422), Korean newspaper contributors impatiently criticized Japan's lenient policy toward the practice (Han 2000, 44). Regardless of the extreme ideological divisions, Korean intellectuals, including old Confucians and new Christians, shared an anti-superstition sentiment (Yi Yong-Bhum 2005, 170).[14] While rebellion was not an option for a population under the yoke of colonization, attacking a scapegoat was perhaps an easier way for most native-born intellectuals to help modernize the country and express their national pride.

SHAMANISM: PRISTINE KOREAN CULTURE

Faced with the dilemma of shedding the image of shamanism as the antithesis of a modern and independent Korea while simultaneously utilizing it in asserting Korean identity, Korean nationalist scholars chose to use it as a way of reconstructing Korea's autonomous past. Their take on shaman-ism was a theoretical tactic meant to offset the "Japanese claims of Korean cultural inferiority" (Allen 1990; Roger Janelli 1986; Tangherlini 1998, 130). Torii Ryūzō (1870–1953) was the first Japanese scholar to perceive Korean shamanistic customs and mores as "vestiges of ancient customs" ([1913] 1976, 347, quoted in Sorensen 1995, 338).[15] Influenced by the British evolu-tionist Edward B. Tylor, as were many other scholars of the time, Torii devoted much attention to the origins of race and culture. In his study "Korean-Japanese Have the 'Same' Origin" (Ni-senjin wa 'tōgen' nari),[16] he argued that Japan's colonization of Korea returned it to its original state and that the Koreans' clamor for independence was pointless (Torii [1920] 1974, 538–39). He postulated that Shinto and Korean shamanism were both derived from Siberian shamanism, but that contemporary Korean sha-manism was a remnant of the primordial Shinto, implying Korea's cultural time lag (Torii [1913]1976, 349).

Ch'oe Nam-sŏn (1890–1957) and Yi Nŭnghwa (1868–1945), known to be the most influential nationalist scholars, laid the foundations of the study of Korean shamanism and established the resilient notion of shamanism as the repository of Korean culture. In 1927, Ch'oe contributed "Notes on Shamanism" (Salman'gyo ch'agi)[17] and Yi "Treatise on Korean Shamanism" (Chosŏn musokko) to a special issue of *Enlightenment* (Kyemyŏng).[18] As indicated by the theme expressed in the subtitle, literature on an old reli-gion (*kogyo munhŏn*), they approached shamanism as an ancient religion and based their studies on literary research.

Well versed in Chinese classics and exposed to Japanese and Western scholarship during his study at Waseda University, Ch'oe used his writ-ings largely for political purposes in response to the colonialist construc-tion of Korean history. In his two related articles, "Notes on Shamanism" and "The Theory of Purham Culture" (Purham munhwaron), published in the same year (1927), he located the importance of shamanism in its assumed status as the origin of Korean and Northeast Asian religion, characterizing it as a grand abstraction. Like the Japanese scholars Ayu-kai Fusanosin and Torii Ryūzō, Ch'oe referred to Korean shamanism as *salman'gyo—salman* is a Tungusic word for "shamans" and *kyo* the Sino-Korean word for "religion"—indicating by the use of the term that he dealt with shamanism as "a distinct religion" (Sorensen 1995, 340). Setting his gaze on Manchuria, which he argued was the central stage of Korea's past, he introduced an exotic view of shamanism irrelevant to contemporary local practice.

In "The Theory of Purham Culture," Ch'oe's theoretical focus was the construction of the geocultural sphere from which the Northeast Asian race and civilization sprang and the sanctioning of the postulated shaman king Tan'gun as the "source and center of all East Asian civilizations" (Ch'oe Nam-sŏn 2013, 55–56; Pai 2000, 68). Utilizing terms and discourse used by Japanese scholars (Choi Seok-Yeong 1999, 52–55), Ch'oe attempted to assert the priority of Korea over Japan. Because the precise location and time of the origin are not provable, Ch'oe was able to overturn Torii's thesis by reversing the direction of diffusion. Echoing Indian nationalists under British rule who emphasized a spiritual concept of the nation (Chatterjee 1986), Ch'oe maintained that Koreans must achieve independence "by way of our spirit," if by no other means (Ch'oe, quoted in Allen 1990, 792). Thus, he turned not only to Korea's prehistory but also to a spiritual character that could live on regardless of territorial losses.

In his seminal work "Treatise on Korean Shamanism," Yi Nŭnghwa referred to the popular religious practice as *musok*, meaning "shamanic customs," instead of *ŭmsa*, the term commonly used among Chosŏn elites.[19] The topic of *ŭmsa* was dealt with in the section on customs in human-geographic books in the Neo-Confucian dynasty, and Yi replaced *p'ung* with *mu*, meaning "shaman" or "shamanic," thus *musok*, avoiding the rather derogatory *ŭmsa*. Yi's neologism *musok* is firmly established as scholarly and popular in present-day South Korea.[20] Chun Kyung-soo (Chŏn Kyŏngsu) maintained that Yi's adoption of the term was a political statement affirming Korea's cultural identity and sovereignty in the face of its dismissal as *misin* by Western missionaries and the Japanese (2012, 35–36). However, Yi himself did not attempt to ennoble the vernacular religion as contemporary practice. For him, *musok* was nothing but residue from the untainted *sin'gyo*, literally meaning "divine teachings" and referring to an idealized prototype Korean religion whose purity had been lost during the expansion of foreign religions such as Confucianism, Buddhism, and Daoism and from which Korean shamanic customs originated.[21] Examining available records related to *musok* was the only means of understanding the ancient Korean religion, which resulted in "Treatise on Korean Shamanism," an assembly of wide-ranging passages from primarily Korean historical sources augmented by his own rather fragmentary commentaries on the excerpts. Although this philological method indeed showed the historical depth of the phenomenon (Sorensen 1995, 341), the various excerpts also reveal much elite denunciation of the practice such as the hypocritical assessment of shamanic taxes and the expulsion of shamans from the capital. According to Yi's devolutionary view, contemporary shamanism was deficient compared to its unadulterated ancient form and lacked religious authenticity. Whereas nineteenth-century European ideas about devolution were an antimodern response to progress (Dundes 1969), Yi's and Ch'oe's backward glances came in response to colonialism.

These frustrated male scholars traced and constructed an ideal form of shamanism by focusing on a there-and-then that was spatially and temporally distant. While claiming native shamanism as fundamental to the Korean *Volksgeist*, they ignored the spiritual world that Korean shamans dealt with on behalf of individual clients. Whereas Ch'oe's interactions with practicing shamans are unknown, Yi consulted several practitioners but only to clarify some passages in old texts. Indeed, Yi was scarcely different from Confucian scholars in perceiving shamans as charlatans and their followers—especially women—as ignoramuses (Yi Nŭnghwa [1927] 2008, 327). The political motivation behind their inquiries left Yi and Ch'oe little room for examining contemporary shamanism.

Though his contributions to Korean shamanism studies are less well known than those of Ch'oe and Yi, Son Chint'ae (b. 1900) produced far more studies on Korean shamanism than did these scholars (Chun 2012). This intellectual giant, whose prolific and eclectic output is too broad to be easily assimilated and thus beyond the scope of this study, was the first Korean scholar who collected shaman songs (*muga*), starting as early as 1923, while still a student at Waseda University High School in Japan.[22] Just as European anthropologists and folklorists attempted to reconstruct national spirits through the oral narratives of peasants, Son felt an urgent need to rescue shaman songs before they completely disappeared in order to explore the folk religion that he perceived was deeply rooted in the hearts of Korean people (*minjung*) (1981, 1:570).

An anecdote in the preface to his 1930 collection illuminates his approach to fieldwork ([1930] 2012, 15–16). During the summer of 1923, while visiting the home of his friend in Hamhŭng (present-day North Korea), Son met a sixty-eight-year-old female shaman named Kim Ssangdol. The encounter, which Son initially thought of as fortuitous, went nowhere, as she was unwilling to talk about anything related to her profession because she did not take pride in it. When she revisited the home after three days, Son and his friend begged again and were rewarded with a song about the creation of heaven and earth, "Ch'angsega." Three years later, as a college student, Son revisited her, this time at her shrine. Impressed that this elite man had traveled all the way from Tokyo and taken the trouble to seek her out, she responded, to Son's great delight, to all his questions, recited chants for him to write down verbatim, and allowed him to take a picture of her in ritual costume.[23]

The novelty of this research event is astonishing in its historical context. Given that transcription is a critical act in cultivating the symbolic capital of narratives and their performers (Bauman 2011), Son's efforts to transform the ephemeral performance of the shaman songs, which had theretofore been denigrated, into a printed record was politically courageous. It was important not only for his academic interests but also for the shaman's pride. Although Son's agenda and presence controlled the situation, the shaman, who understood the impact of her collaboration with the elite man, also exerted her power. Son could transcribe only what she recited in the compromised ethnographic context, but this sufficed, because his primary purpose of salvaging the narratives was to understand fundamental Korean customs and the beliefs they contained.

This view of shamanism as the root of Korean culture prompted Korean scholars to withhold comment on the prevailing allegations against shamanism. Though they, as cultural reformers, might have agreed with many of the criticisms, doing so explicitly would have interfered with their political goal of asserting Korean identity through the folk religion. Their pride in shamanism remained anchored in an imagined prehistorical time, not in the hapless Korea in which they lived. Compared with the long-standing view of shamanism as an odious practice, the sanctification of shamanism as something inherently Korean was so radical that many elites of the time found it perturbing and were not at all eager to support the new perspective (Roger Janelli 1986, 33–34). Perhaps unknown to the vast majority of Cheju people, the polemic view of an idealized shamanism of the past and the degenerate practice of the present is apparent in the work of a Cheju native scholar. In his *True Record of Cheju Island* (Chejudo silgi), Kim Tubong observed that *sin'gyo* held Koreans together in the face of alien influences, but contemporary shamanism was a hindrance to Korea's civilization, and he praised the Presbyterian Church's educational effort to drive out evil customs associated with shamanic shrines (1936, 13). Unlike the newspaper contributors who attempted to discipline the populace by railing against shamanism, nationalist scholars focused on producing "spiritual knowledge" in the sense of historian Andre Schmid's use of the term by reorganizing the past into "a new nationalist framework" (2002, 142). However, the elites, scholars and nonscholars, all approached shamanism primarily in an attempt to alleviate their national agony while paying little attention to contemporary practice.

Presented as the best representative cultural aspect of the colonized, Korean shamanism served Japan's imperial project practically and, more importantly, ideologically. To the young island empire that had the closest cultural and geographic proximity to Korea and had presumably benefited from Korean learning, underscoring the temporal distance between the empire and the colony was important in the creation of its modern identity: "The more Koreans and their culture could be made to appear *temporally* distant from modern Japanese, the more impressive the empire appeared" (Atkins 2010, 57; italics in the original). The folk religion was useful for Japanese scholars in representing Korea as Japan's past and measuring its premodernity against the advances of their home country, thereby allowing them not only to justify its colonialism but also to lament the loss of purity that preindustrial Japan had purportedly enjoyed. This rendered the Japanese ethnographic gaze on colonial Korea full of contradictions.

This primitivist view is easily detected in Japanese scholars' choice of the subject, their research methods, and their interpretations of Korean shamanism. Similar to the GGK employee Murayama ([1929] 1990, 13), Akiba Takashi explained that Korean society was organized on two socioreligious principles—Confucian elite culture and shamanic folk culture—but he emphasized the dominance of the latter (Atkins 2010; Kim Seong-nae 1990; Nam 2006). The first would, of course, not serve well in depicting Koreans as "primitives" and was too reminiscent of China's long-standing influence on Korea's ruling class, which Japan was eager to undermine and replace. However, the "superstitious" folk religion associated with women, illiteracy, and lack of civilization, as Korean elite men themselves described it, suited "the category of primitive" (Atkins 2010, 58).

To Japanese scholars, shaman songs, particularly those from Cheju, were worthy of collection because they contained information about Koreans' uncorrupted lifeways. In his *Korean Shamans* (Chōsen no fugeki), Murayama praises shamanic rituals as an amalgam of primitive art and literature (*wŏnsi munye*) and practitioners as indispensable assets (*kongnoja*) for preserving the pristine quality of a distinctly Korean culture ([1932] 2014, 377–38). In order to illustrate how well the flavor of primitive literature is preserved in shaman songs, he presents two of the many *ponp'uri*, or mythic narratives, salvaged during his field trip to Cheju with Akiba in October 1931. Akiba includes transcriptions of fifteen *ponp'uri* and a *ch'ogamje* (the first segment of a Cheju ritual in which the lead shaman invites the deities to a ritual venue) collected from this trip in the first volume of *Study of Korean Shamanism* (Chōsen fuzoku no kenkyū) that he coauthored with Akamastu Chijō.[24] The volume introduces narratives from Seoul, Osan, and Cheju—with Cheju *ponp'uri* taking up the greatest number of pages, an indication of their particular interest in the region.

These Japanese scholars' attention to Cheju *ponp'uri* as a means of understanding Korea's past is evident in their approach to collecting them. For example, Akiba and Murayama had the principal and a teacher from an elementary school transcribe the narratives recited by Simbang Park Pongch'un of Sŏgwip'o outside the ritual context (Murayama [1932] 2014, 389). Indeed, due to their distinct story lines, *ponp'uri* are relatively easy to detach from a performance context and present in independent narrative form. Endowed with temporal depth, these primitive Cheju myths were considered by researchers to be like museum pieces worthy of collection and preservation (cf. Bauman 2011). However, why and how *simbang* recite them in performance were not within their purview as researchers. The reified Korean thought and culture that Akiba interpreted from his analysis of shamanic song-narratives bespeak his reductionist view of Korean society as feminine, rural, peaceful, and family-centered, a view that is detectable in almost all of his work (Nam 2006). Based on the commonly observed repetitions in the narratives that he saw as befitting agrarians but not urban dwellers, Akiba argued that the genre of *ponp'uri* preserves the most "original" and "primitive" form of shamanic songs ([1950] 1987, 157–58). To the Japanese scholars, *ponp'uri* were objects of both denigration and nostalgic envy.

Their conflicting view of Korean shamanism is most vividly observed in the dismay Akiba expressed at the purportedly growing number of shamans in Seoul who focused on the financial benefit they derived from their work, whom he referred to as "fake" shamans. Even though Akiba's fieldwork-based method allowed him to see shamans as professionals, he still felt that economic profit should not be a primary motive for practitioners: "In a city like Seoul, the number of shaman initiates whose primary aim is economic profit has increased. We can observe here a rather *absurd* phenomenon, the so-called modernization of shamans. This increase in fake shamans who are economically oriented indicates the transformation of a religion into something of a profitable venture and will eventually destroy the religious meaning of shamanism" ([1950] 1987, 82, my emphasis).

This caustic remark expresses Akiba's discomfort with the transformation of the supposedly agrarian practice, in which shamans, he assumes, were disinterested in personal gain. As evidenced by the fact that he took issue primarily with shamans in Seoul, he blamed this degenerative change on modernization. In this interpretive frame, rural shamans are depicted as noble savages, while those in Seoul have been tainted by modernity. Although modernity was often met with contradictory feelings of excitement over newness and anxiety over loss (Atkins 2010; Shields 2017, 9), Korea's modernization was more problematic to the colonial scholar. Akiba provides no clue as to what led him to that conclusion, but judgment seems to have been based on this ambivalence and on his assumption about the rural-urban dichotomy in which the rural represents primeval Korea while Seoul, as an exceptional place, has lost the supposed "primitive" character of the colony. In fact, according to extensive statistics provided to Murayama by police informants in 1930, earning a livelihood was the most common reason shamans nationwide, not just in urban areas, gave for their practice ([1932] 2014, 95–117), thus directly contradicting Akiba's rather procrustean assertion.

Like Akiba, Murayama perceived practitioners' economic interests in an overtly negative light. Cheju is a noteworthy case. According to him, "because the islanders do not perceive shamanism as a superstition, they are easily deceived by female shamans' honeyed words and dedicate food, money, and grain aplenty, hoping that the more they give, the more they will receive from the deities; thus, they are exploited by shamans" ([1932] 2014, 410). Yet reciprocity and sincerity, both of which are intertwined with the quantity and quality of offerings, not only stand at the core of the belief that prompts people to sponsor rituals but also move rituals forward. However, Murayama dismisses the islanders' view on the subject as though they were not capable of comprehending the meaning of ritual giving.

Unlike Korean anti-superstition campaigners and nationalist scholars, Akiba and Murayama associated the prominence of the practitioners' economic motive, not by any means a new issue in Korea (see chap. 1), rather pretentiously to changing times (Murayama [1932] 2014, 148). While aestheticizing shamanism as an undefiled tradition still alive in the colony and thriving particularly on Cheju, they bemoaned its modern contamination: prizing economic gain over primeval purity. Their impulse was to protect the practitioners from the nefarious effects of modernity and keep them well insulated from the societal changes Korea was undergoing due, in no small part, to colonial intervention. Ironically, while Murayama and Akiba were still enamored of the exotic primitives, Vice Governor-General Imaida Kiyonori, in his 1935 report *Thriving Chosen*, made congratulatory comments about the visible progress being made in the transformation of Korea instigated by Japan (Atkins 2010, 78). Whereas the colonial administrator sounded triumphant about Korea's "progress" under Japanese rule, Akiba and Murayama seemed to feel a sense of loss and dissatisfaction with the consequences of colonial development. Whether they were lamenting "a future Korea as contaminated by modernity as Japan itself had become" (Atkins 2010, 101) or the elimination of hierarchical differences between the empire and the colony is uncertain.

What is certain is that Korean and Japanese reformers and scholars alike took issue with ritual consumption, implicitly and explicitly, little considering the perspectives of practitioners or their clients. To them, economic matters associated with shamanic rituals were perceived as trivial or the very antithesis of religious authenticity, a notion that persists in postcolonial studies of Cheju shamanism.

REPUDIATION AND CAPITALIZATION IN POSTCOLONIAL SOUTH KOREA

In South Korea, while the age-old vilification of shamanism as a superstitious and fraudulent practice has persisted, Cheju shamanism has also been championed as the spiritual and cultural underpinning of the region (e.g., Beuchelt 1975a; Kim Seong-nae 2004; Pettid 2000a, 2001). This lofty notion, influenced by scholarship on Korean shamanism from the colonial period, has been fundamental to diverse interpretative and representative efforts. Scholars have been industrious in documenting and transcribing shamanic narratives that they construed as containing the quintessence of Cheju culture, an undertaking that has played a pivotal role in elevating a select local ritual to national heritage status. The view of shamanism as Cheju spirituality has also fueled the imagination of dissident cultural activists, further testifying to the space the popular religion occupied in the local cultural landscape. Different actors have contributed to the redemption of shamanism by purifying and aestheticizing it while shying away from the very sources of its long-standing stigma, such as ritual expense and trust in shamans, which are controversial issues even among ritual participants. In discourses on and enactments of the reified local tradition, the vernacular religion is portrayed as an ethereal entity far removed from the "vulgar materialism" and earthly desires depicted in ethnographic descriptions of *kut*.[25] They have reclaimed the popular religion as a form of regional cultural capital by redefining it in accordance with their ideological needs.

ROOTING OUT SUPERSTITION

The South Korean government maintained its anti-superstition stance until the end of the Park Chung Hee regime (1961–79). The first ROK president, Rhee Syngman (1948–60), retooled the life-improvement movements initiated by the colonial government and launched the New Life Movement (Sin Saenhwal Undong), which led to the destruction of village shrines (Chin Sŏng-gi [1959] 1992, 298). Guided by the notion of modernization and striving to boost economic development, the subsequent Park regime reconstituted it as the New Community Movement (Saemaŭl Undong) in the 1970s (Kim Eun-kyung 2009, 205) and condemned shamanism as an "anti-modern" faith that was "'unscientific, misleading, and thus unethical'" (Chungmoo Choi 1987, 74). From a rational economic perspective predicated on utilitarianism and austerity, the use of money for shamanic rituals was considered sheer waste.

The state-initiated anti-superstition campaign was pursued vigorously on Cheju. Characterizing shamanism as detrimental to "good morals and manners" and vilifying practitioners for being "manipulative," the provincial government ordered ward offices to regulate shamanic activities, even calling for mobilization of the police. On 31 March 1969, agents of the local government destroyed as many as 135 shrines scattered about the island, and in April 1970 they leveled 11 more shrines located in Cheju City (Ch'oe Kil-sŏng 1974, 113–14).

Some unfortunate shamans were arrested for fraud (*sagi*) as described in a local newspaper during the movement's heyday.

The police booked three female shamans—ages twenty-seven, twenty-eight, and thirty; names not given—on charges of fraud and planned to arrest them on 30 March 1972. The arrest of shamans is the first on the island. According to the police, the shamans *deceived* a woman who had lost her mother during the Namyŏng Ferry accident by saying that her mother could not enter the otherworld (*chŏsŭng*) without being consoled through the performance of a *kut* and took 30,000 won [US$30] for ritual offering expenses. When the *kut* was over, they requested an additional 60,000 won [US$60], saying, "Your mother needs money for travel expenses to go to the world of paradise." In addition, they *swindled* two other women by threatening them with family misfortune if they failed to conduct appropriate *kut*. So they obtained, in all, 210,000 won [US$210] by fraud. (*Jeju sinmun*, 31 March 1972; my emphasis)

The Namyŏng Ferry traveling from the Sŏgwi port of Cheju to Pusan (on the southeastern tip of the mainland) sank on 15 December 1970, claiming 322 lives (Kim Pong-ok 2000, 366). For such tragic deaths, bereaved families usually sponsor a ritual for those who have lost their lives in the ocean, to relieve the souls' pent-up grief and to help propel the deceased into the otherworld. Given the scale of this particular tragedy, *simbang* even now refer to the incident in their commemorative chant at the end of *kut*.

The police report mentioned in the article interprets these consoling efforts as a practitioners' trick for exploiting the gullible. However, the accusations most likely originated with the ritual sponsors themselves; otherwise, it would have been difficult for the police to learn the details of the transactions and arrest the shamans. Because a substantial portion of the ritual cost ultimately ends up in the hands of the shamans and the ritual outcomes generally are not immediately obvious, some sponsors may feel cheated and even fault themselves for getting involved with the "superstitious" practice.

Although the government ceased official suppression of shamanism at the end of the Park regime, a broad spectrum of people continued to ridicule shamanism and declare ritual expenses to be wasteful. The charges against shamans came not only from die-hard antagonists, who often singled out ritual expense as a target of the anti-superstition program, but also from erstwhile ritual sponsors. However, eager to defend the tradition, advocates of Cheju shamanism depicted the folk religion and its consumers in a romantic light, suffused with the glow of tradition and mythical origins.

SALVAGING "PRISTINE" TALES

Following the precedents of the colonial-period scholars Son, Akiba, and Murayama, many postcolonial scholars of Cheju shamanism have used ethnographic documentation to salvage shamanic chants, particularly *ponp'uri* that they reified as a vessel for the Cheju Islanders' traditional belief system and thought. Whereas Japanese scholars Akiba and Murayama expressed their discontent with the profit motives of shamans and stressed the economic harm of the practice, South Korean scholars, in company with nationalist scholars during the colonial period, scarcely mention the detrimental economic aspects of the practice. Constructed as the underpinning of local identity and exoticized as the emblem of its cultural difference from the mainland, Cheju shamanism was, in their view, fine and beautiful (cf. Whisnant 1983).

The first-generation scholars of Cheju shamanism played a leading role in studies of Korean shamanism at large (Kim Inhoe 1982, 18–19). Chang Chugŭn (1925–2016) was the first mainland scholar to collect the living indigenous myths. His 2007 essay "Recollection on Studies of Cheju Shamanism" (Chejudo musok yŏn'gu ŭi hoego) offers much insight into his research method and his nostalgic view of the *ponp'uri* and Cheju shamanism, which are, to some extent, similar to those of Akiba and Murayama with respect to "the primordial purity of Korean cultural life" (Atkins 2010, 59). After completing his undergraduate degree in Korean literature at Seoul National University, where Akiba and Akamatsu had worked as faculty during the colonial period, Chang held a position as a full-time lecturer at Cheju National University from 1955 until the spring of 1957. During his tenure, this literary scholar became fascinated with the outlying island's natural beauty and the indigenous myths that, to his astonishment, were still being recited by *simbang* at ritual performances. The "primordial" (*wŏnch'ojŏk*) tales, Chang felt, surpassed the value of their Western rivals *The Iliad* and *The Odyssey*, because their performance in religious ceremonies had continued into modern times.[26]

An anecdote about Chang's fieldwork during the summer of 1962 is particularly telling regarding his approach to *ponp'uri* as oral literature (Chang 2007, 15–16). Chang had Simbang Ko Taejung recite myths at his home and paid him for these recitals performed outside the customary ritual context. In an effort to simulate a ritual setting, the *simbang* set up an offering table, wore ritual attire, and sat on a mat.[27] Each time the *simbang* recited a couplet from a myth, Chang and his research assistants would repeat it while writing it down by hand. The daily sessions lasted more than ten hours, and they kept at it for six days.[28] Through the determined intensity of their labor, they salvaged the "pristine" tales.

Although Chang saw the value of the *ponp'uri* in live performances, he chose to document them in a decontextualized setting. This choice might have been influenced by his literary training, technological limitations, and the availability of ritual performances during his short visit—summer is a slack time for large-scale rituals. However, his fascination with *ponp'uri* was undeniably the primary motivation for his research. In his view, *simbang* are purveyors of the narrative tradition and, like singers of tales, reproduce the myths, and the scholars are collectors of the stories. The *simbang*'s ritual role and the narratives' function in situated contexts were relatively insignificant to Chang.

Chin Sŏng-gi (b. 1936) and Hyŏn Yongjun (1931–2016), the first generation of native Cheju scholars, contributed much to valorizing Cheju shamanism with their exemplary research. Given the complexity of indigenous ritual speeches, their knowledge of the Cheju dialect and idiomatic expressions was an important asset. Eager to preserve their home island's cultural heritage and promote it to the outside world, these scholars have poured a tremendous amount of time and energy into collecting shamanic song-narratives and publishing material on Cheju shamanism. To them, shamanic culture is the spiritual and cultural touchstone of the islanders, and collecting the *ponp'uri*, in which the islanders' "dreams" and "philosophy" are reflected, is a way of restoring the pristine spirit of the islanders and preventing the disappearance of the indigenous tradition in the face of ruinous outside influences (e.g., Chin [1959] 1992, 292–95; Hyŏn Yongjun 1976, 1).

The compilations of Cheju *ponp'uri* and other genres of shamanic chants culled either outside ritual contexts or from ongoing ritual events were produced in great quantity.[29] Reflecting this research convention, which has been predominant in framing scholarly enterprises, *simbang* who had previously worked with other scholars at times instructed me on how to do my fieldwork by telling me, for example, when I should turn my cassette player on and off (cf. Chong 2008, 379). As I recorded their chitchat during coffee breaks, some shamans kindly said, "Miss Yun, this is not important. Turn off the recording machine and come join us in drinking coffee." After a small-scale ritual, a *simbang* told me with a smile that she had recited a longer-than-usual version of a myth especially for me. The compilations can, of course, be dismissed as mechanical and seen as an example of reducing the vast and fluid shamanic world to "an inventory of signature ritual traditions" (Kendall 2009, xx), but this view misses the point of the heroic "salvage" efforts. Transforming shamanic lore into scholarly material by rendering fleeting verbal performances into stable, tangible, and objectifiable data is necessary for further reflection and analysis. This is also an act of valorizing the ritual lore, previously disdained by most elite members of the society. The texts have found favor with a growing audience that has a taste for "vanishing" traditions and embraces time-honored shamanic songs from the exotic island as a way of connecting with their own "primitive selves."

However, while scholars focus on a collective island spirit that they imagine to be contained in the narratives and are preoccupied with their imagined original versions of these narratives, they have been oblivious to the fact that the *simbang* recite the *ponp'uri* in rituals not merely for the sake of maintaining island traditions but for specific rhetorical purposes to achieve ritual efficacy, also a primary concern for ritual sponsors. Spinning out a myth for a large-scale ritual or condensing it into a few sentences for a small-scale ritual would not be considered unusual by either the practitioners or their clients. The disparity between scholarly enterprises and on-the-ground experience cannot be made more obvious than through my own and others' ethnographic research. Scholars are quite focused on verbatim reproduction and word-for-word transcription, while lay participants do not pay much attention to myth recitations in rituals and only a few can reproduce them fully outside ritual contexts (Tangherlini and Park 1990, 85–87, 93). The literary scholarship has inevitably left out concerns for the here and now, an important aspect for individual *simbang* and their clients.

BANKING ON HERITAGE

Transforming the ephemeral oral performances into tangible "text objects" contributed much to the construction of Cheju shamanism as an intangible cultural heritage (Bauman 2011, 6), a project that elevated its status while simultaneously alienating it from its quotidian practice. The Park regime's anti-shaman campaign prompted proponents of shamanism such as scholars and cultural activists to come to its defense. They attempted to "correct" the regime's "distorted" view of a practice that Korean scholars claimed to be deeply entrenched in the tradition and culture of Koreans.[30] These academic plaudits for Korean shamanism, influenced by the nationalist scholarship from the colonial period (Tangherlini 1998), fanned popular enthusiasm for the vernacular religion among those in search of Koreanness and sought its official endorsement as heritage.

Between 1980 and 1996, the government contradicted its previous stance on the popular religion and designated a total of ten communal rituals representing different regions as Important Intangible Cultural Properties (Chungyo Muhyŏng Munhwajae). In 1962, in an attempt to transform his image from a military general who had assumed power by means of a coup into that of a cultural ruler (Chungmoo Choi 1987, 65–74; Jongsung Yang

2003), President Park institutionalized the safeguarding of selected tangible and intangible cultures through the promulgation of the Cultural Property Protection Law (CPPL). Nevertheless, no *kut* was patronized by the government during his presidency due to his disdainful view of the practice.[31] The Yŏngdŭng Kut, a communal ritual performed annually at the Ch'ilmŏri shrine in Cheju City (for details, see chap. 5), was one of the three rituals that earned the title in 1980, thanks to the early scholarly valorization of the local shamanism.

This designation was granted, not coincidentally, just a few months after the presidential inauguration of Chun Doo Hwan, who had seized power through a coup following Park Chung Hee's assassination in 1979 and needed to "claim a legitimizing inheritance of tradition" (Tangherlini 1998, 139). In this modern project of heritage, the designated ritual was selected as an example of the traditional performing arts genre and the skill holder (*kinŭng poyuja*) singled out for his performance skills.[32] While the government patronizes the program, it is primarily folklorists and anthropologists who produce the social knowledge about what constitutes cultural heritage and select items worthy of national recognition. Clients' criteria for what makes a good shaman—such as compassion, ritual efficacy, and "fair" service fees—are scarcely considered in the heritage rationale, although the practice is maintained through the symbiotic relationship between practitioners and their clients.

Members of the Association for the Ch'ilmŏri Shrine Yŏngdŭng Kut Preservation have performed staged versions of the ritual for local, national, and global events, such as the inauguration ceremony of President Rho Tae Woo and the opening ceremony of the 1988 Olympic Games. As many scholars have pointed out, redefining *kut* as performing art and putting them to new uses excludes the religious aspect, that is, the spiritual power of shamans, which is vital to them and their clients.[33] More specifically, the process sanitizes the rituals by emphasizing only the "safe" aspects of Korean shamanism that Chongho Kim characterizes as dealing with "the field of misfortune" while eliminating the "uncanny" and "dangerous" elements (2003).[34] Shamans' artistic skills in singing and dancing, prized in the heritage program, have long been appreciated as entertainment in both household and communal rituals (Keith Howard 1998; Walraven 1999a, 179), but that is not what people primarily seek from shamans. Rather, they have sought their services for their spiritual power, which they also fear. In the enactment of the designated ritual, delicate matters such as fee negotiations and the proper quantity and quality of offerings, important and even points of contention in household rituals, are not an issue between shamans on stage and the audience.

Therefore, despite their ostensible incompatibilities, the heritage program and the earlier anti-shamanism campaign are actually congruent, in that the ROK government did not take issue with *kut* as "folk play or entertainment" (*minsok nori*) despite its attempts to remove the purported medical and economic harm of the "superstition" (Ch'oe Kil-sŏng 1974, 112–13). Even after the official endorsement of the rituals, the long-standing view of shamanism as unscientific and wasteful persists, as does the perception that shamans are exploitative. The double standard could not be more obvious in light of the fact that select shamanic performances are protected under the Cultural Conservation Law, but shamanic healing is illegal under Korean medical law (Chongho Kim 2003, 218)[35] and shamans are occasionally arrested for fraud. The government does not encourage citizens to invest any substantial amount of their household budgets in rituals as a means for resolving personal problems. Although the practitioners may defend their social position by borrowing the heritage rhetoric, because that status is irrelevant to the needs of most clients, shamans remain vulnerable to the old stereotypes related to their ritual roles.[36] The heritage regime, based on the premise that heritage represents "all that is good and important about the past" (Smith 2006, 29), presents contemporary shamans as custodians of the tradition, subjecting them to criticism for not living up to the idealized and imaginary image of shamans from times past (Kendall 2009, 206), when they were supposedly pure and indifferent to economic interests.[37] The effect is the production of incongruent and contradictory messages pertaining to a popular religion that is both celebrated and stigmatized.

RITUALS OF RESISTANCE

While scholars and the government sanctified Cheju shamanism by rather conservative acts such as documenting verbal performances and endorsing the Yŏngdŭng Kut as national heritage, cultural activists opposed its objectification and instead reenacted elements of indigenous rituals in a contemporary sociopolitical context. In 1980, a group of radical students at Cheju National University formed a theatrical group called Sunurŭm.[38] The establishment of the theatrical group was aligned with the *minjung* (subaltern people) cultural movement that emerged early in the 1970s and withered away in the early 1990s. It was led by urban students and elites who were searching for their native Korean cultural roots and attempting to give authority to the underprivileged. Shamans generally promote harmony in rituals, although in-depth ethnographic research has shown that during a séance, *simbang*-mediated lamentations of those who died through tragic historical violence challenge the state's official history, which veiled that violence (Kim Seong-nae 1989a, 1989b). However, the Sunurŭm activists often expressed their own radical political messages through invented shamanistic ritual performances during demonstrations and at on-campus festivals.[39] If not a panacea for all social problems—including neocolonialism, dictatorship, and socioeconomic inequality—activists felt that *kut* could at least be used to "revive the depleted spirit of the nation" (Chungmoo Choi 1995, 109). Sunurŭm shared the general subversive spirit of the cultural movement on the peninsula, but it also opposed the mainland's political and economic domination of Cheju (Kim Seong-nae 1989a, 223–24; Mun 1987a, 207–9). The group's manifesto highlighted Cheju's historical position on the cultural periphery but emphasized its potential to revitalize the mainland's traditional culture, which was threatened by encroaching Western cultures (Mun 1987a, 207).

The cultural activists approached shamanism differently than had the government or academics. Playwright and former Sunurŭm leader Mun Mubyŏng, Hyŏn Yongjun's former graduate student at Cheju National University, vehemently criticized scholars for objectifying *kut*, arguing that they should not be "anatomized as a laboratory frog" (Mun 1987a, 185). In contrast to Hyŏn, whose scholarship on Cheju shamanism was based on traditionalism aligned with the government's cultural policy, Mun observed that, unlike the usual rituals conducted jointly by the *simbang* and their clients so as to resolve a specific problem, *kut* sponsored by the heritage program is performed without an urgent need or a bond between the skill holders (*simbang*) who dance mechanically and the posh onlookers who observe it as though it were a performance of barbaric dances (191). Instead of "fossilizing rituals as a curio" devoid of substance and validity, as the heritage program does (191), he claimed that the activists' task is to solve real-life problems as *simbang* heal patients through a *kut*.

Mun went so far as to assert that activists should identify themselves as humble *simbang* in order to resolve sociostructural problems and build the utopian world (1987a, 218). The fact that cultural activists constructed shamanism in a way that forwarded their own vision, without considering the practitioners' interests or the realities of their trade, came into sharper focus when a former Sunurŭm activist told me of his displeasure with shamans' aggressive contract negotiations. When his organization sponsored a *kut* commemorating and consoling the victims of the April Third Events in 2002, he noted that the lead *simbang* "first brought up the issue of money for the ritual." He seemed to feel that the shamans should accept whatever honorarium they were offered for such a solemn community event. In contrast, I spoke to a star *simbang*, a frequent performer at staged rituals, who criticized the activist's paltry remuneration for a service that involved the careful coordination of many shamans. These two remarks reveal vastly different perspectives on the *simbang*'s social role and professional rights.

In legitimizing their own definition of the island and its shamanism, the guardians of the uncorrupted tradition assumed a mantle of moral superiority as advocates of the oppressed (cf. Tangherlini 1998, 129). However, their vision of the Korean shaman as a "revolutionary or cultural hero who becomes the model of the subaltern class people" (Kim Seong-nae 1989a, 227) overlooks the fact that shamans had long sold their labor and skills to a wide range of people, including privileged court women and politicians (Kendall 1985a, 31; Sarfati 2009; Walraven 1995, 129). Although the activists' interest in reviving the indigenous popular religion was couched in terms of serving the community, in reality it served to augment their moral authority and power as leaders of local activism (cf. Chau 2006, 13; Sun 1991, 177–79).

The anti-superstition campaign condemned the local popular religion and motivated some of the natives to shun the tradition, while scholars, the governments after the Park regime, and cultural activists have elevated Cheju shamanism by constructing it according to their own visions, which, ironically, removed its religious meaning and context, the key to the practice. *Simbang* were revered as purveyors of traditional tales by scholars, as cultural ambassadors by the government, and as art masters by activists, rather than as ritual specialists and spiritual healers. While promoting the popular religion, the elite avoided the issues that stigmatized shamans and the practice, particularly that of ritual expenses, which was important to practitioners and clients, as though these aspects were unimportant and undesirable.

CONCLUSION

On the one hand, on behalf of their evangelical and reform efforts, Catholic missionaries and Korean and Japanese modernizers used the prevalence of shamanic practice on Cheju to emphasize the islanders' backwardness and accuse the local practitioners of financial fraud. On the other hand, proponents of Cheju shamanism extolled it as the epitome of the island's culture for different and, at times, conflicting reasons. The framing of shamanic rituals and songs as the primary living link with prehistorical Korean thought, first developed during the colonial period, resulted in an ongoing temporalization of shamanism in terms of the past in the discourses and enactments of Cheju shamanism in postcolonial South Korea. Validating their survival through a supposedly long history, scholars salvaged Cheju *ponp'uri* with little regard for specific ritual situations or the pragmatic concerns of ritual participants. The controversial aspects of the popular religion, such as the spiritual power of shamans and "extravagant" consumption, for which the government had previously attempted to eradicate the practice in the name of modernization, were neatly eluded in the process of designating and appropriating a Cheju ritual as a national heritage. Critics of the establishment, activists adopted the popular religion for their resistance movement, which idealized shamans as cultural heroes for the disenfranchised.

However, both condemners and supporters undermined the importance of the ritual economy and ignored the perspectives of ritual participants. In the view of critics, shamans' motives are purely profit-driven; thus, any economic investment in their services indicates a lack of financial, intellectual, and moral prudence on the part of the laity. Rather than challenging this charge directly, advocates of Cheju shamanism redefined it in a way that trivialized ritual consumption and romanticized practitioners and consumers. The effect is to inadvertently join the condemners in ignoring their agency and dignity. According to my fieldwork experience, *simbang* care about both their clients' well-being and their own business interests, and consumers are careful in spending their resources on rituals and critical of *simbang* whose personal gain is deemed excessive. The proponents' seemingly redemptive efforts have undoubtedly piqued curiosity about Cheju shamanism but have also helped perpetuate an idealized image of it, in which the motives and interests of individual shamans and their clients are largely ignored.

The value of ritual cannot be measured solely through economic reductionist logic. From the participants' perspective, ritual is undeniably an economic activity that entails delicate negotiations and compromises between the parties involved. Ethical, logical, and economic contradictions arising from ritual consumption can be more fully addressed only by attending to discursive practices within ritual contexts.

3 THE ART OF RITUAL EXCHANGE

ABUNDANT OUTLAYS OF SACRIFICIAL OBJECTS SUCH AS MONEY, food, and cloth are commonplace in *kut* on Cheju, as they are on Korea's mainland. Unlike Confucian, Christian, and modernist critics of ritual expenditure, *simbang* and their clients do not, of course, see it as wasteful, and patrons willingly provide sacrificial objects in anticipation of receiving something of greater value. This pragmatic approach is quite different also from that of South Korean elites who have defended and appropriated indigenous rituals as an icon of the island's identity and spirituality. Sacrifice is a form of exchange of a contractual nature (Hubert and Mauss [1899] 1964, 100; Stewart and Strathern 2008). People make offerings not merely to please deities and spirits but in anticipation of receiving gifts in return— deities granting their wishes (*do ut des*) and forsaken spirits refraining from disturbing the living (*do ut abeas*). Due to the power asymmetry between gods and humans in the Korean shamanic worldview, the powerful gods can demand without feeling obligated to reciprocate (Kendall 2009, 219n14). However, both practitioners and patrons see a ritual fundamentally as an economic activity based on a belief in reciprocity and in the deities' compassion. They tend with care to matters such as the quality and quantity of offerings because these indicate, in their view, the depth of a patron's devotion and sincerity, thus illuminating the nexus of belief and material expenditure in the practice.

While the importance of reciprocity in Korean shamanic rituals is well documented in rural and urban rituals,[1] less explored is *how* the act of sacrifice is made palatable to the recipients by ritual specialists. More than a century ago, Henri Hubert and Marcel Mauss viewed sacrifice as a "highly performative act" in the sense that it changes relationships rather than reflecting them (Stewart and Strathern 2008, xvii, noting Hubert and Mauss [1899] 1964, 99). Shamans and clients strive to please the spirits not only by offering sacrificial objects but also by feasting them and entertaining them with dance and music, in the hope of ensuring a suitable return (Hogarth 2009, 62–83; Seo 2002). The *simbang*'s ritual role is indispensable for this exchange. The specialists *publicly* transform mundane objects into sacrifices acceptable to the deities through their proper performance. For example, legal tender and ordinary goods with use value become possessed of symbolic significance through the *simbang*'s compassionate and competent performance. In contrast to critics' assumptions that shamans use "wicked" words to manipulate gullible people for personal gain, practitioners articulate and enact their compassion with their patrons and their respect for the gods by means of their eloquence.

Exploring the symbolic or moral values of making a sacrifice is pivotal to understanding why making offerings to invisible beings or forces can be understood as a matter of sense, skill, and significance, rather than as irrational, wasteful, or exploitative. The performative power of shamans' verbal artistry (Chungmoo Choi 1987, 1989) in conjunction with ritual exchange is of particular importance. Specific instances of social conduct and symbolic activity illustrate the "practical knowledge" (Bourdieu 1977) that individual practitioners identify as significant in ritual exchange. The best way to learn about the proper modes and meanings of reciprocity is by observing the rituals. In the grand-scale *sin kut* described here, a seasoned shaman, whom I call "Simbang Min," expressed indebtedness to her tutelary spirits for her livelihood. This *simbang*-sponsored ritual usually lasts much longer and costs more than those sponsored by the laity, affirming their own belief in the value of generous ritual spending.

The goods are dedicated through practitioners' verbal communication with supernatural beings. Although scholars have emphasized the primordial beauty and literary value of Cheju *ponp'uri*, *simbang* recite them for immediate rhetorical purposes in concrete ritual situations. The performance of the myth of Saman poignantly illustrates both the cultural logic of sponsoring a ritual and the potency of the narrative recitation in the live performance. By employing their artistic skills in specific contexts—whether ritual speech, narrative, performance, or behavioral action—*simbang* present offerings prepared by patrons to the gods and spirits and negotiate with them on behalf of their clients. The particular kind of reciprocity between humans and the spirits on which rituals are based can be more fully appreciated by paying attention to the intentionality, form, and context of giving.

A RITUAL AT SIMBANG MIN'S

I arrived at Simbang Min's house at dawn on 25 December 2001. The day was quite windy and a bit cloudy; bleak and desolate fields spread out in front of the practitioner's small house, rather isolated from those of her neighbors and marked by a fluttering ritual flag.[2] A huge tent had been attached to the house front, a temporary extension of her narrow home that provided more space for the upcoming performance of a nine-day ritual, which lasted until 2 January 2002. It was the grandest *kut* I have ever witnessed. The interior of the tent was still under construction when I arrived. A long white cloth and other decorations hung from the tent roof. Hard plastic boxes had been inverted, placed on the ground, overlaid with large sheets of Styrofoam, and covered with mats. This arrangement was designed to keep the chill of the cold earth from participants seated on the mats. Two propane stoves had been lit to warm the air inside the tent. One side of the tent allowed entry into the main part of the house, and another connected to an annex, a small room used as a kitchen and for washing up. The privy was located on the opposite side of the house. The main building consisted of a living room, two bedrooms, a walk-in storage space, and a room called *tangju-bang*, where Simbang Min's tutelary ancestors (*tangju*) were enshrined on a built-in table near the back wall. The bedrooms faced one another across the living room, as did the tiny storage space and the *tangju-bang*. All the sliding doors had been removed in an effort to accommodate a large number of participants and ease their movements in the cramped interior.

A group of well-groomed *simbang* (three male and four female) prepared to perform the nine-day ritual inside the house and attached tent. They were hired specifically for the ritual and would take various roles in turn—chanting, singing, dancing, and playing musical instruments. They had moved into Simbang Min's home a day earlier and had already transformed the otherwise rather shabby house into a splendid ritual setting. White and colored paper decorations (*kime*) were attached to the upper walls and hung from the ceilings of the living room and the *tangju-bang*,[3] the latter warmly lit by two candles on the table. Subdued electric lighting hung from the back ceiling behind white paper scissored into geometric patterns.

An array of offerings—including foodstuffs, piles of bundled cloth, and stacks of folded paper to be used as pseudo-money—was laid out in the tent and in the patron's shrine room. In addition to the decorative fake money hanging from the ceiling, folded 10,000-won bills ornamented the tops of rice bowls. Throughout the ritual, at appropriate moments, Simbang Min seemed to spare neither legal tender nor fake money when it was called for. A few bundles of rolled cloth were laid on the offering tables, and additional cloth was stacked in the corners of the tent. The most conspicuous feature of the scene was food, the most basic solace for humans, ancestors, and gods alike. Several tables offered lavish spreads: female *simbang* had meticulously laid out liquor, rice, rice cakes, boiled eggs, cooked fish, various fruits, and commercially packaged hardtack biscuits (*kŏnppang*). Some kinds of food were offered boiled or parched, while others were raw or moist. While there is a degree of flexibility, people still abide by certain rules and forms in regard to what is served and how it should be prepared and displayed in accordance with the understood preferences of the recipients.[4]

The displayed food changed a bit as the ritual proceeded, but it was always abundant, especially in view of Simbang Min's obvious lack of affluence. Several women labored constantly in the tiny kitchen, and the patron saw to it that both the supernatural beings (a range of deities, ancestors, and ghosts) and the humans present (her family, relatives, visitors, the *simbang* who performed the ceremony, and a few scholars who had assembled to witness this rare ritual) were all well fed. Simbang Min, wearing a traditional Korean costume (*hanbok*), seemed to be everywhere as she ensured the proper orchestration of her big event.

The ritual required an enormous investment of time and energy on the part of the patron, the talents and hard work of several *simbang*, and, of course, money. Comparing this ceremony to *chesa*, the lead *simbang* said to me, "There is an old saying that goes like this: You will run out of rice for dinner after *chesa* and a year's worth of food after a *kut*."[5] Although *pujo*, or allowance aid, donated by her relatives, clients, and colleagues would have somewhat alleviated her financial burden, Simbang Min was responsible for the primary expenditure. One of Simbang Min's colleagues told me that Min had asked her for a loan to help fund the exorbitantly expensive ritual.[6] Why would Simbang Min, who usually performs for her clients, sponsor such an extravagant ritual for herself at her own expense? If, as often asserted, shamans collect extortionate fees from clients, how do we explain their own ritual consumption on no client's behalf?

RECIPROCITY BETWEEN *SIMBANG* AND THE GODS

The nine-day event was Simbang Min's third *sin kut*, in which several *simbang* participated and interpreted indigenous Cheju ritual lore, the richness and depth of which, many *simbang* argue, make it nearly impossible to master.[7] Sponsoring such a large event also increases a *simbang*'s professional reputation. But Cheju shamans sponsor *sin kut* primarily for the purpose of expressing gratitude to the gods (*sin*)—including general shamanic deities and spiritual ancestors—for granting them spiritual power and thus a livelihood. They characterize the ritual as one in which *simbang* return to the gods a portion of what they have earned (*sin ege pŏrŏ mŏgŭn yŏkka rŭl pach'inŭn kut*).[8] Explicit here is the idea of reciprocity. Like relationships among humans, a *simbang*'s relationship with the gods is based on both generosity and mutual interest, and the relationship must be nurtured in order to maintain its quality (cf. Chau 2006; Hogarth 2009, 245-47; Mauss [1950] 1990).

Being a *simbang* means that the ritual practitioner is in a close relationship with the gods not only spiritually but also economically. Most Korean shamans depend entirely on religious trade for their livelihoods (Chongho Kim 2003, 50; Tangherlini and Park 1988). Due to social prejudice, poor education, and the perceived threat of supernatural harm if they neglect their vocation, they have little else to fall back on as a means of earning a living (Hwang Ru-shi 2000, 179). Although the image of noted shamans and of the vernacular religion itself has improved greatly in recent decades, the profession still remains stigmatized. As in the myth of Ch'ogong—in which the daughter of Prime Minister Yu becomes the first *simbang* and consequently comes to ruin—contemporary practitioners are commonly perceived as having made a wreck of their lives (*p'alcha rŭl kŭrŭch'ida*) (Mun 1999; Kim Seong-nae 1989a, 179–84). The life stories of *simbang* testify to the many hardships they often endure.[9]

Simbang Min's lot was also a hard one. Born in 1947, she was fifty-five years old and a widow with four grown children (one son and three daughters, all married save the youngest daughter) when I first met her. After the death of Min's father during the April Third Events, when she was two years old, her family moved from a village located on the slope of Mount Halla to the seaside village where her mother's parents had lived. Although a well-known *simbang* in the area, Min's mother, whose father was also a *simbang*, did not want her daughter to follow in her footsteps. However, Min was encouraged to do so by a shaman when she began to have strange dreams and suffered paralysis of her facial muscles at the age of twelve. Within a few years, she began to learn shamanic skills from her mother, her mother's stepbrother, and other senior *simbang*. Her first marriage, about which she was somewhat reluctant to provide details, failed when she was still childless. Her second marriage was with a man from the mainland who had no sympathy for a *simbang*'s profession. Due to childbearing and conflicts with her husband, she was unable to dedicate herself to the practice for about ten years. When she was in her mid-thirties, her husband moved to the mainland, where he lived with another woman; he returned later to Cheju and died rather young, at fifty-five.

Shamanic practice was the only means of survival available to this de facto single mother of four children who was without formal education and could neither read nor write. When she was thirty-one, the people of her village designated her the *tang maein simbang*, the one who performs community rituals for the tutelary gods. Over the years, she performed communal and household rituals in her district and neighboring areas, both as a lead *simbang* and as an assistant. Occasionally, she went to Japan with other *simbang* to perform rituals for migrants from Cheju, which brought her a comfortable income thanks to the favorable exchange rate between Japanese yen and Korean won. Since 1986, she has also worked as a member of the Association for the Ch'ilmŏri Yŏngdŭng Kut Preservation and has received a modest government stipend (a privilege granted only to those with recognized performance skills). In the presence of a few of her close colleagues, she shared her view that *simbang* are able to live on what they earn from their practice if they are not greedy. The others agreed with her.

Indebted to the gods, *simbang* routinely reciprocate what they have received by returning a portion of what they have earned. For example, they dedicate to their gods a small quantity of the food and money that they bring home after performing rituals, and some offer a small-scale ritual for their tutelary gods each year. *Sin kut* is an especially generous reciprocal gift. In terms of form, *sin kut* is a grand-scale (*k'ŭn*) *kut*, comprising major rituals devoted to different deities. Because of the additional rituals performed exclusively at *sin kut*, it is far more elaborate and extensive and accordingly more expensive than those grand-scale rituals sponsored by the laity (Hyŏn Yongjun 1989). In 2001, I was told that the going rate for *sin kut* on Cheju was about 20 million won (US$20,000).[10] Although *simbang* should ideally sponsor *sin kut* three times during their lifetimes, most cannot afford to do so. This was Simbang Min's third, which she had repeatedly postponed; however, her worsening health and a sense that she was down on her luck led her to believe that the time for her third *sin kut* had come.

If the gods are indispensable to *simbang*, so are *simbang* to the gods. *Simbang* help the gods be what and who they are. Thanks to a shaman's intermediary role, the gods can receive offerings from the laity and in return give evidence of their power by exercising it on behalf of humans in need. Thus, the two parties are engaged in a perpetual cycle of exchange. This is clearly reflected in Simbang Min's choice to perform the ritual both as an expression of her gratitude to the gods and in anticipation that the receiving deities would continue to extend their blessing and support to her.

THE ART OF MAKING OFFERINGS

Making offerings is central to Cheju shamanic rituals. Most ritual activities center around altars, "seats of transaction" (Sandstrom 2008, 108), before which ritual participants repeatedly invite, entertain, and entreat supernatural beings. When *simbang* visit their clients' homes, they designate a certain place as a temporary altar and lay out offerings prepared by the patrons on low tables. If the ritual takes place at a shrine, the offerings are placed in front of an altar that could be a stone or an old tree. Participants use the offerings to facilitate their communication with the otherworld. *Kut* is an intense relationship-management event in which sacrificial objects are offered, relationships are established, and favors are asked. People sponsor costly rituals not just to be polite, to maintain a tradition, or to continue a relationship with the gods; they want to get something specific from them. A good relationship allows them to ask a favor from the gods or at least makes it easier and more acceptable to do so. Dedicating sacrificial offerings to the gods is an overture that enables givers to initiate or renew a relationship with the deities (Smith 1970, 546).

What kinds of things are deemed fit to be put on the offering tables, and how do people acquire them? Patrons of indigenous Cheju shamanic rituals by and large use common objects as offerings. As in Simbang Min's *sin kut*, the most fundamental offerings are foodstuffs, cloth, and money. These are considered practical items for the gods, who, like humans, are believed to eat, dress, and spend. Some of these offerings are also used by humans. The offered food is consumed first by supernatural beings, who partake of it by taking in its scent, and is then eaten by humans. Fake money is burned, but real money is taken by the practitioners after the rituals end. Like pseudo-money, cloth made of cheap synthetic materials has only symbolic value to humans these days and is burned after rituals, although cloth, along with rice, once had important use- and exchange-value before cash economies became the norm.[11]

Most of these ritual items are commercially available in Korea today. Fake money and cloth are purchased cheaply and conveniently in shaman supply stores. Although some patrons offer a few food items that they have harvested, such as tangerines and sea products, most sacrificial food and drink comes from nearby grocery stores. Some of the items are Cheju products, but most are imported either from foreign countries (bananas and pineapples) or from the Korean mainland (rice, apples, and pears). Most women do cook vegetables but buy them at their neighborhood stores and at old-style open markets (*chaerae sijang*). Some older women in rural areas make rice cakes at home, but others generally have them made at a mill. In earlier times, Simbang An told me, people raised pigs at home that they would dedicate to rituals; these days, people call a butcher shop (*chŏngyuk chŏm*) and have the dressed carcasses delivered to their homes. On one ritual occasion, I also observed *yangju* (imported Western liquor) used purposefully to placate the spirits of two women involved in escort services who had died in an automobile accident while in the company of their clients. Neither *simbang* nor the laity are strict about the propriety of presenting mass-produced offerings. Rice cakes made in a mill and purchased pork are not necessarily considered less valuable than similar items prepared at home. People perceive store-bought offerings as inevitable, given changing social conditions. The very acts of earmarking household budgets for ritual purchases and buying the necessary items mark their devotion to the deities who require the sacrificial objects.

Like many anthropologists (e.g., Appadurai 1986; Miller 1995, 2001), Cheju Islanders challenge the long-standing anthropological dichotomy between gift as inalienable and commodity as alienable. For ritual participants, the items do not remain purely commodities with their original price tags attached; they become personalized offerings. As with anthropologists who have challenged the boundaries between things and persons since the time of Marcel Mauss (Munn 1983; Strathern 1988; Keane 1994), adherents of Cheju shamanic practice do not separate the two. This is explicit in the word *injŏng*, referring to *human* feelings, especially empathy, that they use exclusively when referring to offerings made in shamanic rituals.

Manner of presentation is as important as the nature of the objects used in building and nurturing relationships. Though Mauss defined reciprocity as an impulse "to give, to receive, and to return" and noted the importance of the duration of the intervals between these actions ([1950] 1990), his articulation makes little mention of the skill involved in this kind of relationship management. It is possible to assume that exchanges that fit the give-receive-return pattern are automatic and to be inattentive to the specifics of *how* an interactional system works. Thus, the so-called rule of reciprocity can obscure potential risks entailed in the practice of gift exchange (cf. Miyazaki 2004, 100).

Simbang are hired because they are specialists who know how to invoke, entertain, and negotiate with the gods "correctly" in the Cheju style, maintaining the appropriate decorum and adhering to the proper etiquette. I once accompanied Simbang An when she performed a small-scale ritual in her neighborhood at the beginning of a lunar new year.[12] When we arrived at the client's home, the patron confessed to the *simbang* that she had tried conducting her own version of the ritual without a *simbang* and subsequently had a nightmare. Though the elderly woman likely dedicated offerings and prayed, silently or audibly, for her wishes, perhaps indeed respectfully, she interpreted the nightmare as a reprimand for her ritual misconduct and decided to offer the ritual again—this time with the help of a professional practitioner. Simbang An replied, "We don't get paid for nothing" (Kong ŭro mŏkchi annŭnda), indicating the inappropriateness of the client's behavior and affirming the value of her own services. This anecdote illuminates the perceived importance of the *way* in which rituals are performed no matter how diverse, flexible, and controversial it may be; it also highlights the indispensable role that *simbang* play in mediating between their clients and the supernatural. Reciprocity is *achieved* by the collaborative work of ritual specialists and sponsors rather than emerging automatically through a context-free rule of reciprocity.

MATERIAL OBJECTS, PERSONS, AND RITUAL SPEECH

Ritual objects "move events and cause actions" and "evoke emotional responses," and thus they themselves become "agentive and constitutive of relationships—thickening ties between clients and their gods and ancestors" (Kendall 2008, 155, 165, citing Gell 1998 and Myers 2001, 8). In Korean shamanic rituals, objects can become fully agentive in conjunction with a practitioner's appropriate words. Shamans expertly manage the dynamic interactions among agents—visible and invisible, living and dead—by means of their spiritual power, ritual knowledge, and performance skills. Clients may offer silent prayers of their own, but shamans are paid to enact petitions both visibly and audibly (Baker 2007, 8). The practitioners articulate the offering of valuables using particular speech patterns and genres that establish connections between *injŏng* and the giver. Only with the proper verbal contextualization can the objects be ritually effective. In this regard, a *simbang*'s words are as valuable as a client's offerings. The following example makes this point particularly clear.

In January 2002, Simbang An performed a ritual sponsored by Mr. Ch'oe, proprietor of a high-end bar that caters to male travelers from Japan and China in the commercial area of Sin-Cheju, a highly urbanized district near Cheju International Airport.[13] At a pre-ritual consultation that I observed, Mr. Ch'oe talked to Simbang An about his previous wife, who had died alone in Japan several months earlier, and about the deaths of two women who had worked for him. He might well have been bothered by a sense of guilt and felt in need of a ritual resolution. His current wife added that their business was not doing well. In short, the couple was looking to contract Simbang An's services in order to comfort the weeping souls of the dead and to receive spiritual support for their business.

During the ritual session to send back the summoned souls, Simbang An offered each of the two deceased hostesses a 10,000-won (US$10) bill and a folded white linen towel that could be used to wipe away their tears and perspiration as they traveled to the otherworld. She divined whether the souls would accept the offerings by throwing coins and two small cups to the floor and examining their placement; at the same time, she engaged the dead through a rhythmic and melodic chant:

> Here is the soul of Xxx[14] with a good name.
> The soul with a good face and a good body tended customers
> And earned money [for Ch'oe].
> You died in a traffic accident.
> Why wouldn't Ch'oe *sajang-nim*[15] remember you?
> Come and receive a cup of liquor.
> [He] offers you *injŏng*.[16]

Here, Simbang An identified one of the souls and succinctly alludes to the nature of her work and her unfortunate death, thus recognizing her grievance. Recalling the circumstances of her death, the *simbang* also spoke for Mr. Ch'oe in order to placate his deceased employee. Further, she invited the deceased escort worker to partake of the liquor that the patron was offering. The *simbang*'s words articulated the meanings of the offerings: who was offering the money, towel, and liquor, and why. Had there been no material offering, Mr. Ch'oe's sincerity and the *simbang*'s words would have felt empty, and the ritual specialist would not have been able to mediate the relationship between the two parties, which had ended abruptly, allowing no time for proper closure. In this regard, as Antonetta Bruno has suggested, material objects and money at shamanic rituals are a "means to create a communicative setting for the participants" (2007, 47).

The spirits of the two women, Simbang An's divination revealed, did indeed "come" to the altar to "receive" the offerings, a move indispensable to redressing the relationship between them and their former employer and for moving the ritual forward. Thus, the objects and the words activate the agency of the invisible.

Although the combination of a layperson's offerings and the *simbang*'s words is considered essential to ritual efficacy, success does not come automatically. Practitioners *work* to achieve the desired ritual goals: as they communicate with the invisible, they diagnose interactive problems and persuade the different parties during emergent ritual situations. For instance, Simbang An learned through her divination that the two women's spirits had accepted the offerings but were still reluctant to stop haunting the proprietor's business premises. After having received several negative responses to her question of whether they would disappear from their former workplace, the *simbang* finally asked, "Shall I offer you a cup of liquor?" Her divination tools then indicated a positive response. When the proprietor's wife tried to get her son to go to a store to fetch a bottle of *soju* (cheap distilled spirits used most commonly at shamanic rituals), Simbang An interrupted and told the client to offer whatever *yangju* she had in the apartment instead. The *simbang* offered the liquor while chanting the following:

> Oh, dear souls, dear spirits,
> Here is liquor that you used to drink, *yangju* that you used to consume.
> The soul of Xxx and the soul of Yyy, receive this *injŏng* and this liquor;
> Leave in a hurry without making a scene in front of Zzz [the bar].

In her speech, the *simbang* marked the *yangju* taken from a cabinet as something personal, *injŏng* that the spirits' erstwhile employer offered especially for them. She used it to induce them to leave the business establishment—a move essential not only to the ritual's progress but also to the proprietor's prosperity, one of his main concerns. As in Webb Keane's examination of wedding gift-exchange in Indonesia, where, for example, cloth and paper money solidified the verbal exchange between the ritual spokespersons (1994, 617), the *yangju* gave the *simbang*'s words the intended gravitas.

If *simbang* comfort lingering ghosts with offerings in order to send them away, they also invite the presence of the gods, who are believed to possess power superior to that of humans, in order to ask for favors on their clients' behalf. When presenting offerings to the gods, as to ghosts, *simbang* link the offerings and the giver through their words, thus making material objects inseparable from the donors (cf. Kim Seong-nae 2002b, 79). However, they do so with much greater care to substantiating the relationship between the two parties. At all rituals, *simbang* declare who is offering the ritual by providing the patron family members' information, such as last names and ages. This is a way of introducing the otherwise unfamiliar donors to the gods, a step in cultivating or renewing a relationship between the family and the gods. The practitioners use melodic narrative to apprise the invoked gods of the specific ritual context, such as the location and date of the ritual (*nal kwa kuk sŏmgim*). They also carefully articulate the motivation for the *kut* (*yŏnyu takkŭm*). Both of these contextualizing narratives are recognized ritual speech genres in the island's indigenous shamanic tradition. When *simbang* begin to recite information about why the patron is offering the ritual proper, they routinely use the following litany, which indicates that the requested reciprocal actions are not precisely in-kind:

> They are not asking for rice. (Pap i ŏpsŏsŏ pap ŭl chupsŏ i kongsŏ
>   to animmeda.)
> They are not asking for clothing. (Ot i ŏpsŏsŏ ot ŭl chupsŏ irŏn yŏnyu
>   to animmeda.)[17]

In the stories that ensue, *simbang* highlight the patron families' dire straits and emotional pain and almost always shed tears in empathy for the family members, both living and dead. Employing artistic and affective verbal performance, they present patrons not so much as needy but as deserving of the gods' compassion and help.

MEASURING SINCERITY

Shamans and the laity believe that sincerity and devotion count more for ritual efficacy than heartless formality or mere number of sacrificial objects. If sincerity is a matter of paramount importance in a ritual context, how can it be gauged, and what is its relationship with the quantity of sacrificial goods? A community ritual that I observed in a fishing village in the northeastern part of the island in spring 2002 clearly shows that quantity alone is insufficient to satisfy the gods. The key devotees were diving women, who work collectively to harvest sea products in the nearby ocean. Their solidarity is essential, as their work involves a great deal of personal risk (An 2008, 136–38). A year before the ritual, discord arose when the women disagreed about a critical decision as they debated the effects of a new fish farm in the area where they worked. Due to mounting tensions, a group of younger women chose not to participate in the ritual. Infuriated by this breach, the gods refused to accept the offerings, as manifested by the *simbang*'s throwing some of the offerings outside the shrine.[18] The anxiety of the attending women was evident in the looks on their faces, and they bowed and begged for the gods' forgiveness. The kinds of material objects dedicated during the ritual might not have differed much from those offered in prior years, but this year they apparently did not represent the unified devotion of the donors.

Although one's sincerity cannot be measured by the sheer amount of material objects, the quantity one is willing to offer, given one's finances, is a crucial indicator of genuine intent and dedication (Hogarth 2009, 243; Kim Seong-nae 2002b, 71). In rituals, *simbang* assess whether the deities are satisfied with the patron family's sincerity through divinations, a process called "weighing the sincerity" (*chŏngsŏng kŭllyang*).[19] If the *injŏng* is revealed to be insufficient, the patron family offers more during the course of the divination. In many Cheju myths, sincerity is measured in proportion to the quantity of offerings. The wishes of characters in the narrative are granted only if the individuals complete the requested consecutive days of prayer, and their offerings (e.g., rice), meet a predetermined weight, typically one hundred *kŭn*.[20] An offering that falls short, even if by only one *kŭn*, signals a lack of effort. In the myth of Ch'ogong, despite praying for one hundred days, the grandmother of the three brothers who became the tutelary gods of *simbang* gave birth to a daughter, their mother, instead of a son, because the weight of her offerings did not reach one hundred *kŭn* (Mun 1998, 119). In the same narrative, in contrast, the daughter of Prime Minister Yu, who became the original *simbang*, was able to perform her first ritual because her heartfelt prayer for ritual instruments and paraphernalia measured up to the required one hundred *kŭn* (Hyŏn Yongjun 1980a, 175; Mun 1998, 147).[21] The number 100 here denotes wholeness rather than an exact number. If patrons mistakenly exclude a portion of a pig carcass, a *simbang* may determine through divination that the god of Kwenwegwi, who should receive a whole pig, will not accept the offering because it does not equal "100." On such occasions, the *simbang* asks the woman of the household whether she has included everything and then watches while she runs into the kitchen to fetch the forgotten part. Given that the idea of sincerity is extremely subjective, setting a definite quantity of satisfactory offerings is as difficult as determining an appropriate gift in a secular context.[22]

Despite the difficulty of quantifying sincerity, it is still construed as quantifiable (cf. Guyer 2004, 12): An acceptable store of sincerity enables successful interaction with the invisible and increases the potential for acceptance of the offerings and the granting of what has been asked for in the ritual context. Thus, quantity plays an important part in establishing the quality of one's sincerity (cf. Bruno 2007a, 57; Hogarth 2009, 107, 243). In other words, it is believed that the more one is willing to sacrifice material wealth, the more one will receive in return. As an elderly *simbang* once told me, "A big *kut* would yield a large field and a small *kut* a small field" (K'ŭn kut hamyŏn k'ŭn pat sago, chagŭn kut hamyŏn chagŭn pat sanda). Simbang An remarked that some people are parsimonious in making offerings because they are ignorant of what ritual is all about. An offering cannot be too small, or it would indicate a lack of sincerity.

MYTH AND THE RITUAL OF EXCHANGE

Cheju is rich in *ponp'uri*—*pon* meaning "root" and *p'uri* "recounting." The term refers to the origin myth in Cheju and some other parts of Korea. *Simbang* recite a range of these narratives in appropriate ritual contexts. However, they can stand alone as independent stories. Therefore scholars have often treated them as oral literature displaced from their religious context, leaning heavily toward analysis of formal structures and motifs in comparison with world myths and other genres with little or no consideration of the perspectives of native Koreans.[23]

South Korean scholars have paid an enormous amount of attention to shamanic narratives and have painstakingly documented, transcribed, and analyzed them, producing an extensive body of published work.[24] Their research treated shamans as purveyors of tradition while obscuring practitioners' verbal talents and affective labor. Fetishized and romanticized ritual texts have served as a legitimate emblem of a group's shared culture, and thus the island's *ponp'uri* are seen as the collective ethos of Cheju Islanders, a point that is quite common to discussions of oral literature (e.g., Chin Sŏng-gi 1991; Hyŏn Yongjun 1980a). Some others highlight subaltern attitudes in the local myths reflecting the quasi-colonial mainland's long-term exploitation of the islanders (Kim Seong-nae 2004; Pettid 2001), which is unsurprising given Cheju's history vis-à-vis the mainland. However, the issue of how the *ponp'uri* make sense to performers and their audiences in a performance setting has been absent from the research.

The myth of Saman, according to the *simbang*, is an account of the principles of *kut* (*kutpŏp*).[25] Indeed, it embodies particularly well the practitioners' view of why people conduct a ritual and how the ritual works. Several Korean scholars have offered comparative analyses of the myth in relation to other Korean myth texts that include similar contents (e.g., Choi Won-oh 2008; Hyŏn Yongjun 2005, 92–98; Kwŏn T'aehyo 2005, 49–97), but few studies have explored how these narratives are used in practice (but see Yun Sunhŭi 2010).

An examination of the myth in its performance context allows us to appreciate the complex integration of belief and practice and the indigenous *simbang's* competence and flexibility in actively managing the verbal resource in specific and unique ritual situations. *Simbang* recite the narrative in a ritual session known as *aengmaegi*, or forestallment (*maegi*) of misfortune (*aek*).[26] Devoted to the messengers of death (*chŏsŭng ch'asa*), *aengmaegi* is performed as a later part of various larger rituals. As is explicit in the name, the primary goal of *aengmaegi* is to prevent deleterious influences from disturbing the perpetuation of life—events such as serious financial loss and the threat of death (illness and accident). The *aengmaegi* examined here was performed on 1 January 2002 by the late Simbang Son as part of the *Siwang maji*, a large-scale ritual that formed part of Simbang Min's *sin kut*. This segment of the larger ritual lasted for about one and a quarter hours, a substantial period of time. Because of the *sin kut's* grandness, and perhaps also due to the presence of scholars documenting the ritual, the lead *simbang's* performance of the *aengmaegi* was more elaborate than on other occasions. Studied in its ritual context, the myth clearly demonstrates that shamanic rituals are attempts by humans to attain their desires and mitigate their uncertain control by persuading the gods through offerings to act on their behalf.

MYTH OF SAMAN

Unlike other Cheju myths, in which the gods are leading protagonists, this myth presents a human named Saman as its main character and portrays how he alters his destined misfortune—poverty and early death—with the help of a Skull Ancestor and the Messengers of Death. The myth establishes themes of reciprocity and relationship management and lays out the rules of gift exchange—to give, receive, and return.

The basic plot, reconstructed here from Simbang Son's recitation at Simbang Min's *sin kut*, is as follows:

> Saman is born into extreme poverty. After losing his parents at an early
> age, he survives as a beggar. Marriage and parental responsibility for
> many children further increase his misery. Although Saman makes an
> effort to alleviate his poverty, he fails. The skull of a one-hundred-year-
> old ancestor (*paengnyŏn chosang*)[27] appears to Saman in the mountains,
> where Saman stayed one night after an unsuccessful hunt. Unable to
> change his own indigent situation, rolling about in the wilderness without
> anyone paying attention, and knowing what Saman needs, the skull
> makes a bargain with Saman: if Saman worships him well, he will make
> him rich. Saman does as he is told and becomes wealthy.
>
> Saman then confronts death. Thirty years is the life span that
> was originally given to Saman and recorded in a document in the
> otherworld. He learns from the skull that the time of his preordained
> death is approaching and that the Messengers of Death serving King
> Yŏmna, are coming to take him away.[28] The ancestor shares his
> knowledge of how to make sacrifices to those who have the power
> to change Saman's fate—the Messengers of Death themselves. As
> instructed, Saman tricks these messengers into taking his offerings.
> Unable to ignore Saman's plea after receiving the offerings, they take
> another person to the otherworld in Saman's place.
>
> However, the Messengers of Death are themselves then at risk of
> punishment by execution for accepting Saman's offerings and taking
> another person. They survive by persuading the secretaries of King
> Yŏmna to revise Saman's original life span to three thousand years.

The plot characteristically begins with Saman's dire straits: being married to the daughter of a high-ranking official and having several children, usually considered blessings, here underscore his material abjection. The man's destitution is attributed to fate, a factor that humans seemingly can neither avoid nor control. Despite her noble birth, Saman's partner also becomes a beggar, since she was born to share his destiny.[29] Although Saman makes an effort to improve his situation, he fails: he is unable to hunt successfully with the gun that he obtained in exchange for his wife's hair, the only item they had to trade for food. Their predetermined destiny can be changed only through the involvement of an extrinsic power.

Luckily for Saman, the one-hundred-year-old ancestor, represented by a skull, appears to him. He initiates a relationship with Saman by telling his own story, highlighting one aspect of their commonality: they have both hunted on the same mountain with the same gun.

> The gun that you hold is one that I used to carry.
> I, the son of Chŏngsŭng Paek,[30]
> came up to Kulmigul-san Nojobang-san Aya-san Sinsan'got,
> was hunting,
> and met a violent gale and died.

Having died alone in the mountains, the ancestor finds himself in a thoroughly miserable state. The pathetic sight of the lost skull rolling around in the wilderness requires no further elaboration—the ancestor simply says, "I am now like *this*." Despite his humiliating circumstances and perhaps frightful appearance, the Skull Ancestor's narrative, which reveals the two men's affinity, appeals to Saman's compassion. If the ancestor's story had not struck an emotional chord and he had not gained Saman's sympathy and trust, Saman might have ignored him or fled from the scene, and the skull would have had to remain as it was. The Skull Ancestor's narrative serves to catalyze social bonding between the two parties, establishes the basis for the obligation to help, and furthers the narrative's development.

Saman cannot change his own indigent situation by himself, and neither can the skull. In this circumstance, the ancestor already knows what Saman needs, and he proposes a bargain: "If you want to become rich, take me and build a big loft in a big storeroom and worship me well. Then I will make you rich within three years." The ancestor's enticing proposal is not a one-sided unconditional offer but rather a reciprocal transaction. Approximating the art of relationship management among humans, the two characters in this myth, one human and one otherworldly, do favors for each other. Saman counteracts his poverty by acting on the prophetic words of the ancestor.

However, Saman then confronts a more fundamental human problem—death. The myth attributes Saman's fated early death to two overlapping factors: (1) it is punishment for Saman's neglect of Confucian ancestor rites for his own parents, which, as in the case of the Skull Ancestor, is a source of grief to them,[31] and (2) like his poverty, Saman's death is ultimately his destiny because thirty years is the life span originally allotted to him and recorded in the otherworld, and the mortal Saman has neither knowledge of its length nor the power to change it.

However, well respected and worshipped by Saman even after Saman becomes wealthy, the ancestor helps Saman beyond his initial promise of material goods. One day, after another unsuccessful hunt, Saman returns home and learns from the Skull Ancestor that the Messengers of Death are coming to take him away. In desperation, he seeks the skull's help, and the ancestor shares his knowledge of how to prolong his life. The only thing that Saman can do is appeal to those who are in charge of his life—those same three Messengers of Death—by creating a situation in which they will be made to feel morally vulnerable should they not help him. The Skull Ancestor advises Saman not only on how to make sacrifices to the messengers but also on how to trick them into seizing offerings that they would otherwise not accept. In contrast to the Skull Ancestor, who was in need of Saman's care, the Messengers of Death do not want anything from Saman apart from his life; there are no grounds for a reciprocal exchange in this relationship. Further, the law of the otherworld is so "clear and just" that breaking it could cost the transgressors their lives. These purportedly austere messengers would never knowingly take the offerings of a mortal Saman, with whom they are not even acquainted.

As instructed by the skull, Saman prepares trays of offerings and leaves them out in the wilderness. He hides himself nearby and observes the messengers as they find and take his offerings:

The messenger who was hungry allayed his hunger,
the messenger who ran out of travel money took money;
the messenger whose shoes were torn changed into new ones.
[*Aside*] *You choke on what you don't repay.*
So they looked at the folding screen
to which was attached
a piece of paper with the three characters *so sa man*.
"Damn it!
We came to summon So Saman
and received his *injŏng*."
They shouted for So Saman,
"So Saman, So Saman, where are you?"
He came out from one hundred steps away.

If the officials of the otherworld should not receive an inappropriate *injŏng* from humans, neither should they neglect to repay what they have received (note the *simbang*'s embedded commentary in italics). The messengers look at the folding screen in order to learn to whom they are indebted. They realize regretfully that they have been caught in Saman's artfully baited trap and try to spirit him away to the otherworld. Having succeeded in putting the messengers in his debt, Saman earns an opportunity to say farewell to his family. As stated in the myth recitation, "Since the messengers received his *injŏng*, they couldn't ignore his plea." The Messengers of Death visit Saman's home and witness another ritual prepared for King Yŏmna, a god of the utmost rectitude as described by Simbang Son. Deflected from their duty by unwittingly incurring obligations and learning that their superior is also receiving the gift of a large-scale ritual, they decide to save Saman's life and take Oman, another villager, as a substitute.[32]

The messengers break the rules of the game rather innocently without knowing Saman's arrangement. However, their punishment for receiving Saman's offerings and returning with the wrong person is severe, according to the laws of the otherworld.[33] They are jailed and sentenced to death. To save themselves, the messengers use their old connections with King Yŏmna's secretaries with whom they studied when they were young. Swayed by their appeal to the brotherhood, the secretaries respond, "How can we save your lives?" The messengers explain:

"This evening,
when King Yŏmna falls asleep,
take out the document of the otherworld,
look for Chunyŏn'guk,
and find the name of So Saman,
who was destined to die at thirty.
Rub down a fine ink stick on a golden inkstone;
with a golden brush
put a bird on the character for 'ten.'"[34]

Editing the record is essential to saving the messengers' lives by legitimizing their charitable yet illegitimate act of leaving Saman behind. Crucially, the editing authorizes the change to Saman's fate, suggesting the possibility of overcoming human destiny by means of making offerings to those who are believed to be in control and to be just but not always upright. Thus, the myth not only depicts the frustrations and anxieties related to life's major challenges, such as extreme poverty and an unexpected death, but also presents proactive tactics designed to overcome them.

A FORESTALLMENT RITUAL

Although the *aengmaegi*, in which the myth of Saman is recited, is performed as a part of large-scale rituals, it can also stand alone. Whereas each ritual has its own structure and emergent elements that belie simple generalizations, all rituals are based on some common premises. Therefore, close attention to the ritual situation offers insight into the interactional dynamics among ritual participants that can be helpful in understanding shamanic rituals in general, one of the primary goals of which is warding off misfortune. Dependent on the mercy and power of the gods, Simbang Min's family makes an effort to show their sincerity and devotion by preparing satisfactory offerings for the pertinent gods and bowing to them at the ritually appropriate moments. The lead *simbang*, dressed in a well-ironed, white, traditional Korean topcoat (*turumagi*), performs the ritual in front of abundant offerings—cloth, rice, liquor, straw shoes, money (both pseudo and real), and open Marlboro cigarette boxes.[35] These sacrificial objects are a means of establishing social interaction with the messengers of death, who are believed to respond to *injŏng*, as are other deities. Simbang Min was present throughout the ritual; most often she sat next to Simbang Son while listening to his speech and tending to ritual chores—bowing to the deities, giving instructions to other ritual participants, or folding paper and cloth for additional offerings.

Both the sincerity of ritual participants (sponsoring family and *simbang*) and the practitioners' verbal dexterity are vital for touching the gods' hearts in the *aengmaegi*, which can influence the patron family's future. Calling attention to the conspicuously displayed sacrificial offerings prepared by the patron family, the *simbang* implores the messengers of death to divert misfortune from the client family and bring them good luck. An examination of Simbang Son's use of the myth and other verbal resources in this performance illuminates that his recitation of the narrative becomes a powerful rhetorical strategy for beseeching the gods to intervene for the patron family's benefit.

Like other rituals, the forestallment ritual is a communicative event in which the practitioner mediates the relationship between the clients and the gods using artistic speech and spiritual authority. In the ritual circumstance, the *simbang*'s words are performative; that is, his utterances have the force of action outlined by the British philosopher of language J. L. Austin ([1962] 1997). Simbang Son first framed the *aengmaegi* session with a meta-communicative statement that refers to the current event itself ("It is time to avert misfortune"),[36] thus guiding the specific gods pertinent to the ritual—the messengers of death—and other ritual participants present at the event. Then he invited the deities to the altar ("Please descend to the forestallment offering trays"). Simbang Son apprised the invoked gods of the location and date of the ritual and named those individuals who made the offerings and thus deserved their care and protection— Simbang Min, her children, and her children's family members. The intention here is to orient the messengers to the ritual event while giving them participatory immediacy in terms of time, space, and social relations. Moreover, in this report to the deities, the *simbang* explained the ritualistic efforts that the *simbang* group and the patron family have made by summarizing what they had performed in previous days and hours. After Simbang Son announced what they were about to do ("[We] would like to offer the forestallment ritual for the messengers of death"), he verbalized the action of offering ("We raise the offering tray to you"). In so doing, he tied the ensuing ritual action—the recitation of the myth of Saman, in which the messengers of death themselves play active roles in staving off Saman's premature death—to the immediate ritual situation.

If speaking for the patron family is the *simbang*'s ritual role as an intermediary, so too is commemorating the gods by telling their stories. As indicated in the passage in which Saman's neglect of his parents' commemoration ritual was in part a cause of his destined early death, neglecting ancestors and the gods is one primary cause of human affliction in the shamanic world (e.g., Janelli and Janelli 1982; Kendall 1985a, 3; Kim Seong-nae 2002b). Simbang An once told me that the main reason for conducting a *kut* is to disentangle the tangled hearts of people and gods by sharing each side's stories with the other (cf. Hogarth 2009, 243). In an interview conducted after the arduous ritual, when asked the purpose of reciting the myth, Simbang Son told me that it was to seek the messengers' help by reminding them of what they did after receiving Saman's *injŏng*. In other words, the act of reciting the myth was intended to invite the messengers' participatory involvement in the current event, in which their charitable action would be as crucial for the patron family as it had been for Saman. The *ponp'uri* "flows over into the reality of the believers for whom" it is chanted (Walraven 2007c, 308).

Simbang Son marked the end of this *ponp'uri* recitation by stepping outside narrative time: "There was a time when this happened." He then contextualized the myth within a broader tradition of offerings by linking it to other old tales in which the protagonists overturn their misfortune by offering sacrificial objects.[37] By constructing discursive continuity between the *ponp'uri* and other tales, the *simbang* established the traditionality of forestalling misfortune and endowed his speech with authority. This is the "work of traditionalization, traditionalization in practice," and at the same time an act of authentication (Bauman 1992, 135). In this example, Simbang Son further authenticated his words by employing the authority of Confucius. To the well-known Korean adage "Sincerity moves heaven" (Chisŏng kamch'ŏn), he added a syntactically parallel phrase—"Piety brings charity" (Karyŏn kongdŏk)—and then claimed these phrases to be Confucius's words.[38] Aside from the fact that shamanic songs are composite genres drawing on different oral and literary sources (Walraven 1994), this interpretive comment lays bare the fact that Simbang Son is asking his divine interlocutors to bestow charity upon the patron family who have shown the gods their sincerity. The invocation of intertextuality and the authority of Confucius is his attempt to persuade the gods to this end by making them feel obligated through the power of precedent.

The *simbang*'s verbal work contextualizes one of the focal points of the ritual, that is, prayer. During the *aengmaegi*, I watched as Simbang Son badgered the gods to keep all misfortunes not only from Simbang Min, her children, and their family members but also from his fellow *simbang* who were collaborating with him on the *sin kut*. In addition, he pleaded with the gods to help Simbang Min be professionally successful by enabling her to attract clients and ritual opportunities. While the lead *simbang* prayed for all of them, the hopeful beneficiaries of his prayer showed their own sincerity. Simbang Min, who heretofore had mostly been sitting, stood up, bowed, and put additional offerings of white paper money and cloth on the offering tables. The patron family and the attending *simbang* also came to the altar and bowed. One of the *simbang* removed bills from her pocket and put them on the tray. As Simbang Son recited the prayer, he shook a bell in his right hand more loudly and more rapidly, creating a sense of urgency. The *simbang* also enumerated the items offered to the gods and bade them to accept the offerings. Kneeling down, Simbang Son and Simbang Min's family then raised up *soji* (blank white folded paper) with both hands in the hope that their unspoken wishes would also be granted by gods allegedly able to perceive even unarticulated human desires. In his litany, Simbang Son invited a range of deities to imbibe the sacrificial liquor, and two female *simbang* each repeatedly dipped an unshelled boiled egg in a small cup of liquor and raised it in the air, an enactment of offering the liquor. When Simbang Son finally prayed to the gods to do them the favor of generously granting their wishes, he lowered his head to the floor.

The fact that divination is subsequent to all these efforts lends participatory immediacy to ritual performance: the gods as well as humans are active players. The gods are believed to respond to the ardent plea via the *simbang*'s divination, which includes an assessment of the deities' satisfaction with the patron family's devotion. Simbang Son stood up and danced, holding a set of *sink'al* and *sanp'an*,[39] to the rhythm of pounding percussion music played by the other *simbang*. Compared to sedentary recitations accompanied only by a ritual bell (*yoryŏng*), this dynamic movement and loud music added a sense of climax to the ritual. Simbang Son then threw the divination tools. The divine response is read in the way the coins and cups point and the directions in which the knives' cutting edges face when they land.

Facing Simbang Min, Simbang Son delivered the gods' message as revealed by the divination. The prospects for the family's luck turned out to be very gloomy, but because of the forestallment ritual they had sponsored, the family was told that they would be able to prevent the worst: they would be safe from the messengers' pending visit to the village either on the third or the seventh, or at any rate within the first fifteen days of the last month of the year. The messengers would take somebody else. The gods also assured Simbang Min that her only son, who makes a living driving a cab on the island, would be safe from deleterious influences. These predictions are assured because the gods have acknowledged the patron's sincerity and accepted the offerings:

> "We can't ignore
> the offered sacrifice.
> As your sincerity was utmost,
> we accepted the sacrifice."

This divination message thus not only affirmed the future safety of the client family but also reiterated the importance of showing sincerity to the gods and the benefit of sponsoring the ritual.

Ending the *aengmaegi*, Simbang Son conveyed to the participating *simbang* that they too would receive protection from dire events in return for their hard work on Simbang Min's behalf. Finally, he offered divination for individual members of the family and relatives. He wrapped up the *aengmaegi* by offering liquor to the underlings of the messengers of death, informing the deities that it was time to have a meal and that the ritual of which the *aengmaegi* is a part would resume after the meal. Simbang Min then thanked Simbang Son for his hard work and shouted that lunch should be served.

CONCLUSION

As ethnographers of popular religion have demonstrated in other regions (e.g., Romberg 2003; Truitt 2013; Weller 1994), Korean shamanism has been in motion. New commodities and extravagant cash offerings are conspicuous in contemporary rituals, which anthropologists have interpreted as indicative of the state of society, particularly the ambivalent attitudes toward rampant consumption and the desire for acquiring more (e.g., Kendall 2009; Jun Hwan Park 2012). But what is the purpose of giving in the first place from the practitioners' perspective, and what do shamans do with the commodities and cash laid out in rituals? Patrons and practitioners on Cheju invest a substantial portion of their assets for which they desire gifts in return. They give up something valuable in the hope of gaining something more valuable (Hogarth 2009, 107; cf. Appadurai 1986).

Although the instrumental use of material offerings is undeniable, the reciprocity between the patron and the gods is premised on their regard for each other. The number of items that make up the offering represents the depth of a sponsor's devotion. *Simbang* themselves make offerings of their wealth as expressions of gratitude for the favor granted them by their gods (e.g., Bruno 2007b; Hogarth 2009; Kim Seong-nae 2002b). Moreover, insincere sacrifices offered by a patron are believed not to yield the desired outcome. By sanctioning material goods as proper offerings and using their communicative competence, shamans work to make the gods and the spirits feel an obligation to grant the patron family's wishes. This reciprocity cannot be arranged as a quid pro quo. The gift the deities provide in return is perceived as a socially sanctioned *gain* that the patron and *simbang* earn through the work of managing a relationship with the invisible. It is construed as the gods' expression of generosity toward the patron family rather than the *mere* cancellation of a debt incurred by their acceptance of the offerings. The power asymmetry between humans and deities makes the exchange of sacrificial objects and the gods' return gift fundamentally incommensurable (cf. Miller 2001). The moral aspect of the exchange suggests that the balance of the transaction between the two parties cannot be calculated with the same exactitude as in the purchase and sale of commodities (Hogarth 2009, 247; Kim Seong-nae 2002b, 74). Thus, the ritual economy is distinguished from other forms of exchange.

The idea of reciprocity entailed in ritual practice should not be romanticized as exclusive to the relatively rural Cheju countryside. It thrives in the crisis of South Korea's present-day precarious capitalism. In particular, Kim Seong-nae's study (2002b) shows the way that capitalism makes use of a culture of reciprocity, a core social value governing relationships in society, both rural and urban.[40] Reciprocal transactions are not merely a leftover from the days when people were less greedy. Before money was used as a common form of currency, ritual sponsors offered cloth and grain, which had both use and exchange value. Would they have done so without some anticipation of return? Ritual sponsors and practitioners have long prayed for the satisfaction of fundamental human needs and desires, although the specifics have changed over time. The popular phrase "seeking this-worldly luck" (*hyŏnse kibok*) is indeed an unpretentious characterization of Korean shamanism. It would also be naive to assume that the relative ritual cost was appreciably less in the past.

However, the reciprocal gift is not guaranteed—the expectation may or may not be realized.[41] As medical doctors cannot cure all their patients,[42] *simbang* cannot always resolve problems that prompt rituals. This, along with other uncertain features, contributes to the controversy over ritual consumption. The gods' reciprocal gift at the conclusion of Simbang Min's ritual was in the form of a promise whose realization requires faith: since its fulfillment is not immediate, it must be awaited in order to be proved. This temporality renders the reciprocity open-ended, and far from assured. Scholars of shamanic rituals highlight the benefits of rituals, such as cure, hope, and confidence, as well as emotional and psychological relief (Bruno 2002; Hogarth 2009, 256–61; Rhi 1970, 1977), but pay far less attention to the undesirable ritual outcomes that occur. Simbang An, who has sponsored three *sin kut* in her lifetime, told me that, in retrospect, she could see that the first had brought a series of disasters into her life. Her experience demonstrates that *simbang* themselves are also bound by the uncertainty of ritual outcomes. The laity are aware that ritual efficacy is not guaranteed and assess outcomes both in positive (*kut tŏk ŭl poda*) and negative ways (*kut tŏk ŭl mot poda*). These phrases literally mean "see ritual benefits" and "not see ritual benefits." When unfortunate consequences follow the performance of *kut*, people comment and speculate about the possible causes, including a bad choice of performer, inadequate ritual procedures, a ritually polluted guest, or lack of sincerity. The awareness of risk also motivates people to try their best to prevent undesirable outcomes and bring about the most auspicious possible results. This hedging also tends to explain the seemingly excessive quantity of ritual offerings because the adherents of shamanic ritual view quantity as an important indicator of one's sincerity, no matter how subjective that might be. For those who disregard the symbolic value of a bountiful quantity of sacrificial objects, such extravagance, of course, constitutes waste.

4 SKILLFUL PERFORMER OR GREEDY ANIMATOR?

RECIPROCITY BETWEEN THE INVISIBLE AND HUMAN REALMS IS CENTRAL
to ritual practice, and ritual sponsors, like practitioners, rely on the social
value of reciprocity and thus the value of making sacrifices to the deities.
However, they have also chastised shamans for demanding high service
fees and encouraging extravagant offerings, a fact that most ethnographers
tend to skim over, perhaps in defense of their shaman informants.[1] Even
a scholarly advocate of shamans referred to the offering money, when
deemed "extravagant," as "the money that shamans extort" (*ttŭdŏ naenŭn
ton*) (Cho Hung-youn 1990, 215).

Most studies of Korean shamanism have treated the claim about "extravagant" ritual consumption as though it were merely prejudice on the part
of critics of the popular religion or have found the conspicuous materialism to be a reflection of a contemporary Korean society that is rampant with
the consequences of capitalism. However, these do not explain why ritual sponsors begrudge shamans the economic gains that they themselves provide or how ritual materialism could have been a problem
since the thirteenth century, well before the development of capitalism.
Some ethnographers of contemporary *kut*, a large-scale shamanic ritual,
have associated extravagant monetary offerings solely with the demands
of greedy gods, notably the Official (Taegam), who became ever greed-
ier, especially during and after the 1997–98 financial crisis (Kendall 2009,
156–59; Kim Seong-nae 2002b, 72; Jun Hwan Park 2012). Others have
acknowledged the practitioners' greed and keen interest in economic gain
(Bruno 2002; Hogarth 2009, 247–48; Chongho Kim 2003, 80). Chungmoo
Choi observed that shamans "calculate financial interest before calculating
the need of the clients" (1987, 193). Instead of playful antics between the
gods and clients during rituals (e.g., Kendall 1985a, 2009), I often witnessed
tension between clients and shamans (Kyoim Yun 2016). Regardless of
whether gods or shamans are the greedy ones, offerings do not disappear
in a puff of smoke.

Challenging the erudite or romantic perceptions of islanders as gullible or compliant in their interactions with shamans, ritual sponsors themselves are careful about spending their assets and watchful of the shaman's demands, which we cannot assume to be a new phenomenon. Although anthropologists have recognized that shamans are professionals (Harvey 1979; Kendall 1985a, x; Chongho Kim 2003, 50) who cater to people's ritual needs and work for payment, the implications in terms of ritual performance have received short shrift. Given that controversy over ritual consumption persists not only among social critics but also ritual participants in Korea, it is important to explore why ritual business is a delicate and contested subject. The laity do not expect shamans to offer their services free of charge, nor do shamans intentionally cheat those laypersons who engage them. What factors, then, make ritual expense such a touchy issue and clients so ambivalent about the economic clout of shamans? Considering these matters helps elucidate how shamans, who are well aware of their clients' feelings, manage ritual affairs, including fee negotiations, ritual speech, and the encouragement of cash offerings. This also allows a deeper appreciation of the agency and dignity of shamans, whose profit motive has been both condemned and neutered.

Despite conflicting attitudes toward shamans, the laity still seeks their help and pays for their ritual services. Why do people put their trust in shamans whom they also inherently distrust? A shaman's ability to mediate between human beings and invisible agents is central to attracting distressed laypersons (Chongho Kim 2003, 35–38; Kwang-Ok Kim 2013, 273; Sorensen 1988, 409). *Kut* is the only religious ritual in Korea in which the living can hear what the spirits say, and such "spirit talk" is essential to Korean shamanism (Chongho Kim 2003, 40). Indeed, a shaman's competent communication with supernatural beings empowers rituals and affects people, even those laypersons who are generally ambivalent about shamans. Although Cheju *simbang* are hereditary shamans, whose so-called medium speech lacks the same kind of dramatic intensity as that of the god-descended shamans (*kangsin mu*), the islanders still consider it to be the kernel of *kut*.

A shaman's ritual power does not necessarily translate into social respect outside the ritual context. For example, Mr. Cho (featured in the introduction to this book) sponsored a three-day *kut* for his son and other family members who had met tragic deaths. He made congenial conversation with the *simbang*, wept profusely, and actively participated by bowing and offering money during the ritual. Nevertheless, he spoke poorly of *simbang* to me when we visited after the ritual: "In the old days, *mudang*[2] [shamans] and *paekchŏng* [butchers] were not even considered human. They were the lowest. People used *panmal* [the low forms of speech] with them because they were *ssangnom* [vulgar people of low birth]. Although I said 'Yes' and 'Yes' [*ye ye*] to them, hoping they would do a good thing for my son, inside I still think it's all right to treat them shabbily because they are *ssangnom*."

Baffled by my commitment to the study of shamanism, this erudite gentleman advised me to stop mingling with shamans, because, in his view, continuing to do so would bring disgrace upon my parents. His advice, which very likely stemmed from genuine concern for me, represents the prevalent double standard regarding the treatment of shamans (Chongho Kim 2003), which is not limited to Korea (e.g., Buyandelger 2013; Pedersen 2011). Money was, in fact, a major reason for Mr. Cho's discontent with the *simbang* who led his ritual.

The ways ritual speech, affective display, and cash management are interwoven in shamanic performances are particularly evident in the *chilch'igi* performed at Mr. Cho's household as part of a large ritual. Literally meaning "clearing up the road," *chilch'igi* is a ritual performed as part of a variety of rituals in which *simbang* symbolically tidy up the pathways to the otherworld.[3] Some Cheju people believe that grieving souls cannot enter the otherworld until a proper number of *chilch'igi* are conducted for them. Cheju native shamans portray the otherworld as composed of realms of different value, such as the high village (*sang maŭl*), the middle village (*chung maŭl*), and the low village (*ha maŭl*) (Hyŏn Yongjun 1980a, 303); dead souls may travel to a higher (better) realm each time *chilch'igi* is conducted.

During this ritual segment, *simbang* deliver the emotionally charged messages of the deceased. This séance is called *yŏngge ullim*—a compound noun composed of *yŏngge*, a local term for *yŏnghon* (souls), and *ullim* (weeping) (Hyŏn Yongjun 1980a, 890). Because the souls speak in a weeping voice, at times even sobbing with intense sorrow and regret, this speech and this part of the ritual is called *yŏngge ullim*, or "the lamentations of the dead."[4] The spirits' mournful messages frequently induce audience members to weep as well.

After this cathartic moment of *yŏngge ullim*, a patron's family offers abundant cash as *injŏng*. At the conclusion of the ritual, the shamans keep the negotiable currency,[5] while the cloth and pseudo-money are burned. *Simbang* encourage members of the sponsor's family to offer satisfactory *injŏng* to a variety of invisible figures: the Ten Kings of the otherworld must be bribed if they are to pass the dead souls to the next realm, the Messengers of Death need to be appeased so that they will be gentle as they take the dead souls to the otherworld, and the deceased themselves should be given "travel money" that can be used for their personal comfort while on the road. Thus, this emotionally heightened stage of the ritual event, often with participants weeping copiously, is juxtaposed to large cash offerings. How are these two actions related? If a ritual is symbolic in nature, shouldn't pseudo-money be adequate for ritual purposes? Why is legal tender necessary as a "ritual prop" (Kendall 2009)? Additionally, the nature of the mediation raises a question: When shamans deliver the messages of the dead, are they working, performing, or simply surrendering themselves to spirits?

This complex issue involves "who is [empowered] to communicate what," with whom, and at what points in a ritual (cf. Kapchan 1995, 498; also see Gal [1931] 1989; Sherzer 1987). Power dynamics between clients and shamans are communicatively mediated and change before, during, and after ritual acts. During the ritual, endowed with the authority of performance (Tangherlini 1998, 132), *simbang* have the upper hand, and patron families comply with the professionals' requests. However, outside the performance frame, patrons put themselves on an equal (if not superior) footing with *simbang*, engage with them on business issues (including bargaining for the service fee), and even discourteously disparage them. Looking closely at the ground rules of performance power allows us to understand (1) how *simbang* use their communication skills to create a performance frame and (2) how clients respond to *simbang* within and outside of this frame.

A ritual sponsored by Mr. Cho, a client whose immediate family's history was marked by numerous tragedies, is illustrative for several reasons. First, both the *simbang* and the household head generously allowed me to videotape the entire event, which provided material required for a detailed analysis of this complex ritual. Mr. Cho's openness toward me was critical to my understanding of what was transpiring before, during, and after the ritual. Further, the performance of *yŏngge ullim* by the female lead *simbang* was particularly poignant. She certainly evoked much emotion among the audience by creating a strong sense of the spirits' presence. However, the collection of money that followed the séance also engendered a subtle tug-of-war between *simbang* and the patron family, thus showing that even a successful ritual performance can lead to contestation over cash offerings and distrust of *simbang*.

RITUAL AT MR. CHO'S

People sponsor a *kut* for specific purposes. What services could be worth the considerable expense? Three generations of misfortune motivated the Cho family to sponsor it. The family's tragic history began during the violence that swept Cheju Island with the turmoil of the April Third Events in 1948. Cho's elder brother, whom Cho characterized as a very clever man, was shot dead by a policeman when he was only twenty-one years old. His wife, Cho's sister-in-law, was also shot as she ran to the mountains with her infant on her back. This occurred just a year after the two were married, and the bereaved couple's families were unable to locate any of the three corpses.

Having lost her eldest son, Cho's mother soon fell gravely ill and died when Cho was only sixteen years old. He was raised by his stepmother, whom he did not much like, and left home. After spending some time on the mainland, he returned to Cheju and married Han, and they lived well on the family property he had inherited. They had three sons and three daughters. However, beginning in his late thirties, Cho suffered from a serious malady that brought him near death on several occasions. His illness continued for almost two decades. In order to pay for his medical treatment, the family sold all their property, and Han had to do all the farm-related work by herself. In addition, her household work for the family included serving her father-in-law. Cho started working as an apiarist, and his eldest son quit his job to help him tend the bees. In his early fifties, Cho was finally cured of his mysterious long-lasting malady.

Another tragedy then struck the family. One summer night, several years before the ritual discussed here, Cho's second son, Ch'ŏlgi, drove out in a pickup truck after receiving a phone call from two friends who were unable to get home because they had missed the last bus. On the way back, one of Ch'ŏlgi's friends was driving carelessly, and they got into an accident. Ch'ŏlgi was the only casualty among the three passengers. On receiving news of the accident, the family drove to the hospital to see Ch'ŏlgi, who was about to undergo a CT scan before major surgery. Though in critical condition, he was still able to talk. However, he succumbed during the CT scan. After hearing about his grandson's death, Cho's father—who had already lost his eldest son long before, had witnessed his wife's death, and now saw his grandson precede him in death—refused to eat or drink and died in a few weeks. Consequently, Cho lost both his son and his father in the same month.

Mr. Cho had experienced six tragic deaths in his family: his older brother, sister-in-law, infant nephew, mother, middle son, and father. According to the Korean shamanic worldview, if a person dies a tragic and untimely death, the soul hovers between life and death, causing misfortune for the family, but a proper ritualistic intervention by the living can allow the dead to enter the otherworld and benefit the bereaved (Bruno 2007c, 326; Kendall 1985a, 155–56; cf. Heonik Kwon 2007, 86).[6] Conforming to the beliefs of their agnatic ancestors, who valued Confucian tradition and considered shamanic tradition vulgar, Mr. Cho and his late father had not sponsored any shamanic rituals. However, like most Cheju natives (including those who do not usually consult shamans), Mr. Cho believed that because he had not sponsored a *sŏngju p'uri* (ritual for settling the household gods into a newly built house), he could not conduct *chesa* in the new home (cf. Kendall 1985a, 119–20).

In order to sanction *chesa*, Mr. Cho decided to sponsor a *sŏngju p'uri* when the family moved into a new house several years after the deaths of his son and father. Since the family had to hire *simbang* anyway, they chose to use the occasion to placate their family members' souls and send them to the otherworld by adding a *Siwang maji* (lit., "receiving the Ten Kings") ceremony.[7] The Ten Kings are believed to decide the length of individual human lives and command messengers to fetch those whose time has come. Then the kings pass judgment on each person's behavior in life and assign the soul to a place in the otherworld (Hyŏn Yongjun 1980a, 883).

During the two-day *Siwang maji*, *simbang* invoke the Ten Kings of the otherworld and appeal to them to intervene on their clients' behalf. Simbang Yang explained the basic scenario of the ritual: "We ask the messengers of death to let Ch'ŏlgi go to the otherworld holding the hands of his grandparents, uncle [*k'ŭn abŏji*], and aunt [*k'ŭn ŏmŏni*]. King Yŏmna decides to which part of the otherworld the souls will be sent. We come to know this through divination. If the divination reveals that the souls won't be able to go to good places, we negotiate with the Ten Kings to send them to good places by offering *injŏng*."

Thus, in mid-October 2001, I accompanied a group of seasoned *simbang* composed of two primary practitioners (husband Yang and wife Kim) and three assistants (two females, O and Kang, and one male, Ko) as they set out to perform a three-day ritual at Mr. Cho's new home.[8] Simbang Yang drove his SUV; the three female *simbang* and I rode along as passengers. Simbang Ko followed us, driving his own SUV loaded with musical instruments, other ritual equipment, and everyone's personal belongings.

When we arrived at the Cho family's home in the early morning, the fine two-story house was marked with a *sot*, a straw rope hung over the gate in order to prevent polluted people (*pujŏnghan saram*) from entering the as-yet-unprotected dwelling.[9] After Simbang Yang removed the rope, we entered the house and were welcomed by Cho and his wife, Han, both in their mid-sixties. The living room was still sparsely furnished. Simbang Yang introduced me to the client couple, explaining the reason for my presence. Before the ritual, I had told Simbang Yang about my plan to donate some *pujo* to the ritual sponsors. He had welcomed the idea and advised me of the appropriate amount to contribute. Following Simbang Yang's verbal cue, I passed Cho an envelope containing the modest sum and thanked him for his willingness to allow my presence at the ritual. After hearing that I was pursuing a doctoral degree in the United States, Cho expressed respect for my education and told me that he would help anyone who wanted to study. As a high school diploma holder (a privileged credential for his generation), Cho was especially knowledgeable about classical Chinese texts, as evidenced by his competence in reading his family genealogy (*chokpo*), which was written in classical Chinese. He treated me congenially throughout the ritual, allowed me to videotape the ceremony, and answered my questions, all of which helped provide a solid basis for my analysis and for which I am very grateful.

POLITICS OF RITUAL FEE NEGOTIATION

The disagreement about the ritual fee described in the introduction to this book arose early in the visit. The outcome of this sort of dispute is crucial—the size of the fee the lead *simbang* is paid influences the patron's household budget and the income of all *simbang* who participate in a given ritual.[10] Mr. Cho, his wife, Han, the lead *simbang*, and an assistant all offered confident assessments of what had been decided in previous discussions. But the difference between the two parties' supposedly agreed-upon amount was 1 million won (US$1,000)—hardly an insignificant sum. In order to understand how such a hitch could have happened, we need to examine how ritual contracts are made. Although a pre-ritual consultation in which the ritual fee is decided is not only routine but also integral to the ritual practice in Korea,[11] relatively little attention has been paid to the matter (but see Chungmoo Choi 1987, 192–93; Chongho Kim 2003, 170–71). One important reason might stem from the fieldwork convention in which both scholars and shamans consider such an event peripheral to a framed ritual performance. Another might lie in the difficulty of obtaining an opportunity to observe pre-ritual consultations, since practitioners themselves may not always know when they will occur—some clients simply walk in, and others make phone calls. I managed to observe only a handful; however, they provided much insight into the economic underpinnings of ritual practice as well as a major source of contention between shamans and the laity.

Along with a *simbang*'s reputation for performance skills and ability to achieve ritual efficacy, the service fee (especially for a large-scale ritual) is a key factor in determining a client's choice of a *simbang*. The total ritual cost, of which the service fee is the most substantial, can also be the reason why some people cannot sponsor a ritual.[12] If financial issues prevent a family in dire need from sponsoring a ritual, *simbang* can avert the imminent misfortune by ritually informing the deities of the family's serious financial straits and promising them a ritual at a later time, usually within a few years, when the family's economic situation has improved. Since there is no standard pricing system for ritual fees, they can vary significantly from one shaman to another and fluctuate depending on the circumstances.[13] In general, the fee that a *simbang* can command is based primarily on the overall length of the ritual to be performed and the *simbang*'s reputation (cf. Bruno 2007a, 49; Chungmoo Choi 1987, 191; Romberg 2003). For example, in summer 1999, a lead *simbang* with a low profile received 800,000 won (US$800), while a lead *simbang* with a high profile received 2 million won (US$2,000), both for performing a one-day *sŏngju p'uri* just a few days apart.[14] Keenly aware of market conditions, *simbang* also adjust their fees. The *simbang* who had received 2 million won in summer 1999 cut the fee for the same ritual almost in half two years later due, according to the *simbang*, to the economic crisis that hit South Korea at the end of 1997.[15]

Both shamans and their clients keep a close eye on the going rates. Knowing that I was also working with other *simbang*, Simbang An once asked how much other *simbang* charged for a particular ritual that she was planning to perform soon. While she would want to receive a "fair" fee, asking for too much could discourage prospective clients. During *haesinje*, an annual community ritual at her seaside village in spring 2002, Simbang An received a phone call from someone in another town, half an hour from An's village by car. Virtually all shamans, like most Koreans, carry cell phones at all times, even during rituals, so as not to risk losing work opportunities. The caller asked whether Simbang An could give a *kwiyang p'uri*, a ritual customarily performed immediately after a funeral in order to console the dead, and how much the ritual would cost. Simbang An said, "Since it is outside [my village], I should receive at least 1.5 million won (US$1,500), in order to pay [assistant shamans]." Later, Simbang An told the story during a break at another ritual, saying to her assistants, "When I did a *haesinje*, someone called to ask me to do *kwiyang p'uri*. I asked for 1.5 million won. After that there was no follow-up phone call. Did I ask for too much?" Her prospective client might have been shopping around for a better price.

Some clients check prices in advance by making a phone call rather than taking the trouble to meet face-to-face with a shaman (when it would be more difficult to refuse a proffer). While clients do not want to pay more than necessary, they also want to avoid the risk of offending a *simbang* or losing face by offering too little. One day in winter 2002, Simbang An smilingly commented on the amount of money that her clients had offered for *chowangje*, a small-scale annual ritual conducted at individual households at the turn of each year. As it is a relatively simple ritual that takes only about an hour or so and is performed by one *simbang* alone, it does not involve a pre-consultation. Thus, ritual fees are not discussed in advance, and *simbang* receive whatever amount they are given at the beginning of the ritual, when the clients stick bills into bowls of uncooked rice as an offering. She surmised that her clients in the town had conspired to fix the price, since every household offered 50,000 won (US$50). Through this collective action, clients might have hoped to avoid the delicate issue of deciding on an appropriate amount so as to avoid embarrassing themselves or offending the *simbang* by tendering less than others.

On the one hand, most *simbang* depend entirely on their religious trade for their livelihoods. Therefore, obtaining a fair fee is critical (Chungmoo Choi 1989, 236). On the other hand, because sponsoring a large-scale ritual can be financially burdensome, clients try to minimize the fees they pay for the shaman's work while attempting to manipulate a *simbang*'s moral sentiments. Due to the conflicting interests of client and *simbang*, fee negotiations often involve haggling, and both parties employ the art of bargaining during these negotiations (cf. Chongho Kim 2003, 170–71).

One particular pre-ritual consultation impressed upon me how contentious a ritual fee negotiation can be. In March 2002, a woman in her late fifties from Kangjŏng, located on the west side of Cheju Island, visited the *simbang* couple Yang and Kim, who had conducted the ritual for Mr. Cho and lived on the opposite side of the island. She brought along her eldest sister, who was in her late sixties. The younger sister wanted to do *chilch'igi* for a total of fourteen souls from four generations among her in-laws and natal family. The client and the *simbang* couple discussed the kinds of rituals to be conducted, the requirements for ritual preparation, and how to group the souls for *chilch'igi*. The elder sister was concerned about having a so-called authentic (*chedaero toen*) *kut* and wanted four separate *chilch'igi* for each generation in the ritual proper. Simbang Kim responded that they could honor the client's request, but it would cost more money to do four *chilch'igi*. She recommended two *chilch'igi* for the souls, and the client agreed. Simbang Kim wrote down a list of necessary ritual items and explained how to prepare some of the ritual foods. As a favor, she offered to accompany the younger sister to the market in Cheju City to buy ritual paraphernalia.

Despite having discussed ritual preparation repeatedly and at length, the parties had still not discussed a contract. They beat around the bush some more before finally bringing up the ritual fee. The younger sister spoke rather mockingly about her observation of rituals performed by migrant shamans from mainland Korea, yet she had a point to make. Migrant shamans, she said, were inexpensive and brought everything, including side dishes, with them. Finally, the elder sister brought up the ritual fee indirectly by saying to her sister, "Now that everything has been written down, what's left is preparing money." Simbang Kim tried to draw her husband, who appeared aloof from these proceedings, into the matter by deferring the matter to him.

The elder of the two sisters, who was older than the *simbang* couple, an advantage in a society in which age hierarchy is still important, led the fee negotiations. A seasoned bargainer, she asked the *simbang* couple to think of the ritual as an opportunity to advertise their skills in the area where she and her sister lived, since people there did not know them. She continued, "Although I know that you [the *simbang*] could ask for extra money because you have the bother of traveling quite a long distance, think of it as if you were going there [her village] for a relaxing business trip." Her younger sister laughed upon hearing her argument.

Simbang Yang said that just one three-day ritual of this type usually costs 6 million to 7 million won (US\$6,000–7,000), but since they wanted to conduct two separate rituals, they would have to pay more.[16] He kindly offered, "I would ask *only* seven [7 million won] for both."

The sisters appeared to be surprised by the proposal. Simbang Yang's wife tried to rationalize the fee by saying, "It [7 million won] includes everything but *injŏng* (*injŏng man ssŭlkkŏ*)."

The younger sister attempted to bargain for a lower fee by referring to her husband, who, she said, saw no value in sponsoring rituals and had no sense of their market value.

Simbang Yang asked how much they were willing to pay. Neither sister responded promptly, and the younger sister said, "Won't it cost a lot even to buy ritual items?"

In turn, Simbang Yang pointed to the current market price of rituals: "So these days, one needs a big one [meaning 10 million won (US$10,000)] for a big (k'ŭn) kut."

The younger sister countered by explaining her dire financial situation and by saying that she would have to borrow money to do the kut and if it cost too much, her husband, who did not support sponsoring shamanic rituals, would be unhappy. The elder sister broke in and urged, "Do it for 5 million won."

Simbang Yang reacted by asserting, "That won't happen."

She responded, "Why not? We'll tell the husband [of her younger sister] that we're paying only 3 million won. If he heard what you asked, he would be shocked and faint (nolla chappajida)." The younger sister supported her sibling by sharing her plan to take care of the remaining cost herself by secretly borrowing small amounts of money from her friends and relatives.

In the face of their insistent bargaining, Simbang Yang lowered the price to 6 million won. The elder sister insisted on 5 million. This time Simbang Kim argued that she and her husband currently had to pay much more money for assistant simbang than they had in the past.

The elder sister, with her sister's pocketbook in mind, asked, "Won't it cost a lot of money to buy clothing for the fourteen souls and the other items necessary for the ritual?"

Simbang Kim responded, "Why, all together it would cost only 400,000 or 500,000 won (US$400 or US$500)."

Observing the tense back and forth, the younger sister hurriedly proposed 5.5 million won (US$5,500). The elder sister tried to fix the fee that her sister had tossed out by saying that her husband was anxiously awaiting her. She made motions as if to leave. The long haggling over the ritual fee was broken off without any real agreement between the two parties. Neither party's substantial verbal skills had won the upper hand in this particular negotiation.

Although I did not observe Mr. Cho's pre-ritual consultation, this example provides some insight into why there was a disagreement over 1 million won on the morning of his ritual. If the ritual fee is agreed upon only verbally and possibly from different perspectives, discord can result. Each party was unwilling to give in easily to the other. A *simbang* might still perform a ritual even if satisfactory payment has not been established, especially after face-to-face conversations with the would-be patrons. Practitioners do not want to discourage their clients by insisting on too "high" a fee, and they must consider the referrals that prospective clients may provide, especially important in light of the competition with other shamans, including migrant shamans from the mainland. Some also make allowances for indigent persons, those who desperately need a ritual but cannot afford an acceptable payment. I observed Simbang An collecting hardly any *injŏng* as an expression of her compassion for the natal family of one of her friends. This *simbang* performed a three-day ritual for only 3 million won, very little considering the scale of the ceremony, for a patron family in a dire situation at that time. However, *simbang* cannot make allowances for all of their clients. When the fee is unsatisfactory, what can a *simbang* do?

In the case of the Cho family, despite the prospect of receiving a much lower ritual fee than the lead *simbang* had expected, Kim and Yang moved on without further ado. They began the large-scale ritual with a daylong *sŏngju p'uri* to let the gods settle in, followed by the two-day *Siwang maji* to petition the Ten Kings on behalf of those who had died. A focus on the affect work that took place during the *yŏngge ullim* and the process of offering cash, both of which were performed as part of the *Siwang maji*, will promote a fuller appreciation of the intersection of the *simbang*'s emotional labor and the politics of money in rituals.

PERFORMATIVE POWER: CREATING PRESENCE AND EVOKING EMOTION

Yŏngge ullim is a locally recognized ritual session in which weeping is expected and culturally sanctioned. Mediating between the dead and the living, *simbang* deliver the lamentations of the dead with varying yet repetitive melodies and rhythms, typically holding a small towel in one hand, which they use to wipe away their own tears.[17] When this ritual event took place at Mr. Cho's, each soul spoke in turn through Simbang Kim, the lead female shaman. Mr. Cho and his wife, their two sons and daughters-in-law, one daughter, and Mr. Cho's two elder sisters, as well as some elderly neighbor women, attended the event. Because *chilch'igi* is the heart of the whole three-day ritual, the clients were at their most attentive during this session and kept their seats throughout the séance.

During many a *yŏngge ullim*, audience members weep along with the ritual specialist and sometimes even wail.[18] Here, I was captivated by a scene in which the clients, some of whom had remained calm and restrained throughout the earlier part of the ritual, became obviously and deeply involved. Han, the quiet-mannered hostess, sobbed loudly, holding a handkerchief in her hands and rocking back and forth when the souls of her father-in-law and son Ch'ŏlgi spoke to her. One of Mr. Cho's elder sisters wailed while poking at the rug where she was sitting. Mr. Cho's daughters-in-law, who had not known the deceased well, also wept softly, wiping away their tears with their hands. Even Mr. Cho and his younger son shed tears—actions rare for men in a public setting in Korea. I too was moved to tears but did not worry about attracting attention because I had set up my camcorder where I would not interfere with the *simbang*'s movements and could make my videotaping as inconspicuous as possible. In general, audience members were so absorbed with their own emotional reactions that they appeared to be unconcerned about my presence. The liberal weeping of the living and the dead (as voiced by the *simbang*) turned the ritual space into a scene of intense grief. Although weeping is expected at the séance, field observations indicate that not all *yŏngge ullim* evoke this level of emotional intensity. The impact of Simbang Kim's performance was profound.

Although this emotional outpouring is considered the mark of a successful séance in Cheju, only a few studies have paid close attention to what provokes the heightened emotional response central to this ritual event. Audience emotion, Hyŏn Yongjun argues, is stimulated by the patron family's belief that *yŏngge ullim* is the *real* utterance of the deceased (1980a, 452, 890). Mun Mubyŏng goes so far as to identify the *simbang* at the moment of *yŏngge ullim* with the departed souls, arguing that *simbang* are not "just playing [the] role of the soul, but *are* the souls" (2001, 20; my emphasis). He bases his assertion on the notion of performance as *acting*, meaning "make-believe, illusion, lying" (Schechner 1982, 62). From his standpoint, the authenticity of a "true" medium comes from the extraordinary quality of being able to *be* the soul, and medium speech then requires little agency on the part of a *simbang* because he or she is merely a voice box for the spirits. In contrast, Kim Seong-nae contends that "*yŏngge ullim* is created by a *simbang*, who composes it based on what she has heard about the dead from his or her family depending on the degree of her recital skill" (1991a, 20).[19] She indicates that *simbang* make choices in their delivery while compiling and arranging information and drawing on past practice. Insofar as Kim's observation gives credit to a *simbang*'s efforts and skills, it does not explain what makes the *yŏngge ullim* so convincing that people believe it to be the utterance of the soul. The apparently opposing perspectives of Mun and Kim reinforce the binary opposition of "being" (real, authentic) versus "performing" (artificial, fake).

Practitioners' comments provide insight into this issue of the authorship of *yŏngge ullim* and help us move beyond polemics. *Simbang* do not deny the influence of spirits. As one *simbang* told me, "We cannot feign weeping when souls do not." No *simbang* would argue that *yŏngge ullim* is crafted solely by them, without spirit involvement. Yet they also take pride in their impact on audiences and the dexterous efforts required for drawing out this emotional response during the *yŏngge ullim*.[20] For instance, although her speech patterns presented the *yŏngge ullim* as the dead's own words when she performed in front of Mr. Cho's family, in the kitchen of her own home Simbang Kim emphasized the labor required for such coordination of mind and feeling: "Do you think the dead come into my body and say things? I feel spiritual inspiration [*yŏnggam*]. But I have to judge what I have to say promptly at the moment, while venting the grief of the deceased and the surviving family and at the same time promoting harmony among the bereaved family members."[21]

Several *simbang* described their role in the *yŏngge ullim* this way. Their comments suggest that whereas their spiritual power is indispensable in the *yŏngge ullim*, their deliberate effort to use empathetic speech is also pivotal (cf. Kendall 2009, chap. 3). However, I suspect that Simbang Kim would not share these comments with her clients, who might then question the speech's authenticity (cf. Schieffelin 1996). A dominant perspective held by ritual sponsors on Cheju Island is that the *yŏngge ullim* is the spirits' own words and weeping, as the term indicates. However, these are made present by the *simbang*, whose performances are evaluated by the audience.[22] *Simbang* therefore walk a tightrope when performing *yŏngge ullim*: they have to make the medium speech sound as if it were emanating from the dead while minimizing the focus on their own performance skills and effort expended to achieve this.

Simbang's view of medium speech is congruent with that of scholars of ritual studies, who have challenged the dichotomy of "theatricality and inspiration" and asserted that it is the delicate balance of the two that makes for a successful shamanic performance (Chungmoo Choi 1989; Kendall 2009, 67; Schieffelin 1996). The spirit séance is a social reality made possible by the *simbang*'s performance. Simbang Kim's comments to me in her kitchen also provide insight into the sociocultural features of emotion that scholars from various disciplines have emphasized, challenging essentialist notions of emotion that place it in an inner realm and instead stressing that it can be public, controlled, constructed or learned, and amenable to sociocultural analysis.[23] In part, then, *simbang* perform what is socially expected from a séance (cf. Ebersole 2000, 243), producing a composition in which cohesive cultural themes prevail. For instance, in the *yŏngge ullim* performance, both the dead and the bereaved are idealized.

During the *yŏngge ullim* discussed here, Simbang Kim labored to exhaustion while controlling social situations by means of her ritual knowledge, experience with spirits and clients, and improvisational skill. Scholars have recognized the emotional transformation that patrons experience during rituals (Bruno 2002; Chungmoo Choi 1989, 240–41) but rarely note the practitioner's labor outlay. A *simbang* does physical labor when she dances intensely and beats drums, she does mental work when she figures out what is needed for the family, and finally she does emotional labor when she manages her own feelings and those of others. A female *simbang* from the southern part of Cheju Island stressed that the intense mental, emotional, and physical expenditures involved in professional ritual performances may have serious long-term costs: "Our eyes go blind earlier than other people's because we shed so many tears. Our ears go deaf earlier because we hear the din of percussion music played at rituals. And our voices get husky because we overuse our throats. Not to mention the mental pain that we suffer [due to our emotional involvement]." After the ritual at Mr. Cho's, even I felt quite spent. Performing a ritual is no small feat.

However, despite the gripping séance and, in part, because of the complex ambiguity of the authorship and emergent features of performance, I was unable to fully grasp Simbang Kim's efforts and multiple talents until I transcribed and analyzed the performed text. The concrete example of Simbang Kim's performance of the *yŏngge ullim* shows how *simbang* move others and socialize the emotions of the ritual participants while utilizing specific linguistic strategies and cultural norms. A refined, controlled, and elaborate style, which at the same time sounds believable in terms of speech style and content, leads to the affective power of the *yŏngge ullim*. The medium frames and performs the *yŏngge ullim* as if the soul speaks by borrowing her mouth, thus discursively surrendering her own subjectivity. Though it may seem that they are possessed, they are certainly not "dispossessed of all agency" (Bauman 2004, 139).[24]

ENACTING THE AUTHORITY OF SOULS' SPEECH

Yŏngge ullim is acknowledged as coming from beings who are in a different realm from the living and to whom the laity have no access under ordinary circumstances. If the *simbang*'s experience with spirits inevitably remains esoteric, examining the performed text of *yŏngge ullim* illuminates *how simbang* render discourse authoritative and what makes spirit medium speech so effective in arousing an audience's emotions. *Simbang* themselves do not openly take credit for their composition or performance of *yŏngge ullim*. However, *yŏngge ullim* is performance in the most fundamental sense; that is, the discursive practice takes place in front of an audience and is evaluated by that audience (Bauman 1977, 1986). *Simbang* make the words of the dead, to whom they are believed to have exclusive access, easily accessible to the public (cf. Bauman 2004, 146). The family members being addressed listen to the messages while sitting and usually remaining silent, heads down, rather than engaging in the conversation. The mediums deliver these messages while standing without musical instruments or ritual paraphernalia such as the hourglass-drum or rattle that often accompany the recitation of other types of shamanic ritual speech. Although the medium speech is intimate and conversational in content and style, it is delivered in a voice louder than that used in ordinary one-on-one conversation. The *simbang*'s voice shifts neither in pitch nor in timbre when conveying the words of men or women.[25] This straightforwardness draws the audience's full attention to the souls' utterances rather than to the "performer."

When conveying each soul's lamentation at Mr. Cho's household, Simbang Kim deliberately manages the lamentations of the dead in ways that seemingly diminished her role. To this end, she employs deliberate communicative means and linguistic strategies that aligned with the conventions expected by her audience. Unlike divination, in which *simbang* consult with the gods and then report the result to their patrons, during *yŏngge ullim*, *simbang* do not relay the souls' lamentations but rather improvise them. As Simbang Kim indicated, mediums figure out what souls want to say immediately and intuitively (*chikkam ŭro*) and articulate those intentions on the spur of the moment, shaping them to match the deceased's emotional state and the bereaved family members' needs. This process is challenging, but it enhances the *yŏngge ullim*'s authenticity, since there is little discursive and temporal gap between "source utterance and target utterance" (Bauman 2004, 139).[26]

Yŏngge ullim is a *simbang*'s solo performance, but the *simbang* plays a variety of participant roles by means of framing and footing (Goffman 1981, 124–59) with the intention of creating a sense of the presence of the dead. Erving Goffman's concept of participant roles, "discriminating, for example, the formulator of an utterance (the author) from the speaker who actually voices it (the animator)" (Bauman 2004, 6), is particularly useful in understanding the communicative dynamics of *yŏngge ullim* that the speaker-hearer dyad cannot explain. Similar to *p'ansori* singers (Chungmoo Choi 1989, 246), the medium enacts each soul's speech and at times plays the role of a narrator who describes the souls' actions in order to contextualize the pertinent messages of the souls.

In her performance for Mr. Cho, for example, Simbang Kim brackets the *yŏngge ullim* by setting it apart from the rest of the ritual while simultaneously establishing a new participant structure using verbal and nonverbal framing devices. To frame the *yŏngge ullim*, Simbang Kim turns her body to the clients, after having sung a libation chant while facing the small offering tables dedicated to the dead souls and the messengers of death.[27] This bodily reorientation is accompanied by her verbal framing work: "Turning back, here are messages [from the souls]. I convey their greetings to you (*tora sŏmŏng punbuwoeda, munan yŏtsummeda*)."[28] The omitted but implied first-person pronouns in the original Korean refer to the *simbang* herself—note that in the Korean language, both written and verbal, personal pronouns are often omitted. This conventional framing phrase establishes that what is to come is from the souls and that she is an *apparent* animator, "the talking machine, a body engaged in acoustic activity" (Goffman 1981, 144). By emphasizing that she is merely an animator, not the principal, she is verbally eliding her subjectivity from the performance.

Simbang Kim's skillful management of framing and footing in accordance with the cultural expectations of the audience is another example of her experienced control over the *yŏngge ullim*. She conveys the deceased's laments in conversational Cheju dialect, making them easy to comprehend. The form of each soul's speech is consistent with that soul's social status. For example, Ch'ŏlgi uses respectful speech (*nop'immal*) when addressing his parents and *panmal* when talking to his younger brother. Coupled with kinship-based terms of direct address, these help audience members recognize which soul is speaking and to whom. The sequence of speakers and addressees is consistent with the family hierarchy. Mr. Cho's father, who holds the highest status in the family, speaks first to Mr. Cho, who holds the highest status among the living. Then Mr. Cho's mother, brother, sister-in-law, and son Ch'ŏlgi speak to the bereaved in accordance with their place in the family.

Ch'ŏlgi, the youngest among the dead, speaks last and longest. Knowing Ch'ŏlgi's importance to the client family (consoling Ch'ŏlgi's soul, after all, was the main reason for sponsoring the ritual), the *simbang* makes an additional effort to frame his lamentation, orienting her audience to Ch'ŏlgi's forthcoming speech:

1. A dear soul is coming in, specifically,
2. The soul of well-named Ch'ŏlgi,
3. Oh, having heard about this ritual,
4. Came to the alley a few days ago.
5. Come, grandfather,
6. The souls of grandmother, uncle, and aunt
7. Beheld his father and mother when they came in; beheld them when they came out,
8. Especially his younger brother, who lives on the second floor.
9. He sat down in the alley and beheld his younger brother when he went down to work;
10. He sat down in the alley and beheld that younger brother when he came back from work.
11. Oh, dear soul.

Describing Ch'ŏlgi's return to this world with older family members who have been long dead, Simbang Kim temporarily narrows the spatial, temporal, and existential gaps between the audience and those that normally inhabit different realms. Taking an omniscient point of view as a third-person narrator and employing parallel structures (lines 7, 9, and 10), she vividly and poetically portrays Ch'ŏlgi's anxious longing to meet with his surviving family through the ritual. By suggesting that Ch'ŏlgi's return has been prompted by his knowledge that the ritual is being held (line 3), the *simbang* also validates the family's decision to engage her services.

Immediately after the description of Ch'ŏlgi coming to the ritual place, Simbang Kim animates Ch'ŏlgi's voice:

Father, father, Ch'ŏlgi has come.
Oh! How have you been meanwhile?
Oh! My father, how did you survive missing me?

The notification of the soul's arrival creates a sensation of co-presence, enhancing emotional engagement. The discursive distance between the *simbang* narrator and the soul in the narrative—constructed partially by the *simbang*'s use of the third-person pronoun in the first eleven lines of the text—is nullified once she starts animating the soul of Ch'ŏlgi. The contrast is immediately evident in the way Ch'ŏlgi greets his father. The personal pronouns in these verses index Mr. Cho (you) and Ch'ŏlgi (my, me).[29] Moreover, the *simbang* speaks not about her own sentiments but about Ch'ŏlgi's. This full "submission to the *form*" (Bauman 2004, 153; italics in the original) of the soul's utterance and to his affect preserves the integrity of the greeting as Ch'ŏlgi's own and leads Mr. Cho and other audience members to surrender to the authority of the message. The care and skill with which *simbang* enact the souls' messages without apparent discursive infiltration help the audience believe that the *simbang* is "being taken over by the spirits" (Chungmoo Choi 1989, 247) and that the messages emanate from the dead.

SHARING EMOTIONS AND MULTIPLE REFLEXIVITY

Simbang render *yŏngge ullim* not only as authoritative but also as affective discourse. The audience's weeping prominent in *yŏngge ullim* is a consequence of the *simbang*'s "intentionally affective work" (Armstrong 1971). In order to generate audience emotions, *simbang* use themes that have emotional potency and linguistic strategies such as direct discourse and conditionals that are effective in making the discourse feel like the intimate communication of the departed. The *simbang*'s empathy with the dead and the living is key to this endeavor (cf. Chungmoo Choi 1989, 240–41). *Simbang* not only grasp but also experience the thoughts, feelings, and attitudes of those whom they portray so artfully. This intensive, multifaceted labor would not be possible if the *simbang* did not engage in empathetic imagination. *Simbang* literally embody empathy for the souls and the surviving family members by weeping for them and thus consoling them in a mourning performance that provides the bereaved with a conventionalized yet specific encounter with the dead. In this regard, the *yŏngge ullim* amounts to a "group therapy session" in which the dead and the living reflect upon their relationships with one another and see each other from the other party's perspective.[30]

Although each spirit has a different message for each living family member, common themes are noticeable. The souls typically open their speeches with heartfelt greetings for their bereaved. The greetings are followed by elegiac lamentations about the souls' pent-up feelings, expressions of regret for their wrongdoings, and descriptions of unsatisfied desires. These messages also often mention the spirits' enduring affection for the bereaved, gratitude for sponsoring the ritual, wishes or advice for the living family, and promises to leave for the otherworld, from which they will look after the well-being of the bereaved. While sharing previously unexpressed feelings, both the deceased and the bereaved disentangle their hearts (*maech'in kasŭm ŭl p'ulda*).

The souls, having been unable to communicate with the bereaved since their deaths, greet the surviving family members with intense emotion, often calling to a family member repeatedly in relational terms and sobbing, frequently interjecting an exclamatory "Oh!" The greetings are mostly directed toward the addressees', not the addressors', emotional conditions and often consist of remarks that penetrate the particular addressee's emotional distress. In this case, Ch'ŏlgi touches upon the sorrow his father experienced as a result of his untimely death: "My father, how did you survive missing me?"[31] This interrogatory remark rhetorically acknowledges his father's pain while poetically embellishing the greeting.

The dead then focus chiefly on the grief left unsaid. For instance, Ch'ŏlgi laments his unfortunate sudden death:

> Elder Brother, if I had been sent to Seoul—
> Oh! If I had been sent to a university hospital to have surgery,
> I might have survived.
> Do doctors care about a dying person?
> Oh! Elder Brother,
> Although they don't care about it,
> How would my brothers forget my death
> Even after ten years and twenty years?
> Elder brother, due to the accident—
> Oh! Didn't my heart get hurt due to the rupture of intestines?
> Didn't my five viscera get hurt?

Having died during a medical procedure, Ch'ŏlgi blames the poor capabilities of the local hospital and wishes for a longer life by using the conditional form. As in this instance, *simbang* often articulate what the dead might have thought by employing the conditional form to conjecture about the dead's unspoken feelings. By contrasting the doctors' indifference with the brothers' bond, he emphasizes his brother's love for him. He also unveils the intense pain that he suffered but was unable to express due to his sudden death. Hearing the vivid descriptions of Ch'ŏlgi's regret and pain, not only his elder brother but also the other members of the audience weep with him.

Words left unsaid are not necessarily due to untimely death alone; they may also have remained unspoken because of reticence. In the following excerpt, Mr. Cho's father reveals his feelings regarding Mr. Cho:

> When I was alive, you were sick.
> Oh, when you got sick often,
> This father, in my heart,
> Oh, worrying "I might lose this son too."
> Oh, although I did not say it,
> Oh, when [I] came
> And saw you were doing well,
> I felt relieved.
> Oh, when [I] came and heard that you were so sick
> That you had gone to a hospital,
> I felt heavy-hearted.

The description is so vivid as to quote the soul's own thoughts: "I might lose this son too." However, as the soul himself indicates, he did not voice such thoughts in life. As in other *yŏngge ullim* that I observed, *simbang* often quote the inner thoughts of the dead, which authenticates their mourning speech without risking infidelity to actual utterances.

Sharing one's intimate feelings—especially between father and adult son—is not common in Korea, even when two people are close. This inhibition about expressing one's emotions is also indicated in Ch'ŏlgi's communication with his father:

> Oh, although my father endured patiently,
> When [my] commemoration date came around, [you] took out my
>   picture.
> Oh, my father burst into tears.
> But, being afraid of getting caught by Mother or Elder Brother,
> Oh, being afraid of getting caught by Younger Brother, [you] wiped away
>   [your] Tears.

Ch'ŏlgi displays his father's emotional agonies by portraying the weeping as though he had directly observed it. In other words, Simbang Kim let Mr. Cho hear his own feelings and thus work out his emotions. Mr. Cho pined for Ch'ŏlgi but endured it until Ch'ŏlgi's commemoration day, when he finally burst into tears. Still, according to Ch'ŏlgi's words, his father's streaming tears would have been an embarrassment to him, so Mr. Cho wiped them away. Here, the *simbang*'s empathy is enacted triply. Imagining what the dead would have felt, she feels empathy for Ch'ŏlgi, who is in turn expressing his empathy for his father. Moreover, the father with whom Ch'ŏlgi feels empathy cares about the feelings the living family members would have experienced had they witnessed his own grief over the loss of Ch'ŏlgi.

The son further elucidates his father's layered thoughts:

Father who thinks,
"When I go out, people might laugh at me:
'Oh, that person lost his son.'"

As illustrated in the doubly quoted form marked by the apt change of pronouns, Ch'ŏlgi exposes Mr. Cho's thus far unrevealed thoughts. He acknowledges how his death might affect his father's place in the world beyond the immediate household, and he expresses sympathy for his father, who in turn is pondering the thoughts of others. As in a number of examples, the medium's empathy is enacted through direct discourse, effectively expressing the dead's intimate feelings by putting herself in others' shoes while rendering their utterances as their own. Thus, both Mr. Cho's father and son, whose deaths in the same month caused Mr. Cho so much pain, console him. Such strong feelings between son and father can easily be shared by the broader audience, including Mr. Cho's neighbors who attended the ritual and perhaps also by this book's readers.

Similar to his observation of his father's mourning on his commemoration day, Ch'ŏlgi articulates his mother's sorrow on his younger brother's wedding day:

On the wedding day of Younger Brother Ch'ŏlsu,
Oh, Mother, [you] started weeping at home
And wept more at the wedding hall, thinking of me.[32]

Thus, Ch'ŏlgi voices his parents' elegiac remembrance of him as though bearing witness to the distress caused by his own death. He lets his parents know that, although he has long been dead, he understands their suffering. Situating the past in the immediate context, he relates his own emotions to those of his parents and powerfully evokes their feelings. This effort to communicate what has been left unsaid and to vent suppressed feelings seems to generate cathartic weeping and in turn to console both the living and the dead.

The *yŏngge ullim* is, in fact, weeping about weeping. Ch'ŏlgi weeps while talking about his parents crying, and his parents weep while listening to Ch'ŏlgi's lamentation. Further, Ch'ŏlgi encourages his mother, whose face is already tear-stained, to weep more:

> Today, you cry your heart out.
> I will also cry my heart out so that
> Later on, Mother, don't think of me.
> Oh, don't think of me.

The patron family's sorrow stems mainly from their remembrance of the dead as those who have not separated completely from the living and thus have not yet entered the otherworld. Like the Japanese who visit spirit mediums at Mount Osore for spirit recollections (J. *kuchiyose*), Mr. Cho and his family are "still in a state of incomplete mourning" (Ivy 1995, 184). Ch'ŏlgi requests that his parents forget him.[33] Paradoxically, they can forget him and in turn stop crying only by weeping to their hearts' content. The *yŏngge ullim* seems to be designed to complete the incomplete state of mourning by letting both the living and the dead communicate and weep. And for this closure, a mediator is indispensable. Only then can the bereaved let go of Ch'ŏlgi and the other deceased who have been invited to the séance; that is, the living can remember them as *dead*. *Simbang* can remove the barriers and shape the proceedings for the benefit of all participants.

Further, only after this ritual can the troubled souls also go to the otherworld and separate safely from the living (cf. Chungmoo Choi 1989, 246; Kendall 1985a, 155), as Ch'ŏlgi announces in the following passage:

> Oh! Mother, don't cry; I will go to the otherworld.
> I will go holding Grandfather's hand and Grandmother's hand.
> Oh! I will go relying on Uncle and Aunt.
> Don't cry anymore, Mother.

To this end, the *simbang* invokes the dead and reconnects, albeit temporarily, the social relationships that were ruptured by death. She is able to fulfill this role because of her spiritual power and linguistic skills. By embodying the feelings of a particular departed person and evoking those feelings in the audience, the ritual specialist organizes the *yŏngge ullim* so that the audience experiences intense emotional engagement.

The *simbang*'s purposeful arousal of the audience's feelings during the *yŏngge ullim* is evident the moment she breaks the performance frame. For instance, after the long and intense period of weeping, Simbang Kim turned to her fellow *simbang* and asked brightly, "Haven't we had dinner yet?" Her question, and the way it was delivered, shattered the somber atmosphere that she herself had created and sustained through her enthralling performance. This sudden shift clearly shows that *simbang* can turn their tears on and off at will, managing their hearts as well as others. The *yŏngge ullim* is the *simbang*'s pragmatic act that allows the audience a "subjective experience of emotion" in Judith T. Irvine's sense (1990, 156). As the audience experiences the empathy doubly, even triply, enacted before them, the living's ability to empathize with and commune with the dead is enhanced and encouraged. The laity craves this "illocutionary" force,[34] or communicative effect of the medium speech, which can be experienced only during a *kut*, more than simple information about the state of the dead obtainable through a consultation with a seer. Indeed, ritual sponsors are not simply present at the *kut*; they are also invited to participate in it.

INTERTEXTUALITY: AUDIENCE AS COAUTHOR

How, then, did Simbang Kim know such details of the family's past and the emotional states of both the dead and the living, knowledge that allowed her to improvise the *yŏngge ullim* so effectively? When the *simbang* conveyed Mr. Cho's late father's unexpressed love, she could not be questioned about the veracity of his belated expression of feelings—after all, as he himself announced through Simbang Kim, he "did not say it." However, other details—Han weeping at the wedding hall and Cho's inner thoughts and his sorrow on Ch'ŏlgi's commemoration days—could have been contested by the patrons, had they not been in agreement with the content of the mediated speech.

In arousing the living's emotions, Simbang Kim drew on her own store of knowledge gained through conversation with and observation of family members as well as her experience with other clients.[35] Before the ritual, Han visited the *simbang* couple (Yang and Kim) for a pre-ritual consultation, which typically includes talk about the family's history and reasons for sponsoring rituals. Soon after the *simbang* arrived at Cho's house, the lead *simbang* conversed with him and elicited detailed biographical information regarding both deceased and living family members. Simbang Kim solicited necessary information by asking direct questions and responding effusively to answers received. Her sympathetic responses encouraged Cho's confessional accounts. In the process, the *simbang* grasped the dynamics of the family relationships and the family's emotional and psychological needs. As the ritual progressed and the *simbang* built rapport, Cho offered several anecdotes during the breaks between ritual sessions. The *simbang* referenced the information he supplied during these conversational gambits time and again in subsequent performances, including the *yŏngge ullim*.[36] Thus, regardless of whether he intended to or not, Mr. Cho took part in the formulation of the *yŏngge ullim*.

However, Mr. Cho's role as source in the earlier dialogue becomes opaque during the *yŏngge ullim*, in which his participant role is reversed and he becomes a discursive target.[37] Using spiritual power and verbal skills, Simbang Kim wove bits of information from earlier dialogue into an emotionally charged, poetic performance on the spur of the moment. The indexical interconnection between what Simbang Kim heard from Cho and what she formulated appears greatly subdued due to the latter's highly stylized form. A *simbang* would not emphasize the dialogic implications of the antecedent discourse in the *yŏngge ullim*, because it would undercut the display of competence and lessen the evocative power of the *yŏngge ullim*.[38]

SANCTIONING THE ECONOMIC VALUE OF RITUAL

Close attention to the *simbang*'s verbal performance reveals that economic calculation is evident in shamanic practice even when the ritual goals are not overtly business oriented (cf. Kendall 2009). Ch'ŏlgi's willingness to leave for the otherworld, an intention affirmed during the *yŏngge ullim*, was a pivotal part of what the family paid for with bank checks before the ritual began. Although friends and kin can provide the bereaved family with emotional support, it cannot be the same as a ritual healing. In this sense, the lamentations of the dead are invested not only with emotional and psychological value but also with economic import,[39] as articulated in Ch'ŏlgi's words:

> Oh! My mother,
> You offer a *chilch'igi* for me,
> *Paying what you would have spent*
> *For my food, clothing, and expenses*
> *And for my wedding*
> *If I had been alive.*
> As you think of me
> And open my heart,
> Mother—
> Oh! Mother, don't cry; I will go to the otherworld.

Indeed, it was Mr. Cho who provided the calculative logic behind sponsoring a grand-scale ritual during an earlier conversation with the *simbang* group: the parents wanted to console their son, who died unmarried, thinking that if things had taken a different course, they would have had to spend money for Ch'ŏlgi's wedding. This comment reflects the fact that they carefully measured the cost of the ritual in light of other factors. The family did not normally value shamanic services, but they were also not entirely free from a general belief in the restless spirits of those who die untimely deaths. Even if they resorted to employing a *simbang*, the desired end would be intangible and the outcome uncertain. Seeking out the most able *simbang* in the area must have seemed the best they could do to achieve an efficacious outcome. By considering the expense as an investment on behalf of their beloved son—an amount they would have had to spend anyway had he lived—they were able to come to terms with their decision. According to Ch'ŏlgi's words expressed through the *simbang*, their calculated wishes seemed to have been realized.

OFFERING MONEY: A BONE OF CONTENTION

Offering money to supernatural entities—a practice that occurs in many other Asian countries—has been the subject of important anthropological inquiries into the relationship between religion and society. Several anthropologists have offered insights into the correspondences or discontinuities between ritual offerings and specific political-economic systems and histories.[40] At the same time, examining the act of offering at a specific ritual is crucial to understanding what is at stake among ritual participants and why it can be thorny. The patron family must be party to extended offerings to supernatural beings over the course of a *kut*. This makes a ritual work but can also lead to implicit and explicit tension between clients and practitioners pertaining to the symbolic and practical value of offerings, particularly that of real money.

At the Cho family's *yŏngge ullim*, after releasing their pent-up feelings, Ch'ŏlgi and the other souls were willing to part with the bereaved and leave for the otherworld. However, not only is the journey to the otherworld arduous and difficult, but the travelers must also stand trial in courts along the way and pass through gates kept by the Ten Kings. Simbang Kim metaphorically tidied up the rugged pathways that the deceased must travel. She enacted this clearance by walking between the rows of bamboo crescents that symbolize the gates of the otherworld, cutting off "weeds" on the road with small ritual knives, and removing the "refuse" with a stick. Assistant Simbang Kang compared these processes to "asphalt paving, cleaning the road, smoothing the rough road." To further smooth the ordeal of passage, the patron family made a concerted effort to work with the *simbang* by offering *injŏng* in order to influence key figures in the otherworld such as the messengers of death and the Ten Kings, in whose clutches the souls have been held hostage (cf. Beuchelt 1975a; Kendall 1985b; Kim T'aegon 1966, 75–76).

The subsequent process of offering money, particularly "real" money, is not without a subtle and complicated battle of mutual assessment between the *simbang* and the host family. The *simbang* encourages the patron family to dedicate copious quantities of money both by inspiring piety with compelling oratory and by literally coaching family members in an orchestrated manner.[41] In general, during the *chilch'igi* at Mr. Cho's, the two female assistant *simbang* rather assertively directed the family to offer *injŏng*, while Simbang Kim softened the tone of the activity. After symbolically smoothing the way, Simbang Kim relayed the departing souls' messages that she had acquired through divination, including the admonition not to grieve anymore and expressions of gratitude for sponsoring the ritual. Simbang Kim then walked around the living room holding a plastic tray on which to collect offerings for the messengers of death. Each family member, including Mr. Cho's eldest grandson, an elementary school student, and the visiting elderly neighbors who had come to observe the ritual, put a bill on the tray. Holding the tray piled with cash, Simbang Kim faced the offering table for the messengers of death and requested, "After having received the *injŏng*, take the souls to the otherworld without being harsh."

In the next ritual segment, Simbang Kim rapidly and graphically depicted the events of the death of the souls, that is, the messengers of death descending to summon them and a representative trial at the court of Hell, in which the dead are interrogated and judged according to their conduct during life. The souls must then pass through each of the ten gates of Hell, which are grotesque, gory, and frightening and where sinful humans are cruelly punished.[42] The *simbang* then pleaded with the Ten Kings, who are believed to be just in their judgments, that amnesty be granted to the dead and that they be sent to better places in the otherworld. It is from this role that the title Simbang, "Judicial Officials of the Gods," stems, and it is why *simbang* refer to themselves as lawyers who work on behalf of their clients (*sin ŭi pyŏnhosa*). In this moment, in which the lot of the souls depends on the deities' mercy, the family members are supposed to offer a range of materials to temper the kings' predilection for justice and punishment. Simbang O showed the patron family how to hang white linen pieces and pseudo-money such as *chijŏn* (blank white paper money) and *tarani* (paper money marked with red coin prints) on the crescent-shaped bamboo rods. When the host family members attempted to hang only one piece of *chijŏn* and *tarani*, the *simbang* encouraged them to be more generous. The amount of *injŏng* offered is a marker of the family's sincerity, which is crucial to ritual efficacy.

When the family tried to sit down after contributing the pseudo-money, Simbang O instructed them: "Don't sit down. Stand up and offer the *injŏng* [i.e., actual cash] now." However, with no demonstration by any *simbang*, the family members seemed unsure about their roles and looked to Simbang Kim for guidance. Her response was somewhat reassuring but also a bit defensive: "After this, we won't ask you to offer any more *injŏng*. It does not have to be a lot of money. But recognize that each row has five [rods]." Although she appeared to make light of the money involved, in actuality *injŏng* cannot be a negligible sum. The fifty rods that she demanded be covered—ten rows symbolizing the ten gates and five columns for the five souls—required a substantial amount of cash. Responding to their hesitation, Simbang Kang bluntly told them: "Although it looks like *simbang* take [the money], this is an allotment for your son's wedding ceremony. It is to console your son." She emphasized the ritualistic significance of the money, while de-emphasizing the shamans' own interests. Although the Korean bills have become infused with symbolic meaning in the performance reality, their ceremonial value is not completely unambiguous. As in every exchange, "symbolic tokens might slip into alternative regimes of value," that is, legal tender "can cross contexts" and be reinterpreted "as cash value" (Keane 2001, 69). While the stacks of folded white paper money lose their use value and are burned after the ritual, the shamans pocket the real bills.

Despite the ambiguity, the patron family has little choice but to offer legal tender in the ritual situation. They did as they were directed. As Han distributed cash to her family members, I recognized the relevance of an earlier exchange between the patron couple and the *simbang* group centered on the need to have additional cash for the ritual. Mr. Cho's excuse that the banks were already closed prompted Simbang Kim's reply, "Then you'd better go and sell honey [to get cash]." As revealed by what he told me later, Mr. Cho had not earmarked the unexpectedly large sum of *injŏng* as part of the ritual cost for his son, and the *simbang* had to make sure the family was prepared for the abundant offerings required. Indeed, as I watched, everyone but the juveniles hung a note on each of the fifty rods—Mr. Cho offered 10,000-won [US$10] bills and the others gave smaller denominations. Simbang Kim allowed Mr. Cho's grandchildren to hang a bill on only the first and last rod, saying sweetly, "How much money could a child have? I will let it pass." Seemingly a generous gesture, this statement indicates her confidence in her control over the family's ritual roles. Having heard through the *simbang*'s divination that the souls are willing to go to the otherworld and having been reminded of the horrifying hells that will soon confront them, the bereaved at any ritual may feel obliged to do whatever they can for the deceased who are, after all, the reason for the ritual in the first place. Therefore, people offer money they might otherwise be unwilling to part with. In addition, the bereaved would not want to appear stingy to their dear dead ones, especially in the presence of living observers.

After the offerings, Simbang Kim prayed on behalf of her patron that the Ten Kings would not make the souls endure the agonies of the Ten Hells. Then, as she passed each row, she divined whether her prayers had been answered. As Simbang Kim received affirmatives at each of the ten gates, the family bowed and offered a libation to the Ten Kings with Simbang Kang's assistance. Simbang O then removed the offerings from each row and pulled down the rods. The money, now infused with multiple meanings, including an expression of the family's care for the dead and a "bribe" to the otherworld officials, seemed to have been well spent.

The sum of money that changes hands during this ritual is substantial; in addition to the cash offered during *chilch'igi*, clients were asked to offer *injŏng* several more times before the entire ritual concluded the next day. At the end of three days, however, Cho remarked to the *simbang*: "It's almost as if you did the *kut* for free." This remark, said sincerely enough, caught me off guard, especially since I had seen the amount of cash offered for *injŏng* over and above the substantial ritual service fee. However, because the *simbang* were present, I did not have an opportunity to ask Mr. Cho what had motivated his comment. Nineteen months later, when I again visited Cho, he rather caustically explained his remark: "At that time, Yang received 5 million or 6 million won. But he still took a lot of *injŏng* at the *chilch'igi*. Since those people are supposed to serve others [*pongsahada*], they shouldn't receive that money; if they took the money offered for *injŏng* in addition to the service fee, then they should be punished. So in order to save them from their punishment, I said 'It's as if you did the *kut* for free.' Although the spirits (*kwisin*) can't see, they can hear."

Mr. Cho had attempted to trick the spirits by speaking aloud in order to save the *simbang* from retribution for their greed. His action also demonstrates his dissatisfaction with their methods. The kernel of Mr. Cho's discontent with the *simbang* group lies in the fact that they took a substantial amount of offering money even though they had already been, from his perspective, handsomely remunerated for their services.

A different ethnographic instance provided me with a clue to the contentious nature of cash offerings involved in rituals. In spring 2002, I was sitting in the backseat of a *simbang*'s car on the way to participate in two *sŏngju p'uri* that would be performed consecutively on the same day. The primary *simbang* claimed that the second household had agreed to an "adequate" ritual fee, but the first had not. I did not understand the implications of this comment until after we had arrived at the first home and I overheard a *simbang*'s conversations with members of the client family.

The assistant *simbang* asked someone to get 5,000-won (US$5) bills ready for offerings. One of the female members of the family responded, "We should've bought *tarani*."

The *simbang* argued, "You should of course offer *tarani*, but you should also offer cash to the ancestors for travel money. Ten-thousand-won bills would do well,[43] but that could be too burdensome." The assistant *simbang* thereby implied that her request had taken the client's financial situation into account. Only after I heard this conversation and observed the offering processes in both rituals did I realize what the lead *simbang* had meant in the car: because the first household had not paid enough up front, the *simbang* would vigorously encourage this family to offer cash during the ritual.

Recall the anecdote about a dispute between the client couple (Cho and Han) and the *simbang* couple (Yang and Kim) before the ritual began. The *simbang* received appreciably less than expected. Clearly, the *simbang* had a reason for the aggressive collection of cash offerings at Mr. Cho's ritual. They had to make up for an inadequate fee in a ritually legitimate way.

CONCLUSION

Contrary to the tenacious assumption that shamans manipulate gullible people, clients utilize shamanic services for specific needs primarily in dealing with a crisis, carefully consider the worth of investing their financial resources in rituals, and aggressively negotiate fees. Although scholars tend to emphasize the benefits of shamanic services based usually on information obtained from clients immediately after a ritual and in the presence of the practitioners (e.g., Bruno 2002, 2007a; Hogarth 2009, 108, 256–61), patrons sometimes become frustrated because of their investment does not bear fruit (Chongho Kim 2003, 81, 171). Not only condemners of shamanism, but also patrons are occasionally critical of ritual expense, particularly "excessive" fees and offering money. This suggests that the controversy over the value of ritual consumption cannot be understood solely on the basis of ideological or theological perspectives. We need to look more carefully at the nature of ritual work and business from the perspectives of practitioners and clients, which neither defenders nor critics have done.

Ritual performance requires intensive emotional and physical labor and multiple talents—verbal, kinetic, and musical—from a *simbang*. In the Cho family's case, Simbang Kim melodically sang the lamentations of the dead souls while weeping and improvising for nearly two hours—quite a feat given the physical difficulty of speaking and weeping simultaneously.

Though the rituals are grueling for practitioners, not all clients appreciate their work. Mr. Kim, a cultural activist and longtime supporter of *simbang*, offered an anecdote illustrating the enigmatic situation that *simbang* face and his discontent with the laity's relentless efforts to lower ritual service fees. A certain wealthy man asked Pablo Picasso to draw a picture, and the artist drew one in fifteen minutes. Taking into account only the time it took for the artist to draw the picture and not the time and effort it took Picasso to develop his skill, the patron complained about the price of the piece.[44] Ritual sponsors often complain about prices, overlooking the time and effort *simbang* invest not only in learning their skills but also in performing a ritual. Unlike the patron in the tale who at least had a concrete piece of "high" art to show for his expenditure, the *simbang*'s patrons do not receive any immediate tangible outcome in return for their payment. The emergent features of performance and the ambiguity of *simbang*'s agency, especially in the *yŏngge ullim* séance, may obscure *simbang*'s emotional labor and delicate skills. An examination of Simbang Kim's virtuoso performance of the lamentations of the dead demonstrates that creating "dazzling" words is laborious work that deserves its due rewards, economic and otherwise. However, this value is difficult to measure. Moved by the *simbang*'s performance, Han wept hard, but when I asked her during a later visit whether the family had benefited from the ritual (*kuttŏk*), she responded with a hesitant "Maybe."

Moreover, the logistics of payment for shamanic services are not as neatly defined as in some other professions. For example, those who avail themselves of medical services are accustomed to surrendering to the authority of an institutionalized price system because they have little control over it. Although there are estimated fee ranges for shamanic services, they are fluid and differ vastly depending on individual shamans and the kind of ritual performed (cf. Hogarth 2009, 102–6). And ritual fees are often negotiated between shamans and clients, that is, patrons are party to the decision on how much money shamans' services are worth. This is likely to create disagreements, as the parties involved have conflicting interests. As a way of remedying this situation, Mr. Kim rather cynically suggested creating a menu listing the names of the different kinds of *kut* and the fee for each.[45] It seems rather doubtful that the standardization of ritual fees would resolve all the quibbles over monetary issues. Given the very personalized nature of shamanic rituals, would it even be possible?

Korean anthropologist An Mi-jeong offers some insight into the issue. Diving women still weigh the sea products that they collect from the ocean on an old-fashioned platform balance (2008, 232), even though digital scales have long been used in most places such as stores and bathhouses. The lack of precision in the analogue measurement can lead to disputes that a digital scale would instantly silence. For all that, An observed, divers continue to use the platform balance as an expression of their desire to participate in the measuring process and, to some degree, impose their own judgment about what is fair.[46] The reader of a platform balance and the observers of the weighing make their own decisions regarding value and thus override the automated digital scales. Whereas the lack of a single extended price system in the vernacular religious market disturbs the quantitative logic that asks only how much, it affords the parties involved room for emotion, engagement, and compromise. As clients try to balance household budgets and avoid losing face (cf. Chongho Kim 2003, 5; Monaghan 2008), *simbang* with great finesse also discreetly weigh their own income against the clients' financial situations. Some might be more generous than others in taking an individual client's circumstances into account. The open, multicentric system embraces elements that cannot easily be given a price. However, it does not eliminate the possibility of contention.

Legal tender offered for ritual purposes can also add to the controversy over the expenditure and a client's doubt about shamans' motives. Although practitioners make the money ritualistically distinct with their speech, it remains sharply differentiated from imitation money. Clients know that the ultimate recipients of the monetary offering are the *simbang*, who collect whatever is offered and seek to gain generous *injŏng*. Further, determining what represents an adequate offering is a delicate matter, politically and economically. Although Simbang Kim mentioned to the two sisters in their pre-ritual consultation that patrons would be responsible for *injŏng*, the amount was not discussed in advance. In fact, it cannot be discussed, for, ideally, it is commensurate with an individual client's devotion. The saying goes, "Whether it be much or little, it all counts as *injŏng*" (Hado injŏng, chogado injŏng). Whereas this cultural logic appears to negate quantity, it also betokens the open-endedness of money offering: there is no fixed upper limit for appropriate *injŏng*. Aware that they do not know how much they will have to offer during the ritual event itself, experienced clients try to negotiate acceptable service fees before the ritual.

Offering *injŏng* is highly contingent on emergent elements of ritual performance, which makes clients vulnerable. The introverted Han settled the debate about the service fee in the patron's favor before the ritual. However, the client family eventually surrendered themselves to the performance situation in which power asymmetries among supernatural beings, *simbang*, and the laity were brought to the fore. Since whether the supernatural functionaries will reciprocate or not is believed to depend in no small part on the clients' participation in their ritual roles, patrons feel obligated to dedicate "sufficient" cash to the authorities for the sake of their kin. Parsimony in offerings can be seen as denoting insufficient devotion, an alleged reason for an unsuccessful ritual outcome. If the gods and the spirits can be influenced by the patrons' devotion as represented by the number and value of offerings, the *simbang* with performance authority can as well.

Patrons may want to encourage *simbang* to make their best efforts by offering additional income (cf. Ch'oe Kil-sŏng 1981, 62). Therefore, although he did not respect them, Mr. Cho reported saying "Yes" and "Yes" to them, in the hope they would do a good thing for his son during the ritual. The man of the house hung 10,000-won bills instead of 1,000-won bills even though Simbang Kang had said to the reluctant family, "You might want to hang 1,000-won bills so that it does not get too burdensome." Patrons, who need to strike a careful balance between honor and household budget and may not fully recognize and appreciate the labor and skills involved in ritual performance, may indeed feel discontent or accuse shamans of greed and trickery—even if they were effectively guided toward catharsis during the performance itself.

5 A *KUT* AS HERITAGE GOODS WITH THE UNESCO BRAND

IN FALL 2009, UNESCO ADDED THE YŎNGDŬNG KUT, PERFORMED annually at Ch'ilmŏri Shrine on Cheju Island, to its Representative List of the Intangible Cultural Heritage of Humanity. Among the ten regional *kut* designated by the South Korean government, this is the first and only one to have earned UNESCO recognition. The inclusion not only gave a boost to the islanders' pride but also presented the island with potential boons, both economic and symbolic. Kim T'ae Hwan (then governor of Cheju) pronounced it a "splendid achievement" (*k'oegŏ*) and announced his heady intention to make use of the internationally sanctioned ritual as a cultural and touristic resource (*munhwa kwanggwang chawŏn*) (Kim Hyŏnjong 2009). Mun Mubyŏng, a well-known scholar of Cheju shamanism, asserted that the local Cheju event should be reborn as a cultural festival designed to attract tourists from all over the world (2009b). According to a national newspaper, Simbang Kim Yunsu, the incumbent skill holder of the ceremony, stated, "I will make a greater effort to pass the tradition down to the next generation and will promote the ritual globally by performing it at international venues" (Hŏ Hojun 2009). He was clearly aware of what was expected of him.

UNESCO seldom discusses the economic issues associated with heritage status, as though economic calculations "might besmirch or spoil the purity of heritage" (Bendix 2009, 258). However, financial factors were a key concern among local and national stakeholders, who initiated the application for UNESCO recognition and have, rather unabashedly, appropriated this patrimony. Given that ritual is a commercial activity (as demonstrated in chaps. 3 and 4), its utilitarian approach to culture may not appear unusual especially in a world dominated by consumer capitalism. However, from a historical perspective, it is quite ironic that the very profit motive, for which shamans have long been denigrated, propels such heritage promotion. Deemed vulgar and damaging to the fiscal health of the citizenry and the nation, shamanic rituals had long been suppressed by reformers. Pressured into the service of the new economy, the purified ritual, packaged as Cheju's indigeneity, has now become heritage goods associated with the prestigious UNESCO brand.

Attaining and maintaining global heritage status involve an economic imperative, and the politics of knowledge and the power relations among shamans, scholars, politicians, and UNESCO reflect the different interests of each party in imagining the role that heritage status will play for Cheju and in the world. Global recognition may have boosted the islanders' pride in their culture and enhanced their hope for economic advancement through heritage tourism, but the much-touted expectation of making Cheju richer and the Yŏngdŭng Kut better known has so far been rather slow in coming. Although the ritual's elevated status ostensibly brought honor to a few shamans, it significantly changed—perhaps even damaged—the social fabric of the major actors and burdened *simbang* who must continue performing a ritual that is no longer relevant to the lives of most community members (cf. Foster 2015a). Moreover, eager to utilize the invested economic good, those in the corridors of power failed to fully take into account the practitioners' principal concern: respect as ritual specialists.

THE YŎNGDŬNG KUT AT THE CH'ILMŎRI SHRINE

The designated ritual is dedicated to Yŏngdŭng, the goddess of wind, who is believed to visit the island during the first half of the second lunar month (on dates that usually fall in March).[1] Although belief in and practices pertaining to this deity are also documented in southern peninsular Korea (Sŏl 1973, 27–28; Song Sŏkha 1960, 91–100), scholars argue that those on Cheju are undeniably distinct (Chang Chugŭn 1983, 95–96; Hwang Ru-shi 1988, 126–27, 95). In the mountainous mainland regions, farming households prayed to Yŏngdŭng, without calling upon shamans, for protection against agricultural calamities. On Cheju some seaside villages hire shamans to conduct an annual rite in order to ensure a good harvest, collective enrichment, and the safety of the diving women and fishermen (e.g., Chang Chugŭn 1983, 99–108; Tangherlini and Park 1988, 1990).

The Yŏngdŭng Kut selected for designation is performed at the Ch'ilmŏri Shrine located on the slopes of Sara Peak in the eastern part of Cheju City. The shrine was originally located on the slope of Kŏnip-dong facing the eastern sea, where seven dragonhead-like boulders once stood, thus giving the shrine its name, Ch'ilmŏri (Seven Heads). Due to construction in the area, the shrine was moved to the vicinity of Port Sanji and then to its current location (Mun and Yi 2008, 17–18). It is marked by three spirit stones placed side by side in an open area ringed by pines; shamanic shrines typically are outdoors in sites without roofs or walls, demarcated by spirit trees or stones.

A rather simple rite is performed on the first day of the month to welcome the goddess and another on a grander scale a fortnight later. Community rituals are usually performed by *tang maein simbang*, who are in charge of the shrine involved, with a few assistants. The rite at the Ch'ilmŏri Shrine is led by Simbang Kim Yunsu, the *tang maein simbang* for the shrine and skill holder of the designated ritual, assisted by many members of the Association for the Ch'ilmŏri Shrine Yŏngdŭng Kut Preservation.[2]

The elaborate annual ritual has a complex procedure (see Association for the Ch'ilmŏri Shrine Yŏngdŭng Kut Preservation 2005, 37–54). Although devoted mainly to the goddess Yŏngdŭng, the ritual embraces all deities. As do all shamanic rituals, it begins with the lead *simbang* inviting deities, including the shrine deities, to the altar. Then the *simbang* entertains them. The next session is devoted to the dragon kings and the goddess Yŏngdŭng. In the session that follows, called "scattering seeds," divers go out into the ocean and scatter millet (representing the seeds of sea products such as seaweed and abalone), and the lead *simbang* offers divinations about the sea harvest. Then the lead *simbang* forestalls village misfortunes, and several other *simbang* offer divinations for each participant's family members. The ensuing antics of the lead *simbang* and seven men representing playful male deities known as Yŏnggam lighten the atmosphere. Following this, shamans sing a song, "Sŏujet-sori," led by the chief shaman, while all participants dance. It is believed that humans and gods can be united through dancing and singing. Then ritual sponsors set miniature straw boats adrift in the sea. Finally, the lead *simbang* sends back all invited deities and spirits.

EXPEDIENCY OF CULTURE

The South Korean government designated the Yŏngdŭng Kut as Important Intangible Cultural Property No. 71 in 1980. Though the stated purpose of both the national and the international effort was to safeguard the ritual, the two heritage designations originated under different circumstances and were appropriated quite differently. Local actors on Cheju, a region long perceived by Koreans as peripheral, wanted to claim national notice for the place and its culture by winning the national title. Romanticized as an authentic folk tradition of the island that had survived the commercialization rampant in all walks of society intact (e.g., Mun 1987a, 1), shamanism was scarcely considered a means of increasing the island's revenue until the dawn of the twenty-first century.

The 2009 UNESCO recognition was closely aligned with what Philip Scher has called "neoliberal nationalism," through which the State capitalizes on national heritage as a way of diversifying the economy while acting as the "legitimate guardian of cultural nationalism" (2010, 200). Under this new moral order, the relentless marketing of culture, whether popular or traditional, came to be seen not as corruptive but as sensible and even virtuous in that it occurred for the sake of the national and local economies. Nation-states now vie for intangible cultural heritage (ICH) designations in order to enhance tourism and develop the heritage industry (Bendix 2009, 258; Hafstein 2009, 106; Kirshenblatt-Gimblett 1998). Although the promise of increased symbolic capital in relation to other nations is certainly an important motivation for pursuing international recognition, financial interest was openly touted in the domestic context.

Several factors contributed to this change at the turn of the century. The establishment of local assemblies in 1991 motivated local governments to enhance each region's brand image by highlighting distinctive local products and cultural items. At the same time that the Kim Young Sam administration implemented a globalization policy in 1995, government support for international festivals and events was spurred on by the nationalist agenda of promoting Korean culture as a constituent of world culture (Shin 2003). In his inaugural speech in February 1998, President Kim Dae Jung, who inherited the Asian economic crisis, emphasized the importance of tourism and culture, along with trade and investment, to South Korea's competitiveness in the new millennium. Echoing this sentiment, the Korean press touted the cultural industry for fueling the national economy, citing futurologists such as Peter Drucker and Alvin Toffler (Shim 2008, 17). Under these circumstances, the Korean Wave (Hallyu)—the unprecedented boom in Korean popular culture in East Asia and beyond—emerged, and cultural festivals came into vogue.

South Korean officials actively used culture as a resource in their push to revamp governance models and bring them in line with neoliberal ideals. This endeavor is particularly pertinent to Cheju, which has the infrastructure for tourism but no other major industry. The establishment of Cheju as a Special Self-Governing Province in July 2006 forced the local government to be more self-sufficient economically when budgetary support from the central government was drastically curtailed. Equating development with publicity, local elected politicians have made efforts to publicize the island by promoting it as a World Heritage site.

A 2011 scandal related to the island's selection as one of the New 7 Wonders of Nature illustrates the provincial and national administrations' desperation to popularize Cheju. The head of the Ministry of Culture, Sports, and Tourism asserted that the selection was not merely a matter for Cheju but part of a national agenda for upgrading the value of the country's brand and making the Republic of Korea a tourism nation.[3] The selection was based purely on Internet and phone votes from people around the world. In order to assure Cheju's selection, the provincial government mobilized its civil servants to urge citizens to participate in the vote. The Cheju Tourism Organization sponsored raffles so that some lucky voters even received prizes for voting. The total administrative "get out the vote" telephone bill was estimated to be as much as 40 billion won (about US$40 million) (Pak Chongch'an 2011). Furthermore, the local government had to pay for the phone calls to the New7Wonders Foundation in order to ensure the validity of the votes (ibid.). Although Cheju eventually accomplished its goal through the self-validating votes, the selection provoked criticism that the state had manipulated people's patriotism while being manipulated itself by the New7Wonders Foundation. The local government's fiscal recklessness in an era of austerity demonstrates their tourism-at-all-costs attitude.

UNESCO's overarching goal of promoting global stability through "heritage tourism and a heritage industry" (Scher 2010, 199) dovetails with the state's interest in marketing cultural patrimony to a global audience. Moreover, the mandate that nominations come from states reinforces the role of nation-states in managing and promoting their own national cultures and engenders a competition between nations. In 2009 alone, five South Korean, thirteen Japanese, and twenty-two Chinese items received a UNESCO designation. Aware of the success neighboring countries had achieved in getting far more items added to the list that year, a heritage administrator informed a national newspaper of South Korea's plan to nominate forty items in 2010. She added, "A rumor has it that China is preparing 200 items for 2010" (Yi Kyŏng-hŭi 2009). Neither the rumored Chinese plans nor the official's proposal materialized.[4] However, the comment bespeaks the fierce competition among East Asian countries to "create" cultural initiatives that will win UNESCO's endorsement and, in turn, attract more consumers of world culture (Pai 2013, xvii; Tangherlini 2008, 81).[5] Once an island destination for exiles, Cheju has entered a new realm of prestige as a natural and cultural heritage destination (Tran 2015),[6] and the Yŏngdŭng Kut has been represented as a highlight of the regional culture.

ON BECOMING A LOCUS OF UNESCO'S INTANGIBLE CULTURAL HERITAGE

An administrator in charge of cultural heritage management at the Cheju Provincial Office observed that the Yŏngdŭng Kut achieved World Heritage status because its uniqueness and scholarly merit was globally recognized (Kim Hoch'ŏn 2013). This popular view assumes that the rite is inherently superior to those other cultural practices that were not selected, even though, in 2003, UNESCO's Convention for the Safeguarding of the Intangible Cultural Heritage changed the Proclamation of Masterpieces of the Oral and Intangible Heritage of Humanity list to the less effusive Representative List of the Intangible Cultural Heritage of Humanity in 2003, in an effort to avoid the elitism and hierarchy connoted by the word "masterpiece" (Blake 2001, 46). However, examining the process by which the ritual won global certification makes it plain that, as many scholars of heritage studies have shown (e.g., Noyes 2006; Smith and Akagawa 2009), World Heritage quality is not inherent but *made*. Only certain cultural practices are included on the list, imbuing those selected with a certain cachet and value (cf. Foster 2015b, 148). At issue, then, is why a particular practice is selected, how it is selected, and who plays a major role in the selection process.

Many traditions die unlamented. Only those who had vested interests in this particular ritual were keen to hold on to it. As in other instances, the inscription of the Cheju rite was almost entirely the result of local efforts (Foster and Gilman 2015). The Republic of Korea's expedient cultural policy, national and local patriotism, aspirations of elected local leaders, and political and economic pressure to market the region helped obtain global recognition for the ritual. Moreover, UNESCO itself emphasizes local participation in order to promote its ideal of "building peace in the minds of men and women" by fostering cultural variation and respect for local autonomy.[7] At the same time, it is unable to observe all the cultural practices in the world with an eye sharp enough to home in on each element's distinctive value.

The power structure ingrained in the system is problematic: local actors petition for global notice, and the international administrative body grants it. The "global judges" (Noyes 2006) examine materials submitted by state parties and decide which cultural forms are worthy of inscription on the Representative List. These judges are members of an intergovernmental committee composed of those "elected by the States Parties meeting in [the] General Assembly according to the principles of equitable geographical representation and rotation."[8] The committee, which has but little in the way of resources for investigating each case on its own merits, makes a decision based on predefined general criteria. This structure influences the entire nomination process at the local level, including what to nominate and how to present nomination materials favorably. Indeed, UNESCO's Intangible Cultural Heritage project is paradoxical in that it represents "an effort to create a global system to stave off the effects of globalization" (Foster 2011, 83, citing Nas 2002, 142, 145).

Despite UNESCO's stated emphasis on community participation, the selection process is not necessarily conducive to promoting the interests of small communities because the nomination is ultimately submitted by nation-states, and it even involves top-down governmental intervention. The nomination of the Cheju ritual encompassed a four-pronged effort by a folklorist, the shamans, the Provincial Government, and the Cultural Heritage Administration, the state-sanctioned governing body that oversees traditional culture in South Korea.[9] However, the shamans themselves did not play a leading role. When I visited the office of the Association for the Ch'ilmŏri Shrine Yŏngdŭng Kut Preservation near the shrine in fall 2010, a Mr. Kim, then the office manager and de facto administrator of the association, emphasized that the nomination had little to do with the association itself, whose main members are *simbang*. Pointing to a local newspaper article preserved in a binder, the office manager told me that the provincial government and the Cultural Heritage Administration had begun planning to submit a nomination to UNESCO in 2000. The Cultural Heritage Administration, he continued, aimed to have all state-designated Important Intangible Cultural Properties receive UNESCO recognition.

It is then not surprising that the Yŏngdŭng Kut performed at the Ch'ilmŏri Shrine, attended by only a small fraction of the neighborhood community members and thus communal in name only, was selected for the international nomination. The decision of the Cultural Heritage Administration was strategic. In fact, performance of the ritual itself is a statement of island Otherness, appealing to both domestic and international audiences. In contrast to Cheju folk songs (*minyŏ*), the other Important Intangible Cultural Property nationally designated in 1989, the communal Yŏngdŭng Kut involves many performers and genres, thus offering a splendid display. These merits predisposed the Cultural Heritage Administration to favor the ritual for nomination and economic cultivation. Like Carnival, its rich material culture—including costumes, masks, decorations, and food offerings—is easily captured and especially photogenic (cf. Bendix 2009, 263). These characteristics are congruent with an existing UNESCO list that privileges exotic and colorful items that underscore "romanticized Western perceptions" (Smith and Akagawa 2009, 4).

Moreover, the know-how obtained in institutionalizing and maintaining national heritage and the rich literature pertaining to the ritual in the Cheju City shrine are conducive to nomination for international recognition. Demonstrating a national effort to safeguard culture is a critical criterion for winning UNESCO recognition.[10] The association had previously rented a rather shabby room with no practice space in the Cheju municipal stadium, and it paid the rent using membership dues and income from public performances. However, in 2004, the organization moved to a handsome and spacious new building that Cheju City had built specifically for the group and permitted it to use rent free. This support, nearly a quarter century after the ritual's national designation, was timely for the government's plan to nominate the ritual for UNESCO recognition. The UNESCO website featuring the ritual includes a photo of the building and another showing several *simbang* standing in front of it. In addition, part of the video submitted the Cultural Heritage Administration was filmed in this building.

As in other parts of the world,[11] most local actors surrendered "control over their own cultural practices" (Hafstein 2015, 296) to cultural "experts" and administrators. Proponents of the ritual characterized shamans as stewards of the rite. However, it was a local Cheju scholar, Mun Mubyŏng, who prepared a Korean-language dossier on the ritual for the Cultural Heritage Administration, which is required to support the nomination. Because Mun had devoted more than three decades to the study of Cheju shamanism, state officials, who were eager to commodify the tradition but lacked expert knowledge, took his view as authoritative. A poet and playwright who led the theatrical movement of the 1980s, in which shamanic rituals were often appropriated for antigovernment demonstrations, Mun had vehemently opposed using Cheju *kut* for any institutional or commercial purpose (Mun 1987a). Seeing himself as the best authority to speak for Cheju shamanism and decide how to use it for the betterment of the island, Mun, no longer shy about expressing his revised view of leveraging the internationally recognized ritual for heritage tourism, collaborated with the Cultural Heritage Administration. Staff members, whose office is in the city of Taejŏn on the mainland, translated the nomination form prepared by

Mun into English. The Cultural Heritage Administration also sent a crew of camera operators and cinematographers to Cheju to film the ritual. The ten-minute film is more or less a visual rendition of the dossier that presented Mun's perspective on the ritual.

Unfamiliar with procedures involving formal protocols, the *simbang* at first showed little interest in nominating the rite for designation by the foreign institution, but neither did they have any particular reason to oppose the initiatives of the state and local elites. The opportunity was difficult for them to pass up since they continued to be taunted, which provided an impetus to keep on seeking official credit (cf. Kendall 2009, 32). The recognition would also allow them to further assert their authenticity in comparison to migrant shamans. Moreover, they wished to see their tradition carried on somehow—even if through someone else's children. There was, in addition, a vague anticipation, especially among those who would benefit most directly from the heritage program, that the more glamorous recognition would benefit the *simbang*'s Association for the Ch'ilmŏri Shrine Yŏngdŭng Kut Preservation in practical matters and allow it to exert more influence in the decision-making process. Thus, despite their uneasiness, they collaborated.

A few weeks before the final UNESCO decision was made at a meeting in Abu Dhabi, members of the association conducted a ceremony to pray for the ritual's election, an event sponsored by the Cheju provincial government. Custodians of the ritual made an effort to generate publicity. The ceremony was scheduled during a weekend at a historical location in downtown Cheju City instead of at the traditional shrine in the suburbs. They also invited two groups of mainland shamans of high stature who performed their own regional ritual repertoire, distinct from the indigenous Cheju rituals. The stellar shaman Kim Kŭmhwa led one of the groups. The poster announcing the event highlighted her *chakttu kŏri*, a ritual session in which a shaman stands on sharp twin blades with bare feet and delivers oracles, the high point of her staged performances both at home and abroad (Chongho Kim 2003, 217; cf. Schein 2000, 271).

Other final preparations were more administrative than dramatic. The skill holder of the Yŏngdŭng Kut and his two trainees accepted the English-language consent form agreeing to the ritual's nomination and conceding their rights to the materials: "We, as the practitioners of the proposed element, give our consent to the nomination of the element for inscription on the Representative List; and cede [our] rights to the documentary materials submitted for the nomination."[12] Though neither in charge nor capable of presenting a nomination of their ritual to UNESCO, the shamans in the end "voluntarily" participated in the nomination (cf. Gilman 2015, 212; Kirshenblatt-Gimblett 2004; Lowthorp 2015, 165).

Although all concerned parties had agreed on nominating the ritual for global recognition, there was little communication among them regarding how it would help safeguard the tradition or how the added value would be collectively beneficial to the nation and especially to the island (cf. Lowthorp 2015, 165). This lack of articulation led to disappointment and tension among the various parties involved in the nomination.

SHAMANISM AS ISLAND AUTHENTICITY

The ritual won UNESCO recognition because the application made claims for certain types of ideologies, historicities, legitimization, and practices of display while excluding others. The textual and visual materials prepared for UNESCO present the ritual as an icon of island authenticity, quite similar to the romantic view of folklore adopted in the discourse of the Republic of Korea's Intangible Cultural Heritage program. The video portrays the island as ultra-rural and isolated by focusing on the surrounding mountains and an ocean filled with fishing boats and diving women, but it omits the numerous hotels and golf courses, mostly owned by mainlanders, that are part of the local landscape as well. The materials also depict Cheju as a timeless shamanic enclave represented by the designated ritual. This self-exotification reinforces the long-standing stereotypical portrayal of the island as a backwater rather than enhancing a nuanced understanding of the rapidly changing society. While shamanism is undeniably more prominent on the island than on the mainland, romantic portrayals often overlook the intricacies of the religious landscape on Cheju, where multiple institutional and vernacular religions coexist (Cho Sung-Youn 2003; Kyoim Yun 2016). Further, shamanism is a controversial practice that does not enjoy unconditional acceptance even among local residents and often descends into a quagmire of altercations.

The homogeneous "traditional" community portrayed in the video bolsters the prevalent concept of tradition as premodern (a rhetorical device deeply rooted in current needs), on which many theorists of modernity rely (Bauman and Briggs 2003, 307–18; Giddens 1994, 62–63). This temporal and conservative notion of tradition provides the ideological basis for most heritage preservation efforts, including UNESCO's, which attempt to safeguard cultural practices and protect them from change or loss (Bauman and Briggs 2003, 306–9). Mun and the visual technicians from the Cultural

Heritage Administration were communicating that the tradition was on the verge of vanishing because of encroaching modernization (cf. Ivy 1995). This construction of threat was key to winning Intangible Cultural Heritage designation. According to the narrator of the UNESCO application video, for example, "After modernization, it [shamanism] was vilified as superstition." While this is undeniable, in actual fact, the stigmatization of shamanism in Korea began much earlier and is documented as far back as the thirteenth century. The early sixteenth-century *Geography of Korea*, cited by the video's narrator to emphasize the ritual's longevity, characterizes shamanic rituals as licentious. Moreover, in 1702 the high-minded Confucian scholar-official Yi had 129 shrines on the island destroyed. It is ironic that while the popular religion was once considered a hindrance to modernization, the heritage discourse construes modernization as a problem for the practice. Lacking firsthand experience with and in-depth historical knowledge of the local culture, the global judges had no choice but to accept the nomination materials in good faith.

The need to protect the ritual is not merely founded on elite rhetoric but comes from dramatically altered circumstances, which the heritage discourse obscures by foregrounding the threat of modernization. In contrast to the proliferation of god-descended shamans, hereditary shamans, including *simbang*, are in steep decline, a national phenomenon that is not confined to Cheju (Hwang Ru-shi 2000, 23–28). This increases the sense of urgency around protecting their lore. Manager Kim told me that, unlike natural heritage, which can be preserved with modern equipment and technology, the lore *simbang* possess goes to the grave with them, and "no *simbang* comes out of a *simbang*'s family anymore." A few shamans have already donated the ritual tools they received from their parents or close kin to museums, and a few others spoke to me of their plans to do the same. Moreover, in recent decades, increasing numbers of nonhereditary shamans from the mainland have come to dominate Cheju's vernacular religious market (Cho Sung-Youn 2003; Kyoim Yun 2016). Their services are in demand among islanders who care more about ritual efficacy than the essentialized sense of local tradition advocated by the social elite. Some *simbang* collaborate with these migrant shamans in an effort to expand their professional opportunities, while others construe them as rivals. Because many are not originally from Cheju, they are disqualified from heritage projects, but their presence gives rise to the dispute over authenticity by which the island's identity and heritage are formulated and defined (cf. Scher 2002, 480; Smith 2006).

Development on the island has also had an impact on the ritual's destiny. Safety and a good catch are the lifelong wishes of diving women, so they are the ones who usually hire shamans and prepare offerings for the Yŏngdŭng deity believed to bring abundant harvest and protect sea workers from danger. However, the number of diving women on Cheju is rapidly decreasing—14,143 were active in 1970, but only 4,415 in 2015, a loss of more than two thirds. Aging is another issue. As of 2015, a mere 1.5 percent of the diving women were under the age of fifty, while 60 percent were in their seventies and eighties; there were none under thirty. Moreover, the diving women, the ritual's "real owners," as identified in the nomination dossier, are not interested in passing their difficult and dangerous job on to their daughters, although they take pride in the autonomy that their capability affords them (Cho Hae-joang 1983). Indeed, this drastic decrease in the number of divers, who have been praised as the strong spirit of Cheju women, has generated an urgent desire to safeguard their culture, which was added to UNESCO's Intangible Cultural Heritage of Humanity list in 2016. However, the narrow and exclusive heritage discourse inevitably conceals the complexities of the current situation on the island (cf. Olwig 1999; Smith 2006).

RITUAL FOR OTHERS

What, then, were the effects of UNESCO recognition? Although the nature of future developments is uncertain, a few points are noteworthy. Immediately after the ritual's inscription on the Representative List, all concerned parties seemed to revel in the global recognition, as though the UNESCO fairy would now magically shower benefits upon the region. Numerous contradictions, however, soon emerged that had been obscured by the initial excitement, dimming the anticipated glory and diffusing the promised economic benefits. One of the local and national stakeholders' primary agendas was to leverage the nomination to gain recognition and symbolic and economic capital for the island and the country (cf. Scher 2002, 465). Unsurprisingly, the most noticeable effort was made toward this end, resulting in intensified other-orientedness (cf. Foster 2011). The imperative was to exhibit and celebrate, for a broader audience, a ritual that is becoming ever more irrelevant to the life of the community. Still, no one disagreed that the ritual's new international standing should be publicized by making it known at various venues and in a variety of contexts; rather, the debates focused mostly on *how* this should be accomplished.

This other-orientedness is neither entirely new nor confined to Cheju sha-manism.[13] According to Hwang Ru-shi, who observed the annual Yŏngdŭng Kut performed at the Ch'ilmŏri Shrine in 1985, just five years after its national designation, it already had incorporated elements of a staged "cul-tural" performance. For instance, after the *simbang* signaled the beginning of the ritual with musical instruments, an emcee abruptly appeared in front of the altar and announced, "The fifth presentation of the Important Intan-gible Cultural Heritage No. 71, the Cheju Ch'ilmŏri Shrine Yŏngdŭng Kut, will now begin." He then introduced participating *simbang*, all standing in a line, and explained the procedure of the ritual (Hwang Ru-shi 1988, 130).

A quarter century later, I observed the ritual for the first time at Ch'ilmŏri Shrine on 29 March 2010 after having seen part of it as an ama-teur onlooker in 1997. Although I do not claim that everything I wit-nessed that day was a direct consequence of UNESCO recognition, it was clear that the designation mattered. When I approached the ceremonial space that morning, the ritual skill holder was facing away from me. I was struck by the fact that his jet-black hair had turned quite gray. His wife, who now referred to her husband as Master (*sŏnsaengnim*), later explained to me, "He stopped dyeing his hair on purpose." The shock of gray hair surely made him look more dignified and thus more appropriate to his newfound status and for what Edward M. Bruner and Barbara Kirshenblatt-Gimblett called "tourist realism" in their study of the Maasai "tribal" dancers in East Africa (1994).

Although camera operators, journalists, and scholars have long been regulars at public rituals, on this occasion their number was almost over-whelming (see fig. 5.1). The Cheju branches of KBS and MBC, two of the most popular nationwide TV stations, were filming the entire ritual with huge cameras, and many scholars and journalists were clicking away with their cameras and recording videos of the performance. In fact, the crowd of journalists and scholars was far more numerous than the dozen or so div-ing women and shipowners' wives present, significantly fewer than the participants from some 150 households who attended in 1981 (Kim Sunam 1983, 18). Shamans are always necessarily attuned to their audience's expec-tations, but under these circumstances, they obviously felt the gaze of an expanded and unknown audience, whether present or imagined. One par-ticular scene made this poignantly apparent. Although it was still March, the sunlight was a bit too strong for those without a place in the shade, so one elderly shaman seated at the front of the stage had made a hat out of

FIG.5.1. Yŏngdŭng Kut at the Ch'ilmŏri Shrine, 2010. Photo by the author

newspapers. The lead shaman instructed her to take it off. While perfectly functional, it was just not aesthetically suitable for the television audience.

The Association for the Ch'ilmŏri Shrine Yŏngdŭng Kut Preservation was prepared for those who were not familiar with the ritual. A few members were selling a book about the ritual, which contained the *simbang*'s recitations of ritual songs, transcribed by folklorist Mun, and detailed the rite's history and performance procedure. Free booklets in three different languages with the UNESCO Intangible Cultural Heritage of Humanity logo were also ready for distribution.

The association was subjected not only to internal but also external pressure to promote the ritual. When a small group of Japanese tourists showed up, members of the association eagerly handed them the Japanese-language version of the booklet. The tourists shouted, "Great!" (*Sgoi!*) but soon disappeared with their tour guide, headed to their next destination. While the Korean- and Japanese-language booklets were handed out occasionally, the English-language versions were all wasted because there were no native English speakers in the audience that year. Still, local culture brokers pressured the association to make the event more inclusive of the imagined global audience. One artist suggested producing booklets in additional languages in order to make the ritual truly global. Manager Kim, who was in charge of all practical matters for the shamans' association, asked, "Where would the money come from [to translate them all]—and for what?" In addition to being criticized for not making the printed material global enough, Manager Kim was also judged for what was seen as insufficient pomp. Noting that only three straw boats were released at the end of the event, one scholar remarked that a global ritual warranted far more—to him, UNESCO status meant that the rite was now of widespread interest. In a rather irritated tone of voice, Manager Kim responded that it was difficult to find straw, since few locals still farmed. As the Yŏngdŭng Kut became gravely compromised through attempts to appeal to outsiders, a local scholar told me in summer 2015 that many of those interested in observing an "authentic" Cheju community ritual had turned their attention to another ritual—one without UNESCO designation—performed in a different village with the active participation of its community members.

HERITAGE ECONOMY

Despite heightened expectations, the ritual at the Ch'ilmŏri Shrine in 2010 attracted only a smattering of visitors beyond the island (cf. Kyoim Yun 2006). Active promotion of the ritual's new status, on which some stakeholders' fame and very existence depend, is necessary. Thus, regional and national decision-making bodies promoted the Cheju *kut* as "a good of morally and economically enhanced valence" (Bendix 2009, 264), which is consistent with the UNESCO ideal of opening up distinctly local practices to the world. In September 2010, for instance, several members of the Association for the Ch'ilmŏri Shrine Yŏngdŭng Kut Preservation performed a small part of the ritual for the Let's Go to See Good event at the Cheju Art Center.[14] Eight groups from the mainland and the island, five of which had been recognized as national intangible cultural treasures, performed in the free ninety-minute event organized by Cheju City and the Korean Cultural Heritage Foundation under the sponsorship of the Cultural Heritage Administration. This heritage-campaign event was meant to show the public that traditional performances such as Buddhist dances (*sŭngmu*) and *p'ansori* are "good" to see, just as *kut* were in the past when few other entertainment opportunities were available.

Although I missed the event, I did hear a few reactions to it. Mun did not conceal his chagrin over the fact that he had not been invited to an affair featuring the ritual he had transformed into an international cultural heritage asset. Manager Kim voiced his displeasure at the high-handed foundation's poor management of the event. Its staff kept requesting that the ritual be shortened to fit the time frame of the whole event, hardly new for staged performances.[15] In the end, *simbang* were given just twenty minutes for their performance, a situation Manager Kim compared with abbreviating Shakespeare's *Romeo and Juliet* to four words: "Oh, Romeo! Oh, Juliet!" From his point of view, it was nearly impossible to show anything meaningful from the daylong ritual in such a short time, and this compromised the shamans' mission of displaying the authentic tradition for an audience. In such a show, Manager Kim said straightforwardly, *simbang* are "used as commodities." He also hinted at ego battles among the star performers. Foundation staff relegated sixteen Cheju *simbang* to a smaller, shabby dressing room and assigned the better, more spacious rooms to groups from the mainland, using the excuse that local performers should yield the better dressing rooms to those from the mainland who ought to be viewed as guests. To Manager Kim, however, the situation subordinated the local shamans to the performers from the mainland.[16]

Several members of the association were also mobilized to perform at the National Center for Korean Traditional Performing Arts in Seoul. Performing condensed versions of annual rituals in a variety of nonritual venues has been routine in South Korea since around 1980, but the UNESCO-recognized ritual earned a rather different treatment. The Yŏngdŭng Kut was part of the center's "2010 Saturday Premium Performances" (T'oyo myŏngp'um kongyŏn) series featuring traditional performing arts. Embedded in the title is a vision of cultural practices as high-quality objects—the Korean word *myŏngp'um* refers to "a fine article, gem, or masterpiece." The host of the series, the National Kugak Center, the main learning institution specializing in traditional Korean music, scheduled performing arts genres recognized by UNESCO for the fourth Saturday of each month, invited the Yŏngdŭng Kut for October, and made an effort to lure diverse audiences to the event. Admission was very reasonable, 10,000 won (about US$10), with various discount options, including a 20 percent reduction for visitors traveling on Korean Air (National Kugak Center 2010a). The center's online media highlighted the convenience of observing the island's ritual without actually having to go there: "Experience the Cheju Ch'ilmŏri Shrine Yŏngdŭng Kut in Seoul" (National Kugak Center 2010b).[17]

These multitudinous efforts by state-sponsored cultural organizations to promote the island's *kut* in nonritual settings ironically accentuate the events' marginality for the general public. In fact, about half the approximately three hundred seats in the rather small hall were empty for the performance in Seoul. This pales in comparison to the audience present at the famous shaman Kim Kŭmhwa's performance at the Seoul Arts Centre Opera House, supported by the government and free of charge, which attracted more than 1,500 including those "standing in the corridors or sitting on the floor" (Chongho Kim 2003, 215). Although Simbang Chŏng Kongch'ŏl, who often served as emcee at public performances, described the ritual as an event in which the audience and the performers interact, most onlookers seemed puzzled. They were trying to grasp what was happening onstage by reading digital subtitles on a monitor hung high on the front wall. Although shamans perform for their clients, the latter's collaboration is indispensable for a ritual's progress, but the audiences at staged performances watch with little emotional involvement. The ideology supporting the heritage program is aligned with a particular presentation of the ritual, similar to Vimbuze, a UNESCO-recognized Malawian healing ritual performed as a dance in nonritual settings "divorced from spirits" (Gilman 2015, 209). The way the ritual is displayed onstage necessarily undermines shamanic agency by veiling the spiritual powers of the *simbang*—powers that entail uncanny and discomforting elements—instead of validating them. Therefore, it is unlikely that onlookers would learn much about what *simbang* do for their clients at rituals or respect them for their affective work as spiritual healers.[18]

As no one in the audience volunteered to come to the stage for an exorcism, the female *simbang* had to rely on one of her own young performers, an expedient I had never seen before. In an effort to help, I went onstage and served as a living prop during the performance of the exorcism. At the finale, the spectators were invited to join the performers onstage for singing and dancing in order to generate a sense of the "lost communitas (*kongdongch'e*) of a village ritual" (Kendall 2009, 14), but most audience members remained in their seats. Some young female students were amused when a male student of the same age moved his arms and shoulders like the performers. This awkward scene was in stark contrast to the enthusiasm aroused by the music and dance routines of K-pop singers. For these young cosmopolitans, a *kut*, which appealed to urban elites at the end of the twentieth century,[19] seems to have lost its attraction. In the age of consumer electronics, when many other forms of entertainment distract Koreans from the charm that *kut* once held, there appears to be a mismatch between sellers and buyers of the cultural product.

Nonetheless, stakeholders cannot squander their hard-earned opportunity: if consumers lack interest in their investment, it needs to be cultivated. In February 2013, Cheju Province announced its plan to build a *chŏnsugwan* (lit., "a hall for passing on heritage"), to be used for training, exhibitions, and performances, with facilities appropriate for these three activities, as well as office space. Simbang Kim's remark reported in a local newspaper immediately after the rite achieved world recognition, might also have been related to his wish for a new hall: "The proximity of the Ch'ilmŏri Shrine should be improved, but regretfully nothing can be done because it is in the park area" (Chin Sŏnhŭi 2009). The provincial administration went so far as to lift development constraints to allow the new construction. This is striking given the history of the shrine. Earlier shrines of the same name were destroyed in 1702 during Yi Hyŏngsang's tenure as governor and again in 1970 during the Park regime's anti-superstition campaign, and more recently the shrine succumbed to development. The heritage regime was at least now prepared to alter the cultural and physical landscape for the purpose of highlighting the ritual that takes place there.

News of the new building came replete with an optimistic preservation discourse. Conceptualized almost as a museum in which to preserve objects, the building was construed as a locus for safeguarding the ritual's future and promoting the excellence of Cheju's shamanic culture (Kim Hoch'ŏn 2013; Hwang Kyŏng-gŭn 2013). The question remains, however, exactly for whom the building will safeguard the ritual and how. Cultural pundits and commentators focus on the transmission of objectified ritual lore and skills from old to young *simbang* but often ignore the very nature of shamanic training. *Simbang* learn their multifaceted skills by observing the performances of more experienced *simbang* and their clients' behavior, as well as by performing their assigned roles in a variety of ritual situations. The general decrease in demand for the *simbang*'s rituals deprives apprentice *simbang* of these opportunities, leaving them ill equipped to perform healing rituals that are usually conducted in a domestic space. To remedy this, the Association for the Ch'ilmŏri Shrine Yŏngdŭng Kut Preservation collaborated with Mun, who published transcribed texts of *simbang*'s oral performances in 1998 and, as Chungmoo Choi predicted earlier (1991, 60), began videotaping senior *simbang*'s performances in 2002 for the benefit of younger practitioners. However, context-sensitive interactional skills with clients and with the supernatural cannot be learned in a training hall with the aid of texts and videos. Still, given that the association's members have performed a modified and condensed version of the annual ritual more frequently onstage than at the city shrine since the ritual was granted national designation in 1980, such a hall is perhaps necessary.

No small wonder then that the formerly *simbang*-only organization has become more flexible about its membership. In fact, some of the young members are not shamans at all but performers trained in traditional music, dance, and acting. Neither interested nor competent in mediating between this world and the otherworld, these members are not hired by individual clients for household rituals. However, these local talents do augment their performance repertoire by learning the artistic elements of Cheju's traditional ritual from a famous *simbang* master. Further, their facility in acting, singing, dancing, and playing instruments is conducive to *kut*-turned-spectacle performances, especially in the face of the dwindling number of *simbang*. The new hall can be helpful for teaching a younger generation these external skills if not the deeper spiritual competence necessary for the healing arts.

What is expected from this endeavor can be inferred in the Cultural Heritage Administration's nationwide Living Cultural Assets Project (Saeng Saeng Munhwajae Saŏp), implemented in 2008 with the goal of revitalizing the local economy through heritage tourism. The Cheju municipal government won funding four times between 2012 and 2014 to have the Association for the Ch'ilmŏri Shrine Yŏngdŭng Kut Preservation run a range of programs related to the Yŏngdŭng Kut for islanders and tourists. In March 2013, the Cultural Heritage Administration announced that the Living Cultural Assets Project had given an economic jolt to service sectors, such as transportation, lodging, and food, increasing it by as much as 3.3 times the original investment (Cultural Heritage Administration of Korea 2013b).[20] Although how they reached this conclusion is unknown, the Cultural Heritage Administration apparently found it necessary to show that it knew how to promote the project successfully. This calculative logic focused on revenue is missing a discussion of *intangible* benefits such as the ways people have appreciated *simbang* and the ritual.

AN UNCERTAIN HONOR

When news of the ritual's UNESCO recognition became public in 2009, *simbang* reacted to it enthusiastically. Members of the Association for the Ch'ilmŏri Shrine Yŏngdŭng Kut Preservation conducted a celebratory ceremony, and in an interview with a national newspaper, the association's president Simbang Kim Yunsu exulted, "I am so happy that I can't believe it" (Hŏ Hojun 2009). Though not a member of the association, Simbang An said to me rather cathartically: "When I heard the news, I was so happy that I wept." The designated skill holder of the ritual, who seemed to enjoy basking in the media attention, recounted the social ostracism that he had experienced as a young *simbang* and expressed his hope that the global recognition would change people's attitude toward *simbang* (Chin Sŏnhŭi 2009).

After the performance in Seoul in fall 2009, I asked the designated skill holder what benefit the recognition had brought him and was told, "Just an honor (*myŏngye*), nothing else." His response not only befitted his stature but was also true financially. Unlike national recognition, the international and supposedly more glamorous UNESCO designation was not accompanied by any form of direct financial assistance to purveyors of the tradition. When I pressed him, he calmly mentioned that the provincial office was now more willing to help them with matters like moving the association's office. The UNESCO endorsement surely eased the group's access to funds and afforded the head *simbang* far greater social and political control than before. The new hall was one of the material benefits that the association received from local government and the Cultural Heritage Administration after UNESCO recognition.[21]

So have *simbang*, as Simbang Kim wished, acquired new dignity through UNESCO's validation of the ritual? Not necessarily. In March 2011, a local assemblyman from the ruling Grand National Party decried as superstitious the shamanic ritual to be performed by *simbang* at the memorial service for the April Third Events. This politician's insensitive remarks speak to the tenacity of public prejudice against shamanism and its practitioners (see also Kendall 2009, 24). Nevertheless, the UNESCO designation did offer some aid in response to public denunciations: the assemblyman's comments sparked an outcry from several local organizations, including the association (Yi Sŭngnok 2011). These organizations issued a lengthy statement condemning his affront to the memory of the uprising's victims and arguing that his dismissal of a *kut* that has become a heritage of the world's people (*illyu yusan*) was seriously out of line and that the politician himself was out of touch.

The fact that the defenders of the popular religion borrowed the authority of a supranational institution underscores the operation of the hierarchy of value. The ritual's added value comes precisely from the high stature of the global institution that granted it recognition. This was palpable in my phone conversation with a staff member of the National Center for Korean Traditional Performing Arts in Seoul in fall 2010, when I called for information on the time and place of the Yŏngdŭng Kut. Unfamiliar with the ritual's official name, usually printed as one word while spoken with a pause between the words for "shrine" (ch'ilmŏritang) and "ritual "(yŏngdŭngkut), he read the ritual's official name rather awkwardly in Korean, pausing in the wrong place between ch'ilmŏri and tangyŏngdŭngkut. As a result, he referred to the ritual by an incorrect name. But he volunteered the information that it was "a masterpiece of UNESCO-designated world intangible culture." For him, and perhaps for most Koreans, the international recognition was paramount, more important than the content, function, or even the correct name of the ritual itself. In fact, as a result of the ritual's recognition, the name UNESCO came to be known to a wide spectrum of Cheju residents, many of whom had probably never before heard of the organization (cf. Gilman 2015, 207, 212; Lowthorp 2015, 164).

However, its prestige did little to erase the stigma associated with the vernacular religious practice on the ground. The former association manager Kim noted rather cynically that the only benefit was that the ritual's official name has gotten longer, becoming UNESCO World Intangible Cultural Heritage, Important Intangible Cultural Heritage No. 71, Cheju Ch'ilmŏri Shrine Yŏngdŭng Kut. Indeed, the ideology supporting the new status, similar to that of the national heritage system, rests on a double standard. The ritual was ennobled precisely because its presentation has been severed from specters of spirits, the fundamental source of stigma and power associated with the practitioners. In this regard, the simbang's lot is quite different from that of professional entertainers who specialize in traditional music and dance, often after university-based training, and aspire to become respected artists (yesurin) through the intangible cultural heritage program (Chungmoo Choi 1991, 57, 74). To these artists, performing onstage fulfills their professional goals, but for shamans, doing so involves a grave compromise as it eliminates their magico-religious role, the core of their trade. Further, the honor can abet the simbang's estrangement from his professional role as a healer. For example, it has brought some financial disadvantages to the lead shaman, whose wife complained to me, "People don't hire him anymore because they assume he will be too expensive now that he is a world-famous shaman. This is so unfair that I should write a letter to UNESCO." She indicated that assumptions about his higher fees are false and that, instead, UNESCO had cost him a significant portion of his livelihood.

Referring to a non-*simbang* member of the association who was pursuing a doctoral degree in Korean studies at Cheju National University, a local intellectual commented to me in 2010, "Who would want to become a *simbang*?" His off-the-cuff remark, which he would never make publicly, is a telling example of the persistent ambivalence toward *simbang* on the part of even their strongest advocates despite UNESCO recognition. More importantly, *simbang* do not want their offspring to follow in their footsteps,[22] and the UNESCO designation will not readily change their minds in this regard. Though they themselves had no choice but to accept their path, a *simbang* of high stature told me, their children inhabit a vastly different world in which more attractive career opportunities abound.

In the extreme, the ritual's global recognition strips the shamans and the community of the option to cease performing the ritual, as many seaside villages on Cheju have already done, because the reason for its very existence has weakened. Although the incumbent skill holder has reached the pinnacle of his profession thanks to the ritual, Manager Kim pointed out that maintaining it as something more than a perfunctory display will be a serious challenge to future generations. In fact, the state has become an ever more significant patron for the annual rite since its national designation. In 2010, the Cultural Heritage Administration and the provincial government granted the Association for the Ch'ilmŏri Shrine Yŏngdŭng Kut Preservation 2 million won (about US$2,000), and due to lack of interest among lay community members, the association provided participating diving women with a modest sum to aid with the cost of their food offerings.[23] The sincerity of the faithful locals, crucial to ritual efficacy, was thereby diluted. However, as is true of most safeguarded heritage practices, the mission is to keep the show going.

The association is also left to further revamp its resources toward curation of the ritual for the general public by performing the core functions of a museum—collection, conservation, exhibition, and education—in its new facility, which is part and parcel of the push for heritage tourism. In June 2015, I visited the association's office to learn about the new preservation hall. In the old office, I met Manager Kim's replacement, a sturdy young man with an undergraduate degree in police administration, a degree he described as not well suited to his job (*saengttung matta*). The new manager took me to the nearly completed two-story building across from the old hall.[24] The multifunction building includes not only an office and a storeroom for ritual tools but also a separate space for exhibiting material objects and photos and a theater that can seat a large audience.

The incumbent skill holder now has to meet the expected functions of the hall with neither Manager Kim, who acted as the association's administrator, nor Simbang Chŏng, who played an active role in the public performances. After working from 2000 to 2013 during his prime, from his early thirties to his mid-forties, Kim left the association due to growing internal political strife, financial pressure (his salary was too meager to support his family), and difficulty dealing with the complexities, uncertainties, and dilemmas associated with working for the organization. Most decisively, the death of Simbang Chŏng gave added impetus to Kim's decision to leave the organization. For Korean shamans, becoming a "state-certified performer" (Tangherlini 1998, 141) is a Cinderella story, and many have campaigned for such a position (Chungmoo Choi 1991; Chongho Kim 2003, 208). UNESCO recognition of the Yŏngdŭng Kut seems to have intensified the old conflict over selecting the next skill holder, a position that is considerably more prestigious than that for a ritual having only national recognition. Manager Kim and the folklorist Mun backed Simbang Chŏng. All three had been involved in the theatrical movement of the 1980s, in which they used *madang kut*, an open-air folk drama that incorporated *kut* to awaken popular consciousness (Namhee Lee 2003; Mun 1987a, 208). Chŏng performed as an actor the first shamanic ritual officially commemorating the victims of the April Third Events in a theater in Cheju City in 1989, at a time when performing such a ritual was seen as a challenge to the state itself. Due to pressure, the state-certified Simbang An Sain (1928–1990), who was supposed to perform it, withdrew, and Chŏng stepped in on Simbang An's behalf.

Chŏng's experience with that performance affected him deeply, and rather than continue to "act" like a *simbang*, he decided to become a *simbang*. He joined the Association for the Ch'ilmŏri Shrine Yŏngdŭng Kut Preservation to learn the shamanic arts, worked as its first office manager from 1993 to 1997, and became an official trainee (*isuja*) for the Ch'ilmŏri Shrine Yŏngdŭng Kut in 2002 (Park Kyŏnghun 2013). While the former cultural activist's trajectory can be seen as a process of becoming a "true" *simbang*, it can also be seen as a compromise because the theatrical movement in which Chŏng had been involved opposed the government's intangible cultural heritage program. Although Chŏng became a professional shaman, most shamans without college degrees, some with no formal education at all, undermined his authenticity as a *simbang* by characterizing him as a shaman who was *made* rather than born. Due to internal politics, by no means unique to Cheju shamans (cf. Chungmoo Choi 1991), this intellectual shaman left the association to join another *simbang* group that was much smaller and lower-profile than the association. In 2011, he was reborn as a "true" *simbang* by sponsoring a seventeen-day *sin kut*. He also worked as an office manager for the group. Unfortunately, Simbang Chŏng died unexpectedly of laryngeal cancer in 2013 at the age of fifty-three and was commemorated as a *minjung simbang*, a shaman for the (subaltern) people, and an artist from the periphery. Witnessing the politicization of Simbang Chŏng's death by various groups pained Manager Kim so greatly, he told me, that he traveled to the mainland to avoid the shaman's funeral.

UNESCO recognition may have been the source of power that earned the association its new building, but it is also the source of much of the turmoil that may limit its effectiveness. Moreover, while shamans' magical intervention continues to be sought privately by a wide range of Koreans living in an exceedingly uncertain contemporary society,[25] the general public seems to be far less interested in the wonders of a staged *kut* as a cultural entertainment. It remains unclear just how the rosy economic benefits the Yŏngdŭng Kut's elevated status was expected to bring to the island and the nation are to be realized.

CONCLUSION

Writing of bringing a Guggenheim Museum to Bilbao in northern Spain, the Basque anthropologist Joseba Zulaika compared globalizers with Don Juan, seducing and abandoning local sweethearts: when he says he loves you, he really means it at the time but quickly forgets and turns his attention elsewhere (2005, 152).[26] From the perspective of the former association manager Kim, there were many Don Juan–like figures who came and went, each with his or her ideas of where and how the ritual fits in the Cheju narrative. Journalists move around from one attention-catching topic to another. Enchanted with "the politics of cultural and financial seduction" (Zulaika 2005, 154), state cultural agencies obtained the ritual's World Heritage status and advertised its inclusion on UNESCO's Representative List primarily to generate publicity for the island and in hopes of material rewards. Since the performance of elected local leaders and officials is "directly associated with the amount and the quality of the publicity that their city receives," they are pressured "to show something off" within their four-year tenure and thus "put more weight on public *image* than on issues inside their communities" (Oh 2014, 2145, my emphasis). The ritual's new status may not bring Cheju the rapid and extensive publicity that comes of drama tourism, but its symbolic capital could be more sustainable than publicity, though the long-term outcome is not certain. At the same time, the local government continues to proceed with development plans, hindering the work of divers and disturbing the sustainability of the environment that had fostered the practice and belief. Left to carry on the ritual in the face of these inevitable but contradictory policies, the members of the Association for the Ch'ilmŏri Shrine Yŏngdŭng Kut Preservation may well feel that they have been abandoned.

According to Kim, scholars only take care of their research interests and accomplishments (*chagi pap kŭrut man ch'aengginda* [lit., "only looking after one's own rice bowl"]). Indeed, since the colonial period, scholars have generated a plethora of studies on Cheju shamanism. Their canonized representation and interpretation of it has often been parroted in newspapers, magazines, and governmental and nongovernmental heritage literature for a variety of audiences. Thus, they have exerted considerable discursive power and contributed much to elevating the popular religion and the practitioners. Associating with scholars has lent *simbang* a certain cachet (cf. Chungmoo Choi 1991; Romberg 2003, 134), but *simbang* are also keenly and critically aware of the structured power differentials between scholars and themselves. After a local cultural festival in the fall of 2001, I had an opportunity to sit at a temporary bar under a tent with a folklorist and two male *simbang* who had led staged rituals. When the folklorist introduced me, one of the *simbang* reported what he had told a well-known specialist in Cheju shamanism who had retired from a university faculty position and who had been his middle school classmate: "Huh, we both studied what *simbang* do [*simbang kongbu*], but one became a *simbang* and the other a scholar." This remark made me painfully aware of the differences in social position and the hierarchical nature of the relationship, in which one is representing the other.

To *simbang* who had long been ostracized, the seduction of gaining symbolic and political empowerment through UNESCO's Intangible Cultural Heritage convention must have been hard to resist. As did many others, they assumed that the world organization's approval of the ritual would enhance their social position. Indeed, international recognition has further ennobled select *simbang* as performers of spectacles and offered ever more options to some *simbang* and non-*simbang* artists to display heritage goods. However, in the purified and exoticized image of the ritual presented and enacted by the heritage program, the uncanny element of practitioners' magico-religious role and the unsavory issues associated with the ritual economy are inevitably neutered. Given that these constitute the rituals' potency, as well as cause for controversy, the sanitization has paradoxically denied the core of the practice and the *simbang*'s professional role. In this sense, the ennoblement is rather negative. Unsurprisingly, outside the heritage field, the practice retains much of its former stigma. Efforts on the part of the elite, apparently intended to protect and defend *simbang*, ironically have better served their own moral, academic, and political goals.

CONCLUSION

THIS BOOK BEGAN WITH MY RATHER UNCOMFORTABLE OBSERVA-
tion of a dispute over the service fee between a client couple and *simbang*
before the commencement of a ritual held at the patrons' home. My personal reaction was related to paradigmatic narratives—both academic and
popular—of Cheju shamanism that condemn or ignore practitioners' economic interests. The prevailing moralistic framework either dismissed or
trivialized ritual expenditure as an element that defiles the religious purity
of the practice. The seemingly contradictory representations of shamans
either as altruistic healers or as deceitful swindlers are not as contradictory as they seem in that they both come from the deep-rooted historical
legacy of construing shamans' economic interests as immoral. This view is
resilient and powerful. Even shamans who might demand handsome fees
and propel clients toward abundant monetary offerings often claim a lack
of self-interest as a means of affirming their authenticity while criticizing
other shamans for their greed (e.g., Kim Kŭmhwa 1995, 253–59; Kim Paeksun 2000, 156–61; Sin Myŏnggi 2001, 266–67).

Though not unique to Cheju, this dominant view is particularly salient
in discussions about the popular religion of the region, romanticized as a
homeland of the gods due to its flourishing and distinctive shamanism.
Sociohistorical research reveals the way that elites constructed ritual consumption over the past several centuries. Regardless of their position—
whether hostile, sympathetic, or ambivalent—they all discounted the symbolic
value of cash and ordinary goods and the shaman's work in transforming
them into sacrificial objects indispensable for efficacy. They have regarded
economic issues as degrading to the religious integrity of shamanism or at
best as peripheral to the practice. Attending to the ways that *simbang* and
their clients perform, justify, interpret, and experience a variety of transactions affords insight into their process of giving meaning to the financial
investments. It also demonstrates how a ritual is constituted economically

and why ritual affairs are inevitably thorny. The notion of ritual economy—that is, an understanding of ritual itself as an economic event filled with cultural meanings such as reciprocity, devotion, and sincerity—and the recognition of the delicate nature of ritual transactions shed new light on the long-standing controversy over the value of shamanic services and the concomitant distrust of shamans. Further, this ethnographic research lays bare the multifaceted labor and skills exercised by these ritual specialists.

Preoccupied with their own agendas, elite groups constructed a chimera of Cheju shamanism composed of (in)congruent parts that each group imagined differently but that had little grounding in reality. Despite their different ideologies, reformers have attempted to eradicate the popular religion, ostensibly to protect "unenlightened" people from shamanic manipulation. However, the groups were often more interested in enhancing their reformative goals by constructing the popular religion as a foil for their own ideals. For example, Governor Yi Hyŏngsang, who strove to Confucianize the island, portrayed local shamans as little better than robbers and laid waste to 129 shrines in 1702. During the Chosŏn dynasty, Confucian scholar-officials, endowed with ritual hegemony, perceived shamanic rituals as illegitimate, and exaggerating practitioners' economic clout was an effective way of justifying Yi's reform. However, his reforms did not survive beyond his term because he focused solely on policy changes with little consideration for the islanders' perspective.

The zealous Roman Catholic priest Kim Wŏnyŏng, arriving on the island at the end of the nineteenth century, chose shamanism as the primary target of his criticism. Kim's belligerent proselytization combined with the economic and political plight of the islanders, aggravated by new taxes imposed by the centrally appointed commissioner, infuriated the islanders, who had long maintained a strong sense of regional identity. The church excused the abuses of native Catholics, who had converted primarily to avoid the tyranny of corrupt officials and seek the privileges associated with the church (Son 2006), and turned on shamans using the traditional rhetoric of Confucian scholars—shamans exploit the innocent. A variety of modernizers in the twentieth century demonstrated their identity by characterizing shamanism as an impediment to their reform agendas and accentuating its financial harm. Because opponents devalued shamanic rituals, they regarded expenditures on service fees and offerings as extravagant regardless of the actual sums involved.

At the same time, proponents of Cheju shamanism in postwar South Korea defended it by eschewing the issue of ritual consumption and redefining the popular religion as they wished it to be. They were undoubtedly influenced by scholarship on Korean shamanism produced during the colonial period, when Japanese and Korean scholars turned the subject into a heated debate over ethnic identity. While valuing Korean shamanism as a repository of Korean thought and prizing the primordial beauty of Cheju *ponp'uri*, or mythic narratives, as indigenous oral literature, Japanese colonial scholars explicitly criticized the practitioners' economic interests. They did not recognize the ritual work involved in creating reciprocity between clients and deities. In an attempt to counter the Japanese assertion of Korean inferiority, nationalist scholars wished to proclaim a distinctive Korean identity through the notion of a Tan'gun-centered shamanism as the origin of Northeast Asian culture (Pai 2000, 68). In need of shedding the stigma associated with the vernacular religion, they remained silent on the critical view of ritual consumption and shamanic exploitation that was prevalent among Confucian elites during the Chosŏn dynasty and among their contemporaries, the Korean and Japanese modernizers.

An assortment of gatekeepers of Cheju shamanism in South Korea romanticized the popular religion as the epitome of an as-yet-undefiled distinctive local culture, which aided the government's cultural heritage program. Similar to their mainland forebears yet unlike Japanese scholars, they avoided such topics as shamans' self-interest and ritual expenditure that disrupted the idealized image of shamanism. Scholars, heritage experts, and cultural activists, who might not necessarily have believed in "the efficacy of shamanic ritual" (Kwang-Ok Kim 1994, 197), portrayed *simbang* as reciters of "pristine" tales, artistic theatrical performers, or cultural icons working for the disadvantaged. However, they ignored the centrality of economic negotiations in ritual practice and the uncomfortable story of shamans dealing with the prevalent ambivalence toward the value of their services. Proponents of Cheju shamanism disregarded the views of sponsors and practitioners, as did the reformers.

Because elites are more interested in how to appropriate the popular religion for their own agendas, their discourses and policies have been replete with incongruities. Governor Yi, known for his purge of Cheju shamanic shrines in the early eighteenth century, pointed out the state's hypocritical policy on shamanism by borrowing the voice of local practitioners who purportedly asserted to him that they continued their trade purely because of the heavy shamanic tax imposed on them. In fact, the Neo-Confucian government tacitly allowed the practice for the revenues generated by the shamanic tax while officially discrediting it, allegedly to protect innocent people from shamanic exploitation. Moreover, although the Confucian state officially marginalized the practitioners, it had them perform rituals for rain and care for the sick in the government's medical facilities through the first half of the Chosŏn dynasty (Choi Jong Seong 2002, 124–25, 142; Walraven 1999a, 173).

Several centuries later, the South Korean government promoted purified and aestheticized *kut* as a traditional performing art, while undermining the magico-religious role of shamans, and discouraging healing rituals as superstitious (Chongho Kim 2003, 217–21; Harvey 1979, 11). Contradicting earlier policy, the central and local governments integrated the Yŏngdŭng Kut, an improper and irrational ceremony of yesteryear, into the economy of cultural tourism through sanctification by UNESCO and appropriation as heritage goods. An activist-turned-folklorist who previously opposed the "corruptive" act of commodifying the unsullied local tradition teamed up with officials to ensure the success of the endeavor. If the profit motive of practitioners has long been faulted as an indication of the loss of religious integrity, theirs was justified in the name of local and national economic benefits.

The *simbang* had no reason not to welcome an opportunity to elevate Cheju shamanism by assisting in transcribing *ponp'uri* into print and transforming the Yŏngdŭng Kut into national and international heritage in the hope of satisfying their personal and professional ambitions. These efforts have, to some degree, helped remove the stigma from the practitioners and elevate select *simbang* to the status of local celebrities (cf. Chungmoo Choi 1991). However, because the heritage economy sanitizes both *simbang* and their rituals in order to make them more salable cultural commodities, the practitioners' principal concern—receiving respect as well as payment for what they do professionally—is not addressed. In the heritage discourse and presentation, delicate and often contentious issues related to the ritual economy, which matter to shamans and their clients and are critical to making rituals move and work, are perforce omitted. The spiritual power and work of *simbang*, like those that deeply moved Mr. Cho's family members, are not displayable at staged rituals (*kongyŏn*). In other words, shamans are ennobled at the cost of their profession's vitality. Thus, not despite, but because of, the sanitization, the redemptive discourse has inadvertently done a disservice to the practitioners by denying their standing as professionals and in effect making them more vulnerable to the deep-seated insult that shamans are only out for money.

The performance skills valued for staged rituals and the images praised by the elite are not what clients seek from shamanic services. Both *simbang* and the laity distinguish two categories of rituals—one practiced for efficacy and the other displayed as local tradition (cf. Chongho Kim 2003, 219). Because the essentialist cultural narratives or distinctions are not based on the lived experiences of patrons and the official status of purveyors of intangible cultural heritage is bestowed upon a coterie of *simbang*, they exert little discursive power over the laity, including *simbang*'s clientele. Thus, even after "superstition" was elevated to "religion" and "culture" (Kendall 2009, 1), the contradictory appraisals of shamanism, in which it is both vilified and extolled, prevail in public discourse. It is not surprising, then, that despite the full-spectrum elevation of the popular religion, most *simbang* still live with stigma and the occasional insult as social others, bearing the brunt of doubt and suspicion related to their economic interests. This is true not only for Cheju *simbang* but also for most Korean shamans at large (e.g., Kendall 2009, 24, 32; Chongho Kim 2003).

This dichotomous view has persisted well into the present time. In the fall of 2016, prejudice against shamans was loudly and openly expressed in connection with the cronyism scandal involving South Korea's former president Park Geun-hye. When the news first broke, foreign and domestic media sensationalized the apparently perplexing scandal by associating it with shamanism, and South Korean politicians, celebrities, and populace referred to Park's confidante Choi Sunsil as a shaman.[1] Although Choi performed neither rituals nor divinations, she was associated with shamanism because she manipulated Park for personal gain, at times resorting to mysterious powers. Several shamans defended themselves against the unfounded and contemptuous association that they saw as religious discrimination by emphasizing their social role as selfless healers.[2] The writer Hwang Taegwŏn supported their cause by contributing the article "Don't Insult Shamanism" to a daily newspaper (2016). He contended that shamanism has been part of Koreans' valuable worldview (*uri minjok ŭi sojunghan kach'igwan*) and grassroots religion (*kijŏ sinang*) since ancient times (*t'aego*) and that genuine shamans do not have selfish motives (*sasim*). Citing this author, who found shamanism's most important function to be healing (*ch'iyu*), Son Sŏkhŭi, a nationally known television news anchor, suggested that it might be time to perform a *kut* for Koreans who were feeling distressed and lost due to the shocking scandal (JTBC *Nyusŭrum*, 9 November 2016). In defending shamans, both Hwang and Son paid little heed to practitioners' economic interests. Moreover, by rendering shamans' self-interest and healing irreconcilable, they inadvertently devalued the (economic) worth of shamanic labor and skills. This resilient view affords little room for critical or productive examination of the ritual economy that is at the core of the practice and central to the controversy around it.

Scholars of shamanism have played no small part in perpetuating the double standard. Although they may have assumed that their interests were congruent with those of shamans, they have not only otherized shamans in their writings and theories but also patronized them. When practitioners betray their idealized image, for example by charging high fees and encouraging lavish offerings of money, some join their opponents in faulting practitioners for being more interested in money than in their spiritual role (e.g., Cho Hǔng-yun 1990, 215; 1997b, 110). Many scholar-advocates tend to see the conspicuous ritual materialism and practitioners' self-interest in urban areas as degeneration brought about by outside influences such as capitalism and modernization on Korean society and culture (e.g., Akiba [1950] 1987, 82; Cho Hǔng-yun 1990, 216; Hwang Ru-shi 1988, 19–31).

Even when the changes are not viewed as a sign of deterioration, most scholars emphasizing the changes relate them to the system of modern capitalism under which South Koreans now live.[3] A study of rituals conducted in Seoul after the 1997–98 Asian economic crisis showed that the belief that luck (*chaesu*) and fortune (*pok*) bring about actual wealth was not inherent in the folk belief of wishing for blessings (*kibok sinang*) but was instead related to the phantasmagoric nature of a capitalistic market economy (Kim Seong-nae 2002b, 72). This focus on the capitalist economy can alleviate, to some degree, the idea of shamans as inherently deceitful by highlighting external economic influences on the religion. However, such a view ignores the fact that "excessive" ritual consumption and the practitioners' desire for personal gain have encouraged widespread elite denigration of the practice since the beginning of the thirteenth century, well before the advent of modernization. The lack of historical records of patrons' views on ritual expenditure makes it impossible to conclude that the laity in the past were less prudent with ritual expenditure or less interested in enhancing their economic well-being by sponsoring rituals.

The nostalgic view that shamans and patrons were once purer than they are now amounts to an attempt to keep brilliantly adaptive shamans in the past (Kendall 2009, 33) and to objectify the practitioners "as signs of rural authenticity" prominent in "the story of Korean modernity" (32). This criticism is especially applicable to constructions of Cheju shamanism.

Underscoring "isolation" as a significant feature of the island, many studies have portrayed Cheju shamanism as pristine and coherent, as though the island were less hospitable to change than the mainland (but see Oh 2014; Tran 2015; Kyoim Yun 2016). In contrast to Seoul-based ethnographic studies that are full of descriptions of shamans in motion,[4] studies of Cheju shamanism often perpetuate the image of Cheju *simbang* as caretakers of a disappearing tradition. One of the most popular academic endeavors related to Cheju shamanism since the 1930s has been the transcription of indigenous *ponp'uri* recited by several well-known *simbang* outside ritual contexts. While Cheju *ponp'uri* fully deserve continued academic attention, the disproportionate attention to preservation unwittingly undermines the potency of narrative performances and the *simbang*'s professional role at rituals. More importantly, this academic practice relegates ritual consumption to the periphery of scholarly inquiry. An "extravagant" ritual price is rarely noted, and if it is, it is only mentioned in passing to explain the desperate situation of a patron family and to emphasize that the potential benefits of the ritual warrant the expense (Kim Seong-nae 1989b, 160–61).

However, *simbang* and patrons themselves are quite practical-minded when it comes to rituals regardless of the primary purpose for sponsoring them (healing, prosperity, and harmony) or the occupations of the patrons' families (e.g., beekeepers, diving ladies, and small-business owners). As on the mainland, ritual materialism is conspicuous in contemporary Cheju, a region that, apart from its two large cities, Cheju and Sŏgwip'o, remains relatively less urbanized. The laity often seek shamanic services in the hope of resolving pressing financial problems and enhancing economic prosperity, which are both closely related to the physical, mental, and financial health of their households. At the same time, they see ritual itself as an economic affair. Indeed, sponsoring a *kut* demands an extravagant financial outlay, in addition to considerable time and labor, on the part of patrons. Unlike critics who have devalued ritual consumption as mere squandering, they perceive it as a worthy investment despite the risk of not getting what they hope for.

Further, practitioners and patrons do not necessarily construe economy as an external element that spoils the otherwise pure spiritual practice, a perspective resolutely held by elite advocates of Cheju shamanism. Instead, they perceive economic matters to be at the heart of the practice. For them, a ritual is itself an economic activity based on reciprocity between humans and the spirits, in which the dedication of offerings is of primary importance. The practitioners infuse mundane goods with their patrons' sincerity through the use of their affective language and negotiate with the spirits and deities on their clients' behalf. Thus, both sacrificial objects and *simbang's* eloquent presentations play a critical role in rituals. In the act of making a sacrifice, the quantity and quality of sacrificial objects indicate the degree of a sponsor's devotion. For this reason, belief and material expenditure are inextricable.

The belief in reciprocity manifests most vividly in the myth of Saman, a *ponp'uri* that *simbang* recite during a ritual for the purpose of enhancing efficacy and which highlights an exchange-based relationship between humans and the spirits. The idea that a kind of reciprocity is at the center of a ritual is particularly clear from the perspective of Cheju *simbang*. They themselves sponsor the most elaborate and grandest-scale *kut*, investing far more than patrons would, both to express their gratitude to their tutelary gods for granting them their livelihoods and in the hope that the deities will continue to support their ritual business.

Nonetheless, not all patrons are unquestioning devotees of the practice, a fact rarely noted by scholars. As ideological opponents of shamanism, they can also doubt practitioners' motives and complain about their pecuniary interests. Financial issues related to ritual affairs can turn into a quagmire for several interrelated reasons. First, patrons and practitioners have different perspectives on the value of shamanic services. *Simbang* selling their services for a living are deeply concerned about "proper" remuneration for their labor and skills, as well as their patrons' welfare. Patrons carefully weigh the worth of their investment, a substantial amount of which becomes a *simbang's* income, and at times haggle aggressively with shamans at pre-ritual contract sessions to settle on a "fair" fee.

More importantly, ritual transactions are fraught with ambiguity about the ownership of sacrificial objects and what is bought and sold. This ambiguity, exacerbated by the fact that ritual contracts are verbal, can lead to discord between service providers and consumers. Despite its accepted value and quite contrary to the romantic perceptions of reciprocity (e.g., Chun 2012; Hogarth 2009), it is not entirely a non-calculative exchange, and the appropriate amount for an offering is a subjective matter. Further, it is not immediately apparent that the hoped-for gifts will be bestowed in return; in other words, reciprocity is not a given. Although some emphasize the gods' demands for cash and other offerings (Kendall 2009. 218n14), critics of shamanism, such as self-righteous Confucians, missionaries, and nationalist reformers, have long disparaged shamans for their cupidity but have exempted the shamanic deities from criticism. The issue of who ultimately benefits from the cash offerings, *simbang* or deity, if not the matter of who is demanding the money during a ritual, can seem ambiguous to clients. Therefore, patrons who willingly abide by *simbang's* authority and are affected by their cathartic performance can resent the amount of ritual expenditure, especially when there is disagreement over remuneration and/or the expected outcomes do not materialize. However, clients do not automatically construe shamans' economic interest as a sign that their religious role has been defiled but rather as an ordinary matter of business.

Moreover, although performing a ritual requires multifarious tangible and intangible skills and intensive emotional, mental, and physical labor on the part of *simbang*, these are hard to measure. Anti-shaman commentators have long frowned on shamanic ritual performances as distasteful, despite their power to attract the laity, and considered the pragmatic and tactful business strategies shamans employed manipulative or even wicked. Supporters of Cheju shamanism, who essentialized the image of *simbang* as selfless healers and purveyors of a distinctive local tradition, also undermined the grueling labor and delicate skills involved in the often messy and discordant reality of performance situations. For some manual laborers, what *simbang* do during rituals is not "proper" work. For example, an elderly diving woman, who used to participate in shamanic rituals, told me that "*simbang* earn a living with their mouths while sitting on a cushion." Moreover, *simbang* themselves have to downplay their own agency at times. Although patrons appreciate the *yŏngge ullim*, the lamentations of the dead, practitioners cannot overtly draw attention to their skills and the deliberate effort involved in their performance. Doing so would jeopardize their authenticity as spiritual mediums, as the expectation is that they are conveying the words of spirits. While studies of shamanism in Korea and elsewhere have demonstrated the practitioners' performance competence and the transformative power of rituals,[5] they have paid far less attention to the laboriousness of their care work. Detailed analysis of the *yŏngge ullim* performed by a seasoned *simbang* who brought catharsis to Mr. Cho's family (see chap. 4) illustrates the skillful *and* labor-intensive nature of their affect work. Nonetheless, the cathartic moment created by *simbang* is ephemeral, and the value of their work is not easily measurable.

The perspectives of patrons and *simbang* on the subject of ritual economy not only enhance our understanding of consumption associated with Korean shamanism but also allow us to see how economic matters are intimately and intricately built into the religious practice. Although anthropologists and sociologists have long paid attention to the intersection of religion and economy,[6] fewer studies have approached ritual itself as economic (e.g., Wells and McAnany 2008). It is undoubtedly important to consider the ties between changes in ritual offerings and broader socioeconomic transformations and how new commodities speak to the ambivalence contemporary South Koreans feel toward heightened materialism and consumption (Kendall 2009; Kim Seong-nae 2002b; Jun Hwan Park 2012). However, the seemingly excessive expenditures and patrons' ambivalence toward the value of shamanic services cannot be fully explained by the capitalist ethos or economic conditions. For a deeper understanding of ritual economy and a more nuanced appreciation of shamanic agency, it is important to examine how values and beliefs are communicated through discursive practices that are both historical and contemporary. The gestalt of the popular religion is complex and fluid, and its value is contingent on multilayered cultural idioms and pragmatic considerations.

GLOSSARY

Abbreviations

C. Chinese
J. Japanese
alt. alternative

aek 액(厄) malevolent influence
aengmaegi 액(厄)맥이 forestalling misfortune

chaehwa 재화(災禍) misfortune
chaerae sijang 재래시장(在來市場) old-style open market
chaesu 재수(財數) luck
chakttu kŏri 작두거리 ritual session in which a shaman stands on sharp twin blades with bare feet and delivers oracles
chamnyŏ 잠녀(潛女) diving women
changgye 장계(狀啓) official's formal letter to a king
charyojip 자료집(資料集) collected materials
ch'asa (alt. **ch'esa, ch'ŏsa, ch'ŏsŏ** on Cheju) 차사(差使) messenger
chemul 제물(祭物) ceremonial goods
chesa 제사(祭祀) Confucian ancestor rites
chijŏn 지전(紙錢) paper money
chikkam 직감(直感) intuition
chilch'igi 질치기 ritual in which *simbang* symbolically clear pathways to the otherworld (lit., "clearing up the road")
Ch'ilmŏri 칠(七)머리 the name of a shrine (lit., "Seven Heads")
chinjŏk kut 진적굿 *kut* sponsored by shamans to bring luck and prosperity
chinogwi kut (alt. **ogu, ogi,** or **ogwi kut**) 지노귀 굿 ritual in which the dead are sent off to the otherworld
chiok 지옥(地獄) a hell
chisok 지속(誌俗) records of customs
chisŏng kamch'ŏn 지성감천(至誠感天) sincerity moves heaven
chisŏng kamsin 지성감신(至誠感神) sincerity moves the gods
ch'iyu 치유(治癒) healing
ch'ogamje 초감제(初監祭) the first segment of a Cheju *kut* in which the deities are invited to the ritual venue

ch'ohon 초혼(招魂) invocation of the spirits of the dead

chokpo 족보(族譜) family genealogy

chŏksu konggwŏn 적수공권(赤手空拳) empty hands and naked fists

ch'ŏndoje 천도제(遷度祭) Buddhist ritual in which the dead are sent off
to paradise

ch'ŏngbaengni 청백리(淸白吏) literally, "clean-handed official"

chŏngsŏng 정성(精誠) sincerity

chŏngsŏng kŭllyang 정성근량(精誠斤量) weighing the sincerity

Chŏngsŭng 정승(政丞) prime minister in the Kingdom of Korea

chŏngyukchŏm 정육점(精肉店) butcher shop

chŏnsugwan 전수관(傳受館) hall for passing on heritage

chosang 조상(祖上) ancestors

chŏsŭng 저승 the otherworld

chŏsŭng ch'asa 저승차사(差使) messengers of death in the otherworld

chowangje 조왕제(竈王祭) small-scale annual ritual conducted at individual
households at the turn of each year

chujan kwŏnjan 주잔권잔(酒盞權盞) offering drinks to deities and spirits

chung maŭl 중(中)마을 middle village

Chungyo Muhyŏng Munhwajae 중요무형문화재(重要無形文化財) Important Intangible
Cultural Property

ha maŭl 하(下)마을 low village

haengjang 행장(行狀) account of conduct

haenyŏ 해녀(海女) diving women

haeoe 해외(海外) overseas

haesinje 해신제(海神祭) a community ritual performed at seaside villages

Hallyu 한류(韓流) Korean Wave, the unprecedented boom in Korean popular culture
in East Asia and beyond

Han'gŭl 한글 vernacular Korean script

Hanbok 한복(韓服) traditional Korean costume

hokse mumin 혹세무민(惑世誣民) delude the world and deceive the people

hŭi 희(戱) entertaining or theatrical plays

hwangguk sinmin 황국신민(皇國臣民) subordinate citizens of the
Japanese empire

hyanggyo 향교(鄕校) public schools during the Chosŏn dynasty

hyangni 향리(鄕吏) local clerks

hyŏn 현(縣) lesser county

hyŏnse kibok 현세기복(現世祈福) seeking this-worldly luck

idan 이단(異端) heterodoxy or heresy

illyu yusan 인류유산(人類遺産) heritage of the world's people

injŏng 인정(人情) human feelings (C. renqing; J. ninjō) and ritual offerings

ipch'un 입춘(立春) one of the twenty-four seasonal divisions

Ipch'un Kut 입춘(立春)굿 communal kut celebrating the onset of spring on
Cheju Island

isuja 이수자(履修者) master artist
itako (J.) イタコ blind medium and healer, typically a woman

kabo 갑오(甲午) name of a year in the sixty-year cycle (e.g., 1894)
kach'igwan 가치관(價値觀) attitudes or worldview
kajŏn 가전(加錢) cash offerings collected by shamans
kangsin mu 강신무(降神巫) god-descended shamans
kibok sinang 기복 신앙(祈福 信仰) belief in wishing for blessings
kijŏ sinang 기저 신앙(基底 信仰) grassroots religion
kime 기메 paper decorations used in rituals
kinŭng poyuja 기능 보유자(技能 保有者) skill holder
k'oegŏ 쾌거(快擧) splendid achievement
kogyo munhŏn 고교 문헌(古敎 文獻) literature on an old religion
kongdongch'e 공동체(共同體) community
kongnoja 공로자(功勞者) asset
kongsu 공수 oracles
kongyŏn 공연(公演) public performance
kŏnppang 건(乾)빵 hardtack biscuits
kosa 고사(告祀) small-scale rituals
kuchiyose (J.) 口寄せ spirit recollections
kŭllyang 근량(斤量) weighing
kun 군(郡) county
kŭn 근(斤) unit of weight, 1.323 pounds
k'ŭn 큰 large, grand, great
k'ŭn abŏji 큰아버지 father's older brother
k'ŭn ŏmŏni 큰어머니 father's older brother's wife
kut 굿 large-scale shamanic rituals
kutpŏp 굿법(法) the principles of *kut*
kuttang 굿당(堂) commercial ritual halls
kuttŏk 굿덕(德) benefit of ritual or ritual efficacy
kwanch'alsa 관찰사(觀察使) top commander
kwi 귀(鬼) ghosts
kwisin 귀신(鬼神) spirits
kwiyang p'uri 귀양푸리 a ritual performed following the interment of a corpse
kye 계(契) financial association
kyo 교(敎) religion
kyoan 교안(敎案) religious disturbance
kyŏngse chemin 경세제민(經世濟民) administering the state to relieve the suffering of
the people

li 리(里) smallest administrative unit of the government
li (alt. **i**) 리 (이) (理) propriety

madang kut 마당굿 open-air folk drama that incorporates indigenous shamanic rituals
maegi 맥이 forestallment

mansin 만신(萬神) honorific term referring to mainland shamans
minjok 민족(民族) nation, ethnicity, race
minjŏn 민전(民田) people's land
minjung 민중(民衆) people; mass
minsok nori 민속(民俗)놀이 folk play or entertainment
minyo 민요(民謠) folk song
misin 미신(迷信) superstition (C. *mixin*; J. *meishin*)
misin t'ap'a 미신 타파(迷信 打破) eradication of superstition
mok 목(牧) special county
moksa 목사(牧使) magistrate of a special county
mu 무(巫) shaman
muan 무안(巫案) rosters or tax register of shamans
mudang 무당(巫堂) derogatory term referring to shamans
muga 무가(巫歌) shaman songs
mugyo 무교(巫敎) shamanism (lit., "the teachings of shamans")
mugyŏk 무격(巫覡) shamans
muhyŏng munhwajae 무형문화재(無形文化財) intangible cultural assets
muijŭm 무(巫)이즘 shamanism
munhwa kwanggwang chawŏn 문화관광자원(文化觀光資願) cultural and touristic
    resource
munjŏn ch'ŏlgari 문전철갈이 small-scale ritual devoted to household deities conducted
    at the beginning of the year
muŏpse 무업세(巫業稅) taxes collected from shamans for performing rituals
muse 무세(巫稅) shamanic tax
musok 무속(巫俗) shamanic customs or practice
myŏngye 명예(名譽) honor
myŏngp'um 명품(名品) masterpiece

nahŭi or **naryehŭi** 나희(儺戱) or 나례희(儺禮戱) theatrical exorcism
nal kwa kuk sŏmgim 날과 국 섬김 informing deities of the location and date of a
    ritual
namgyŏk yŏmu 남격여무(男覡女巫) male and female shamans
nan 난(亂) disturbance
narye 나례(儺禮) exorcism
noemul 뇌물(賂物) bribes
Nongch'on Chinhŭng Undong 농촌진흥운동(農村振興運動) Rural Revitalization
    Campaign
nongmin 농민(農民) peasants
nongmin ponggi 농민봉기(農民蜂起) peasants' uprising
nop'immal 높임말 respectful speech
noro (J.) ノロ Okinawan priests
nunch'i 눈치 intuition

orŭm 오름 small volcanic craters

paekchŏng 백정(白丁) butchers

paengnyŏn chosang 백년조상(百年祖上) one-hundred-year-old ancestor

pan mal 반(半) the low forms of speech

p'ansori 판소리 solo musical drama

pison 비손 small-scale ritual

pok 복(福) luck

ponggi 봉기(蜂起) uprising

pongsa hada 봉사(奉仕)하다 serve others

ponp'uri 본(本)풀이 mythic narratives recited by *simbang*

posal 보살(菩薩) god-descended female shamans (lit., "bodhisattva")

pujo 부조(扶助) allowance aid

pujŏng 부정(不淨) pollution

pujŏnghan saram 부정(不淨)한 사람 polluted people

Pultto maji 불도(佛道)맞이 literally, "receiving Birth Spirit Grandmother"

p'umasi 품앗이 reciprocal labor-exchange practiced in agrarian society

p'ungsok 풍속(風俗) customs

p'ung-un-noe-u-je 풍운뇌우제 (風雲雷雨祭) ritual devoted to the gods of wind, clouds, thunder, and rain

pyŏlbi 별비(別費) cash offerings collected by shamans (lit., "additional costs")

pyŏnhosa 변호사(辯護士) attorney or lawyer

ri or li 리(里) the smallest administrative unit of the government

ruiji shūkyō (J.) 類似宗教 pseudo-religion

Saemaŭl Undong 새마을운동(運動) New Village (Community) Movement

Saeng Saeng Munhwajae Saŏp 생생문화재사업(生生 文化財事業) Living Cultural Assets Project

saengttung matta 생뚱맞다 off the wall

sagi 사기(詐欺) fraud

sagikkun 사기(詐欺)꾼 fraud

Sahŏnbu 사헌부(司憲府) Office of the Inspector General

sajang-nim 사장(社長)님 honorific term used in addressing a business owner

sajeja 사제자(司祭者) priests

Saman 사만(四萬) name of the protagonist in the myth of Saman (lit., "Forty Thousand")

sang 상(尙) respect

sang maŭl 상(上)마을 high village

sang ŭmsa 상음사(尙淫祀) respecting licentious rituals

sangp'ije 상피제(相避制) laws to prevent appointing officials to their town of origin

sanp'an 산판(算版) divination tools consisting of a disk, two small cups, and coins

Sasam Sakkŏn 사삼사건(四三事件) the April Third Events

sasim 사심(私心) self-interest

sasŭl (alt. sasil) seugi 사슬 or 사실 세우기 balancing an animal carcass on the prongs of a trident in order to determine the gods' satisfaction with the offering

sesŭp mu 세습무(世襲巫) hereditary shamans

shyamŏn 샤먼 Korean rendering of "shaman"

shyamŏnijŭm 샤머니즘 Korean rendering of "shamanism"

Sillok 실록(實錄) *Veritable Records*

simbang 심방 Cheju indigenous shamans

Simsin Chakhŭng Undong 심신작흥운동(心身作興運動) Mind Cultivation Movement

simyak 심약(審藥) medical official of the Chosŏn dynasty

sin 신(神) gods, deities

Sin Saenghwal Undong 신생활운동(新生活運動) New Life Movement

sin ŭi ai 신(神)의 아이 servant children of the gods

sin ŭi hyŏngbang 신(神)의 형방(刑房) judicial officials of the gods

sinang 신앙(信仰) beliefs

sinbang 신방(神房) literally, "judicial officials of the gods" (contracted from *sin ŭi hyŏngbang*)

sinch'uk 신축(辛丑) name of a year in the sixty-year cycle (e.g., 1901)

sindang 신당(神堂) shamanic shrine

sindang t'oemulse 신당퇴물세(神堂退物稅) tax on the ceremonial goods left over after rituals

sindangse 신당세(神堂稅) property taxes for shrines or taxes for property associated with shrines

sin'gyo 신교(神敎) literally, "divine teachings"; idealized prototype Korean religion

sink'al 신(神)칼 divine knife

sin kut 신(神)굿 *kut* sponsored by shamans

sinsep'o 신세포(神稅布) shamanic tax paid in cloth

Sirhak 실학(實學) Practical Learning

Siwang maji 시왕(十王)맞이 receiving the Ten Kings of the otherworld

soji 소지(燒紙) blank white folded paper used for petitions to the gods

soju 소주(燒酒) cheap distilled spirits

sojung han 소중(所重)한 valuable

Sok taejŏn 속대전(續大典) *Continuation of the Great Code*

sŏlsoe 설쇠 a metal percussion instrument used in Cheju shamanic rituals

sŏngju p'uri 성주풀이 ritual for settling the household gods into a newly built house

sŏnmul 선물(膳物) gifts

sŏnsaengnim 선생(先生)님 a polite term for addressing and referring to teachers

sot (Cheju dialect) 솟 a straw rope hung over the gate of a house before a ritual to prevent polluted people from entering, *kŭmjul* 금(禁)줄 in standard Korean

sŏwŏn 서원(書院) private Confucian academy

ssangnom 쌍놈 vulgar people of low birth

Ssikkim kut 썻김굿 *kut* for the dead common in the Chŏlla Province coastal region

Sukchong sillok 肅宗實錄 *Veritable Records of Sukchong*

sullyŏkto 巡歷圖 inspection tour

sŭngmu 僧舞 Buddhist dances

sunulda (Cheju dialect) 수눌다 to reciprocate labor

Sunurŭm (Cheju dialect) 수눌음 a noun form of *sunulda*, *p'umasi* in standard Korean

sup'yo 수표(手票) bank checks

suryŏng 수령(守令) magistrates

t'aego 태고(太古) ancient times

t'aenghwa 탱화(幀畵) portraits of shamanic deities

tang 당(堂) shrine

tang maein simbang 당(堂) 매인 심방 *simbang* who performs community rituals for the tutelary gods

tang chip 당(堂)집 shrine house

tanghan 당한(堂漢) old term referring to *simbang* on Cheju Island

tangju 당주(堂主) *simbang*'s tutelary ancestors

tangju-bang 당주방(堂主房) room where the *simbang*'s tutelary ancestors are enshrined

tan'gol 단골 *simbang*'s clients

tan'gol 당골 hereditary shamans in Chŏlla Province

tangp'a 당파(黨派) political factions

tangsin 당신(堂神) shrine deities

Tano 단오(端午) Fifth Day of the Fifth Lunar Month

tarani 다라니(陀羅尼) paper money marked with red coin prints; imitation paper money

t'ogwan 토관(土官) indigenous officials

t'oho 토호(土豪) indigenous power holders

T'oyo Myŏngp'um Kongyŏn 토요명품공연(土曜名品公演) Saturday Premium Performances

turumagi 두루마기 traditional Korean topcoat

ŭi 의 of

ullim 울림 weeping

ŭmsa 음사(淫祠) illicit or licentious shrines (C. *yinci*)

ŭmsa 음사(淫祀) illicit or licentious rituals (C. *yinsi*)

ŭmsa mubok 음사무복(淫祀無福) licentious rituals bring no luck

ŭnhye 은혜(恩惠) grace

ŭp 읍(邑) town(ship)

uri 우리 we or our

ŭro 으로 by means of

wŏnch'ojŏk 원초적(原初的) primordial

wŏnsi munye 원시문예(原始文藝) primitive art and literature

yangban 양반(兩班) ruling aristocrats

yangju 양주(洋酒) Western liquor

Yangmahŭi 약마희(躍馬戱) playful raft race performed at the end of the Yŏngdŭng Kut on Cheju Island (lit., "the play of jumping horses")

yeak 예악(禮樂) ritual and music

yesurin 예술인(藝術人) artists

Yŏmna Taewang 엄라대왕(閻羅大王) King Yŏmna [of the otherworld]

Yŏngdŭng 영등(燃燈) goddess of the wind

yŏnggam 영감(靈鑑) spiritual inspiration

yŏngge (Cheju dialect) 영게 souls

yŏngge ullim 영계울림 lamentations of the dead on Cheju

Yongwang maji 용왕(龍王)맞이 receiving Dragon Kings

yŏnyu takkŭm 연유(緣由)닦음 informing deities of the reason for a *kut*

yoryŏng 요령(鐃鈴) ritual bell

yukchi-nom 육지(陸地)놈 mainland bastards

yusaeng 유생(儒生) Confucian scholars

yuta (J.) ユタ Okinawan female mediums or shamans

NOTES

Introduction

1. Unlike the practice in many peninsular regions, where clients pay shamans to purchase offerings before the ritual (e.g., Chungmoo Choi 1987, 195; Hogarth 2009; Chongho Kim 2003), clients on Cheju Island prepare ritual offerings, including clothes, food, and money (real and imitation), and then hand over a service fee just before the ritual begins.

2. Korean women keep their maiden names after marriage.

3. For a similar observation about Mongolia, see Pederson 2011.

4. For example, see Chungmoo Choi 1989, 1991; Kendall 2003, 2009; Kim Seong-nae 2002b; and Jun Hwan Park 2012.

5. This is not unique to shamanism. Observing Confucian lineage rituals, the Janellis noted, "Real-world social goals, rather than beliefs about the afterlife, prompt the offerings of lineage rituals" (Janelli and Janelli 1982,122). However, pragmatic matters are more openly discussed in shamanic practice.

6. The term "Ch'ŏngdam" refers to Ch'ŏngdam-dong, a wealthy district of Kangnam in Seoul. Originally a Buddhist term, *posal* refers to bodhisattvas or lay Buddhist women, but in the Korean shamanic context, it is commonly used to indicate female shamans. *Posal* are also sometimes called "fortune-tellers." For various usages of *posal*, see Bruno 2002, 76; Kendall 1985a, 126, 132; and Kim Chongho 2003, 23.

7. In the most recent case of which I am aware, a Seoul municipal court acquitted a shaman who was accused of fraudulently earning 500 million won from one client for performing five hundred rituals in the course of five years (e.g., *Kyŏnghyang sinmun*, 30 August 2017, http://news.khan.co.kr/kh_news/khan_art_view.html?artid=201708301002001&code=940100).

8. For example, see Appadurai 1986; Befu 1968; Keane 1994, 2001; and Miller 1995, 2001.

9. Gates 1987; Kendall 2009; Kim Seong-nae 2002b; Heonik Kwon 2007; Truitt 2013; Weller 1994; and Mayfair Yang 2000.

10. See Chongho Kim 2003, 170–72; Harvey 1979, 197; Kendall 1985a, 31; and Yim, Janelli, and Janelli, 1993, 55–56.

11. For example, see Feuchtwang 2001; Jackson 1999; Charles Jones 2003; Heonik Kwon 2007; Jun Hwan Park 2012; and Mayfair Mei-hui Yang 2000.

12. See Bruno 2007a; Chun 1984, 111; Hogarth 2009; Kim Seong-nae 2002b, 76–78; Park Il-Young 1990, 129–34; and Seo 2002, 4.

13. I have not heard people in Cheju refer to offerings dedicated to *chesa* (Confucian ancestor rites) as *injŏng*. Though the use is more dominant than in the peninsular regions in present-day Korea, this meaning of *injŏng* is not exclusive to Cheju Island (Byun Jisun [Pyŏn Chisŏn], personal communication, 4 May 2011).

14. For example, see Befu 1968; Janelli with Yim 1993; Rupp 2003; and Mayfair Mei-hui Yang 1994.

15. The managers of the company where the author did his fieldwork tactfully accommodated gifts and made occasional allowances with trade partners with a view to the long-term benefits for both parties. They reckoned *injŏng* to be humane and beneficial in commercial matters.

16. The term *p'umasi* originally meant an exchange of labor on a quid pro quo basis.

17. See Brandt 1971; Chun 1984; Hogarth 2009, 220–31; Janelli 1993; and Jesook Song 2014, 52.

18. This is one of the common phrases *simbang* recite when they make sacrifices. Similarly, shamans on the mainland chant, "Pray accept this devotion," rather than "Pray accept our gift" (Hogarth 2009, 263; cf. Bruno 2007a, 55).

19. See Geschiere 2013, 30–31; Keane 1994; LiPuma and Lee 2008; Mauss (1950) 1990; and Miyazaki 2004, 100.

20. The island remained a subdivision of Chŏlla Province until 1946. It was then upgraded to a province when South Korea was under the trusteeship of the U.S. military government (Kim Pong-ok 2000, 301).

21. The Chosŏn elite also referred it to as "overseas," as evidenced by Governor Yi Hyŏngsang's letter to the king in 1702.

22. This local crop was a popular tribute for the central government as early as 1052 and became a cash crop beginning in the mid-1960s (Sŏgwip'o Citrus Museum).

23. According to the kingdom's foundation myth, it was founded by three brothers representing the three legendary ancestral clans: Ko, Yang, and Pu.

24. Most previous studies have interpreted the change in Cheju's administrative status and the subsequent dispatch of centrally appointed officials to the island as signifying the loss of its political independence. Cheju-born historians Kim Iru (2000) and Yi Yŏnggwŏn (2005) have challenged this dominant view. According to them, regardless of changes to Cheju's administrative units, Cheju was under Koryŏ's political system in the early years of the dynasty. Well aware that isolation from the Koryŏ central government meant political and economic death for Cheju, local leaders made efforts to promote the island to a different status in order to enhance Cheju's political position.

25. See Chejudoji P'yŏnch'an Wiwŏnhoe 2006, 332–35, 403–6, 508–18, 588–609; Merrill 1980, 141; and Yi Yŏnggwŏn 2005, 158–189. During the Chosŏn dynasty, more than two hundred scholar-officials were exiled on Cheju. William Sands observed that the island was "used by Seoul as a penal colony for political prisoners" ([1931] 1904, 167).

26. For example, Ch'oe Pu, author of *A Record of Drifting across the Sea* (P'yohaerok), was appointed commissioner of registers for Cheju in 1487 for such a mission (Ch'oe Pu [1488] 2004, 110).

27. See Committee for the Compilation of the *Gazetteer of Cheju Island* 2006, 378–83; Kim Sanghŏn (1601) 1992, 55, 62; Yi Hyŏngsang (1704) 2009, 155–58; and Yi Yŏnggwŏn 2005, 140–42.

28. See Baik 2007, 96–97; Cumings 2005, 219–21; Hun Joon Kim 2014; and Merrill 1980.

29. See Hyun Hye-Kyung 2005, 2008; Kang So-Jeon 2004; Kim Seong-nae 1989a, 1989b, 1991a, 2000b; and Heonik Kwon 2009.

30. As of January 2016, the population of the Republic of Korea was 51,826,287, of which 667,337 lived on Cheju. Statistics of Korea, http://kostat.go.kr/wnsearch/search.jsp (accessed 8 February 2019).

31. See Ha 2003; Hyŏn Yongjun 1976, 1980a; Ko Haegyeong 2001; Mun 1998, 2001; and Yi Suja 2004.

32. Boudewijn Walraven notes that the term *simbang* "is found in an early *han'gŭl* text, a 1461 vernacular-Korean translation of the *Śūraṃgama-sūtra* (Nŭngŏmgyŏng ŏnhae), and apparently at that time was in use on the mainland as well" (2007b, 285). During the Chosŏn dynasty, scholars from the mainland referred to Cheju shamans as *mudang* or *mugyŏk*, but colonial and postcolonial scholars have used the term *simbang* exclusively for Cheju's indigenous shamans.

33. *Simbang* divide their *tan'gol* into three categories in terms of sincerity: utmost (*sang*), mediocre (*chung*), and least desirable (*ha*). Note that in Chŏlla Province, hereditary shamans, not clients, are called *tanggol* (Ch'oe Kil-sŏng 1978, 18).

34. This issue has been one of the focal subjects in the study of Korean shamanism. For example, see Ch'oe Kil-sŏng 1978, 1981; Kim Seong-nae 1998, 2002a; Kim T'aegon 1981; Jongsung Yang 2004; and Yim Suk-jay 1971.

35. In this regard, their séances are comparable to Japanese blind female spirit mediums (*itako*) (Ivy 1995, 175), although *simbang*'s séances are far more elaborate and lengthy.

36. Further, pointing to the fact that hereditary practitioners work for a particular community, he compared them to Okinawan priests (*noro*), distinguishing them from Okinawan shamans (*yuta*) (Ch'oe Kil-sŏng 1978, 19), who are believed to possess "preternatural powers of possession, seeing, and hearing" (Lebra 1966, 74) and are called upon by individuals when the necessity arises (74–87).

37. For god-descended shamans, see Bruno 2002; Chungmoo Choi 1987; Harvey 1979; Hogarth 2009; Kendall 1985a, 2009; and Seo 2002. For hereditary shamans, see Keith Howard 1998; Kim Seong-nae 1989a, 1989b; and Mills 2007.

38. I never heard the more respectful term *mansin*, referring to shamans on the mainland, used on the island.

39. This hinders outsiders' understanding and therefore transcripts of shamanic songs (*muga*) are replete with annotations by experts.

40. See, for example, Chang 2001; Chin 1968, 1991; Hyŏn Yongjun 1976, 1980a; and Mun 1998.

41. Several of these narratives have been translated into English (e.g., Choi Won-oh 2008; Seo Dae-seok and Peter H. Lee 2000; Walraven 2007b).

42. See An 2008, 195; Hwang Ru-shi 1988, 129; Kang So-Jeon 2005, 37; National Research Institute of Cultural Heritage 2008, 169–93. For small-scale rituals

performed by a village *simbang* alone, women usually contribute their own food and monetary offerings (Chang 1983, 105).

43. For example, Harvey 1979; Howard 1991; Janelli and Janelli 1982; Kendall 1985a, 1988; Pettid 2000b; Sorensen 1988; and Walraven 2007b.

44. I am grateful to Clark Sorensen for drawing my attention to Beuchelt's study of Cheju shamanism and generously providing me with his English translation of the article.

45. On commodification, see Bruno 2007a; Chungmoo Choi 1989, 1991; Hogarth 2009; Kendall 2003, 2009; Kim Seong-nae 2002b; and Jun Hwan Park 2012. On corruption by Western influence, see, for example, Cho Hung-youn 1990, 216; Hwang Ru-shi 1988, 2000; Mun 2001, 16; and Sin Myŏnggi 2001, 266–67.

46. For Christianity, see Baker 1998; for Buddhism, see Buswell 1998.

47. I concur with Korean native anthropologist Chongho Kim that Korean shamanism is not popular in the sense that it is well liked by ordinary people (2003, 189). I refer to it as such because shamanism is a noninstitutionalized religion and a broad range of people resort to its services.

1. A Neo-Confucian Reformer's 1702 Purge

1. For instance, in his seminal *Admonitions on Governing the People* (Mongmin simsŏ), Chŏng Yagyong (1762–1836), whose development of Practical Learning was influenced by Yi Hyŏngsang, noted that Yi's destruction of Cheju's famous Kwangyang Shrine was an act praised by those who heard of it ([1818] 2010, 452). I am grateful to Don Baker for calling my attention to Chŏng's mention of Yi's purge.

2. Yi Ik related a different story: The islanders felt bewildered when they learned of the survival of the governor, who they had thought would be drowned during his return trip to the mainland as punishment for his iconoclastic destruction of the shrines (1977, 2:80). Similarly, the insult to a local deity by Governor Sŏ Ryŏn, who was appointed to Cheju in 1513 and died of illness there in 1515, also engendered two opposing interpretations. According to a legend, Sŏ fell from his horse and died on the way home after killing a gigantic snake dwelling in the Kimnyŏng Cave that demanded an annual offering of a virgin. While this legend manifests the belief that his death was the revenge of the snake god, an important deity on Cheju, he has also been commemorated for a heroic action that others did not dare perform (Kim Seong-nae 1989a, 88–90; Yi Yŏnggwŏn 2005, 252–53).

3. For example, see Cho and Pak 1998; Kim Seong-nae 1989a, 86–88; Pettid 2001, 174; Yi Yŏnggwŏn 2005, 251–56; and Walraven 1999a, 177.

4. The Chosŏn government was well aware of this and, beginning in 1423, assigned appointees to Cheju, along with northern peripheral regions, for only thirty months, half the regular term for centrally appointed officials. However, the 286 Cheju *moksa*'s actual tenure averaged only twenty-two months (Chejudoji P'yŏnch'an Wiwŏnhoe 2006, 345).

5. The government founded public schools (*hyanggyo*) for Cheju Mok in 1394 and for Taejŏng and Chŏngŭi Hyŏn in 1420 (*T'aejo sillok*, 27 March 1394; *Sejong sillok*, 15

November 1420). Although the number of *hyangni* gradually increased, they initially engaged mostly in trade, fishing, hunting, and tending land reserved for the army (*Sejong sillok*, 10 June 1427).

6. The central government prevented the appointment of officials to their town of origin by the "laws of avoidance" (*sangp'ije*).

7. The general public thus bore the brunt of the consequences arising from the collaboration of these two groups, and this often triggered rebellions among desperate local residents, particularly during the late dynasty (Committee for the Compilation of the *Gazetteer of Cheju Island* 2006, 532–53; Kim Iru 2000, 244–51; Kim Seong-nae 1989a, 92–104; Merrill 1980, 141–48; Walraven 2009, 5; Yi Yŏnggwŏn 2005, 163).

8. This contrasts with characterizations of people in other regions recorded in *Geography of Korea*. For instance, it praised residents of Kangnŭng as "courteous and learned" (*Sinjŭng Tongguk yŏji sŭngnam* [1530] 1969, 5:480) and those of Ch'unch'ŏn as "pure-minded and beautiful" (6:26). *Geography of Korea* was published in 1530 "in its definitive form," although its primary text "dates to 1486" (Walraven 1999a, 268n84).

9. Kim Chŏnghŭi was exiled in Cheju for almost nine years, from 1840 to 1848. Like most political offenders, he was sent to Cheju due to the clique politics of the Chosŏn dynasty. This excerpt is from a letter written to his friend Kwŏn Tonin (Yi Yŏnggwŏn 2005, 158–59, 212).

10. Westerners commonly referred to the island as Quelpaert (with various spellings) beginning in the late seventeenth century and continuing until the early twentieth century (Griffis 1889; Nemeth 1984, 325; Sands [1904] 1931). According to A. E. Sokol, Quelpaert was a common Dutch name for a particular type of ship, but exactly why Western navigators chose it for the island has yet to be revealed. Although the name is found on charts some five years before Hamel's shipwreck, the publication of his journal, in which he referred to the island as "Quelpaert," gradually made this the commonly accepted name among Westerners (Sokol 1948, 233). Based on the rather distant similarity of the common Korean pronunciation of "Quelpaert" and Kap'a-do, a small island located off the southwestern tip of the main island, the folklorist Chin Sŏng-gi conjectures that Hamel's ship actually came to grief on Kap'a-do ([1959] 1992, 248).

11. The term *nahŭi*, derived from the compound noun *naryehŭi*—*narye* (exorcism) and *hŭi* (entertaining play) refers to a ceremony conducted to cast out sundry evil spirits and entails theatrical performances (Pihl 1994, 22; Lee Du-hyun 2003, 89). All dates in this chapter are according to the lunar calendar.

12. *Yangmahŭi* literally means "the play of jumping horses." Hyŏn surmised that it referred to the playful raft race conducted as part of the Yŏngdŭng Kut, a shamanic ritual dedicated to the goddess of wind (Yŏngdŭng). At the end of the ritual, each man took his raft, carrying a miniature rice-straw boat laden with sacrificial objects, out to sea and set it on the waves to float away as the deity made her departure from the island. The one who steered his raft fastest and set the miniature boat out to sail first was the winner, and it was believed that he would have the largest catch of fish during the year (Hyŏn Yongjun 1980b). As fishermen

no longer use the old-fashioned rafts, only a few miniature boats are set afloat these days.

13. The standard pronunciation of the Chinese characters 燃燈 in the original text would be "yŏndŭng," but this is both written and pronounced "yŏngdŭng" in the shamanic context on Cheju today.

14. The term ŭmsa is also translated as "lewd rituals" (Kendall 1985a, 31). The lax boundaries between sexes and alcohol consumption during rituals were often cited when criticizing the practice. Confucian scholars were contemptuous of the mingling of men and women who were said to spend the night together in shrines for ritual purposes. Since separate spheres and social norms for the genders were among the basic tenets of Neo-Confucian education, unaffiliated men and women sleeping together in the same place was construed as morally corrupt.

15. In 1410, the government established the Office for the Establishment of Ceremonies (Ŭirye Sangjŏngso) and, in 1474, created the first official manual of state rituals, *The Manual of the Five State Rites* (Kukcho oryeŭi), prescribing "which spirits could and should be worshiped, as well as when, how, and by whom" (Baker 2008, 67).

16. Although Buddhist rites were eliminated from the manual, they were not treated as a local custom, as shamanic practice was. Hostile toward Buddhism, Neo-Confucians took measures against it. However, they did not perceive Buddhism to be as vulgar as shamanism because it had been, after all, the philosophical and intellectual foundation of the previous dynasty's elites.

17. Kim Chŏng was exiled to Cheju in August 1520 and died there in October 1521 when King Chungjong forced him to drink poison. *Cheju Topography*, written during his time in exile, comprises Kim's answers to his nephew's queries about the island (Kim Iru 2007, 11–12).

18. Yi was dismissed because he let his friend O Sibok, who had been under house arrest in Taejŏng, stay in an official building in Cheju (*Sukchong sillok*, 5 March 1703). Although he was appointed in March, he resided on Cheju from June 1702 to June 1703, due to travel time (Yu Hongjun 2012, 269).

19. His work was collectively designated Treasure No. 652-6 by the South Korean Government in 1972 (Yi Sang-gyu 2009, 9–10).

20. Although the island's official name was Cheju during the Chosŏn dynasty, T'amna was more commonly used. Given the island's distance from Chŏlla, Cheju governors, who assumed to a large degree the role of Chŏlla provincial governors, took on military responsibility as top commander (kwanch'alsa) and carried out inspection tours of Cheju twice each year. *T'amna Inspections* consists of one map of Cheju and its sundry islets and artist Kim Namil's forty color paintings, which include twenty-eight pictures portraying events that occurred during such a tour from 29 October to 19 November 1702. The remainder of the book comprises eleven pieces from other expeditions before and after Yi's three-week tour and a landscape of Mount Halla and its surroundings as viewed from Pogil Island, Chŏlla Province. For each piece, Yi inserted a four-syllable title at the top and, except for this landscape, a succinct explanation of the image at the lower right.

21. Yi dedicated *Various Things* to Yun Tusŏ, his older brother's son-in-law and close scholarly colleague, who expressed interest in the island's particulars. Natural history was one of their common interests (Yi Hyŏngsang [1704] 2009, 10–17).

22. Others noted much earlier than Yi Hyŏngsang the islanders' preference for turning to shamans instead of medicine: the exile Kim Chŏng in 1521, a royal inspector Kim Sanghŏn in 1601, and a governor Yi Wŏnjin in 1653. This indicates that the polemics between medicine and healing is not necessarily a modern construction, as argued by some (e.g., Kendall 2009, 3).

23. Contrary to what might be assumed, there was laxity among scholar-officials with regard to Confucian ritual observance, which increased even in the capital toward the end of the dynasty. They often attempted to avoid their duties by hiding, bribing, throwing tantrums, or ignoring prescribed ritual abstentions (Lee Wook 2008).

24. During his tenure as governor of Cheju (October 1704–May 1706), Song Chŏnggyu had gongs and bells confiscated from shamans made into weapons (Kim Ch'anhŭp 2002, 331).

25. Yi quoted from a local gazetteer, Kim Chŏng's *Cheju Topography*, and Kim Sanghŏn's *Travel Writings on Cheju Island* (Namsarok).

26. He wrote the letter while perhaps still unaware that he had been disqualified from submitting such a document to the throne.

27. See Kim Seong-nae 1989a, 86–88; Lee Wook 2009, 54–59; Pettid 2001, 174; and Yi Yŏnggwŏn 2005, 251–56.

28. For this reason, the elite vociferously attacked Buddhism as well on the basis that it "undermined the political authority and economic prosperity of the state" (Buswell 1999, 136).

29. The poem "Lay of the Old Shaman" (Nomup'yŏn) in *Collected Works of (Prime) Minister Yi of Korea* (Tongguk Yi Sangguk chip), presumably written sometime between 1210 and 1230, illustrates most fully and vividly the negative view of shamans held by Confucian scholars of the period. In the 1230s, the author of the book, Yi Kyubo, served as the supervisor of the Ministry of Rites, the body of officials whose primary function was directing state rituals and interpreting decorum for the dynasty. For the full translation of the poem and a succinct overview of its sociohistorical background, see McBride 2007.

30. According to this *changgye*, the island, comparable in size to a midsize town (*ŭp*) in Kyŏnggi Province, was required to pay a tribute one hundred times the amount paid by a major county (*kun*) in Kyŏngsang Province.

31. Kŏnp'o is an abbreviation of Kŏnipp'o, which is located in present-day Cheju City. Its full name is written at the lower left side of the illustration.

32. The first private Confucian academy (*sŏwŏn*) on Cheju was founded in 1665. On mainland Korea, such academies, strongholds of rural scholars, appeared in the middle of the sixteenth century. In 1682, in response to the request of local Confucian scholars (*yusaeng*), King Sukchong bestowed a wooden plaque bearing the name of the academy, Kyullim Sŏwŏn, in his own calligraphy on the school (Yu Hongjun 2012, 257–61).

33. Some Cheju villages have more than one shrine.

34. Walraven notes this only in passing (1999a, 172).

35. As a result of the reform enacted under Japanese auspices, shamans were freed from their lowborn status and ostensibly acquired the same status as the aristocratic elite class (*yangban*).

36. In Kangwŏn and Hamgil (present-day Hamgyŏng) Provinces, the government also required the laity to pay tax in cloth (*sinsep'o*) for sponsoring shamanic rituals, which doubly burdened them as they had to prepare cloth both to offer as a sacrifice and to pay the tax. Whereas patron families were supposed to offer only the amount they could afford for sacrificial purposes, all households, including those that did not patronize shamans, were taxed one roll of cloth (*Munjong sillok*, 12 April 1451).

37. Other goods, including thread, fruit, lamp oil, safflower seeds, and grains such as millet and rice, were also collected in some regions (Rim 1993, 109–10). *Continuation of the Great Code* (Sok taejŏn), published in 1746, records the logistical details of collecting taxes from shamans during the dynasty (Yi Nŭnghwa [1927] 2008, 171). William Woodville Rockhill, who resided in Seoul for four months in 1886–87 as the United States chargé d' affaires, described the tax collected by the Board of Revenue from shamans arriving in the capital as one of "the most curious taxes levied on trades people." Shamans (or sorceresses, as he called them) had to pay "a certain number of logs or sticks of wood," though he noted that the tax was no longer being collected. (1891, 178).

38. See the *P'aegwan chapki* in Peter Lee 1989, 124.

39. See Cho Hung-youn 1997b, 75, 80; Kim Inhoe 1982, 1–30; Kim Iru 2000; Mun 1998; Yi Yŏnggwŏn 2005; and Yu Tongsik 1975.

40. For his several *changgye* written while on Cheju, see Yi Hyŏngsang 1990, 181–95.

2. Cultural Politics of Cheju Shamanism in the Twentieth Century

1. The rebellion has been given several different names, among them, the Disturbance of Yi Chaesu (Yi Chaesu ŭi Nan), the Religious Disturbances of the Year *Sinch'uk* (Sinch'uk Kyoan), and the Cheju Peasants' Uprising of 1901 (1901 Cheju Nongmin Ponggi), reflecting varying perspectives on the event. For representative studies of the rebellion, see the following: in Korean, Park Chan-Sik 2013, Yu Hongyŏl 1962, and Kim Okhŭi 1980; and in English, Walraven 2009 and Son 2006, chap. 8.

2. Peynet's letter to Bishop Mutel in Seoul on 28 May 1899 (*Charyojip* 4:21); Kim's letter to Mutel on 27 July 1899 (*Charyojip* 4:51).

3. At that time, such slanderous tales about Catholic priests seemed to be widespread beyond the shores of Cheju, as Mutel himself acknowledged. The Chinese Boxers defamed Franciscan missionaries for "carving out the hearts and eyes of Chinese children" (quoted in Anthony Clark 2015, 11).

4. According to Peynet's letter to the bishop dated 13 March 1900 and sent from Chemulp'o (present-day Inch'ŏn), Kim had written to Peynet to say that he was "fighting well with devils" (*Charyojip* 4:45).

5. Missionary accounts at the turn of the century transliterated the Korean equivalent to shamans as either *mudang* or *mutang* (adding "s" for the plural) and sometimes translated it as "sorceress." The Roman Catholic Church undiscerningly

followed this common practice, ignoring the Cheju native term *simbang*. Eli Barr Landis, MD (1865–1898), of the Church of England, was one of the first missionaries who used the term "shamanism" (Walraven 1998, 72n25), in his 1895 article "Notes on the Exorcism of Spirits in Korea."

6. See Hyaeweol Choi 2009, 147; Kendall 2009, 4–8; Michael Robinson 1988, 35; Schmid 2002, 47–48; and Sorensen 1995, 330.

7. The church also defended them by arguing that the events in question took place before they joined the church (*Charyojip* 2:29–51; Park Chan-Sik 2013, 75–76, 130), which suggests that it attracted many of society's bad apples. However, it later admitted that not all Catholics were deserving of their membership in the church (Ch'oi Sŏnhong 1935, 178–79).

8. T'osan is located in southern Cheju.

9. This negative view of Korean shamans was widely shared by Protestant missionaries in Korea (e.g., Hulbert 1906, 413; Moose 1911, 192, 195–96).

10. Recognizing the power shift, shamans turned to Japanese authorities for help in easing the restraints being imposed on them. Politically savvy shamans in Seoul resorted to Japanese power brokers to found shaman organizations (Walraven 1995). When the Japanese scholar Akiba Takashi went to Cheju for his fieldwork in 1931, Simbang Ko Imsaeng, the former head of the Cheju branch of the shaman organization Spirit Worshippers' Association (Sungsin-in Chohap), requested that he revive the branch (Akiba [1950] 1987, 178).

11. Japan's censorship began on 20 August 1904, and all Korean newspapers were forced to close in 1910 (Schmid 2002, 53–54). After the 1919 March First Uprising, the Government General of Korea allowed publication of Korean newspapers and journals until 1940, when it forced the closure of all publications. Most Japanese-language newspapers published in Korea remained open for (reduced) business even after Korean-language newspapers were shut down (Mizuno 2007, 259).

12. In contrast, precolonial newspapers rarely used the neologism "superstition," although the word "superstitious" occasionally appeared in *The Independent*, the English-language newspaper targeting foreigners residing in Korea. Even at a time when most elites deliberately avoided the Chosŏn lexicon (Schmid 2002, 13), neither *Tongnip sinmun* nor *Taehan maeil sinbo*, published in the vernacular, used *misin*, the Sino-Korean equivalent of "superstition" (cf. Yi Yong-Bhum 2005, 155n4). Further, *Hwangsŏng sinmun*, published in a combination of the vernacular and Chinese characters, frequently resorted to Confucian idioms in denouncing shamans as those who "delude the world and deceive the people" (*hokse mumin*) and characterizing shamanic rituals as useless, saying "licentious rituals bring no luck" (*ŭmsa mubok*).

13. Nearly all articles in *Tongnip sinmun*, the first vernacular Korean newspaper circulated during the precolonial period (1896–99) and staffed mostly by pro-Christian metropolitan male elites, emphasized the economic harm associated with the practice and suggested that the primary motivation in becoming a shaman was economic (Yi Yong-Bhum 2005, 161, 166). Between 27 April 1920 and 7 August 1940, *Tonga ilbo*, one of the major Korean newspapers during the colonial period, published a total of 519 articles dealing with this topic, clearly indicating its rhetorical and conceptual usefulness in advocating new ideas.

14. The ideology of the Mind Cultivation Movement resonated with the core Confucian ideal of self-cultivation, thus garnering support from some Confucian local leaders in rural areas (Kim Kwang-Ok 2013, 281).

15. The original source was his 1913 "Korean Shamans" (Chōsen no fugeki), published in Tōa no hikari (Sorensen 1995, 352n53).

16. His study was originally published in 1920 in the inaugural issue of Tōgen (lit., "the same origin").

17. Salman'gyo means "shamanism" and ch'agi refers to a sort of summary note. Indeed, his piece is not much more than a distilled translation of the Polish cultural anthropologist Marie Czaplicka's 1914 Aboriginal Siberia augmented with Torii's studies on shamanism, as Ch'oe acknowledges at the end of the essay (Chun 2012, 22).

18. Ch'oe's essay was published in Korean with Chinese characters and Yi's was entirely in classical Chinese. Yi's study was translated into Japanese and published in eight issues of the GGK magazine Chōsen from May 1928 to January 1929, extensively cited in Murayama's 1932 Korean Shamans (Chōsen no fugeki).

19. During the Chosŏn dynasty, the word musok was used only on one occasion, in a letter the poet Yun Sŏndo (1587–1671) sent to his son in 1678 (Chun 2012, 34).

20. Mu (e.g., Cho Hung-youn 1990, 1997a, 1997b), mugyo (e.g., Kim Seong-nae 2002a; Yu Tongsik 1975), muijŭm (Yim Suk-Jay 1971), and shyamŏnijŭm (the Korean rendering of the English-language term "shamanism") have also been used but have not been as popular as musok among Korean scholars and the populace.

21. Before Yi did so, in Mudang Chronicles (Mudang naeryŏk), most likely published in 1885, according to Seo Dae-seok (1996, 5), an author using the pen name Nan'gok also found the origin of Korean shamanic rituals and beliefs in sin'gyo passed down by the shaman king Tan'gun (30).

22. Shaman songs incorporated into p'ansori were collected in the nineteenth century (Pihl 1994; Walraven 1994). The narratives Son collected over a period of several years in different regions of the peninsula were published in 1930 by a reputable Japanese publisher in Tokyo. The book featured both Korean and Japanese transcriptions augmented by his introduction to each piece and his footnotes in Japanese.

23. Son expressed his desire to devote this book to Kim Ssangdol ([1930] 2012, 16).

24. Based on the authors' nationwide fieldwork conducted during 1930–33 and supported by the Japanese Imperial Academy (Teikoku Gakushiin), the first volume (1937) of Study of Korean Shamanism is a collection of shamanic narratives, and the second (1938) is a collection of their analyses of various topics related to Korean shamanism. Neither Akiba nor Akamatsu was fluent in Korean (Walraven 1999b, 230; Chun 2012, 29). Several Korean junior scholars, notably Son Chint'ae, assisted with their recording and translations (Akiba and Akamatsu [1937] 1991, 6). In the second volume, they wrote one chapter together and the rest separately—Akiba contributed eight chapters and Akamatsu three. Akiba rehashed all the chapters for the University of Tokyo (PhD diss.) in 1941 and in his monograph Ethnographic Research of Korean Shamanism (Chōsen muzoku no genchi kenkyū) in 1950.

25. See Kendall 2009; Kim Seong-nae 2002b; Sarfati 2009; and Kyoim Yun 2016.

26. Chang Chugŭn, interviewed by Hŏ Yŏngsŏn, 28 December 2010, Seirye at'ŭsent'ŏ, http://cafe.daum.net/sayre/LOjY/147?docid=Kn1tLOjY14720101202221940 (accessed 2 June 2012).

27. This setting is still being simulated in recent research efforts to document Cheju *ponp'uri* as recited by prominent *simbang* (e.g., see the book covers of Hŏ Namch'un et al. 2009, 2010, 2013, 2015).

28. These recitations are included in Chang 2001.

29. For example, see Chang 2001; Chin Sŏng-gi 1991; Hŏ Namch'un et al. 2009, 2010, 2013, 2015; Hyŏn Yongjun 1976, 1980a; and Mun 1998, 2001.

30. See Cho Hung-youn 1983; Ch'oe Kil-sŏng 1978; Kim T'aegon 1981; Kim Yŏl-gyu 1977; Yim Suk-jay 1970, 1971; and Yu Tongsik 1975.

31. However, a few shamans won awards for their virtuoso singing and dancing in government-sponsored traditional *arts* competitions during the Park regime (Chongho Kim 2003, 204; Keith Howard 1989; Jongsung Yang 2003). The Tano Festival (Tanoje) in Kangnŭng, Kwangwŏn Province, in which shamans play an indispensable role, earned the designation Important Intangible Cultural Treasure in 1967. A leading Korean folklorist saw the selection as a highly satisfactory way of tricking the government into recognizing the festival, as opposed to *kut*, and protected East Coast shamans (Walraven 1993, 16). However, the Tano Festival is a fusion of Confucian and shamanic rituals and includes some nonreligious elements (Hwang Ru-shi 2000, 242–58; Nam 2008; Saeji 2018). This festival was added to UNESCO's Representative List of the Intangible Cultural Heritage of Humanity in 2005.

32. Skill holders enjoy a number of benefits, including fame and government stipends, in return for giving public performances and training apprentices, the most promising of whom also receive stipends.

33. See Chungmoo Choi 1987, 74; Harvey 1979, 11; Keith Howard 1998, 194; Kendall 2009; Chongho Kim 2003, 96; 215–18; and Tangherlini 1998, 141, 194.

34. Many scholars of Korean shamanism have confessed that they had to overcome the stigma associated with working with shamans and their fear of shamans, uncanny spirits, and becoming shamans themselves (e.g., Chungmoo Choi 1987, 8-9; Chun 2012, 8; Chongho Kim 2003, 55; Kim Seong-nae 1989a, 28). I am not an exception.

35. As of 2018, this law is still in effect.

36. This state of affairs is depicted in the 2009 comedy *Fortune Salon*. Offended by a client's rudeness during a consultation, a young, attractive, and affluent female shaman throws her fee in the air and walks out of her studio. As though a shaman had no right to get upset, the fictional client angrily comments, "How dare that shaman [*mudang*] storm out during a session?" One of the shaman's colleagues counters with, "Who dares to talk like that these days when shamans have become [national] intangible cultural assets [*muhyŏng munhwajae*]?"

37. For an idealized view, see Cho Hŭng-yun 1990, 216; Hwang Ru-shi 1988, 2000; Mun 2001, 16; and Sin Myŏnggi 2001, 266–67.

38. The group's name, Sunurŭm, is the noun form of the verb *sunulda* and refers in the local dialect to *p'umasi*, the reciprocal labor-exchange practiced in agrarian society (Hyŏn P'yŏngho et al. 1995, 326). The group was dissolved due to its radical political messages but reorganized as two different groups in 1983 (Mun 1987a, 210). Since

then, Cheju theatrical groups with different names have continued to incorporate indigenous Cheju shamanic elements into their performances.

39. For the political use of shamanic rituals in South Korea, see Chungmoo Choi 1995; Kwang-Ok Kim 1994; Nam-hee Lee 2003; Sorensen 1995; Sun 1991; Tangherlini 1998; and Jongsung Yang 2003.

3. The Art of Ritual Exchange

1. See Bruno 2007a; Chun 1984, 111; Hogarth 2009; Kim Seong-nae 2002b, 76–78; Park Il-Young 1990, 129–34; and Seo 2002, 4.

2. Keith Howard also observed that several shamans lived in houses separated from the center of the village where he did fieldwork (1989, 205). Chongho Kim interpreted the remote locations of shamans' residences, often a distant corner of their villages, as indicative of their paradoxical position in Korean society, in which they are both ostracized and needed (2003, 63). However, Simbang Min's isolated residence was actually rather exceptional, as I knew other Cheju *simbang* who lived within their communities.

3. For details on the kinds of *kime* and their ritual functions, see Hyŏn Yongjun 1969; Kang So-Jeon (Sojŏn) 2006; and Mun 2009a.

4. National Research Institute of Cultural Heritage 2008. For a comparison with the mainland, see Bruno 2007a, 57; Hogarth 2009, 62–71; and Jun Hwan Park 2012, 47.

5. The magnitude of financial expenditure involved in sponsoring a *kut* as opposed to a Confucian rite is by no means unique to present-day Cheju, although *kut* are usually held far less frequently than Confucian rites. According to a report by Roger L. Janelli and Dawnhee Yim Janelli, the cost of a *kut* in a village in Kyŏnggi Province in 1978 was "about twenty times the expense of a typical death-day offering" (1982, 148).

6. Going into debt to support such an extravagant ritual is exclusive neither to Simbang Min (see, e.g., Mun 2001) nor to Cheju *simbang* (Hogarth 2009, 246). The cost of a three-day *chinjŏk kut* that a top-tier shaman in Seoul sponsored for her tutelary gods was about 20 million to 25 million won in 2010. Due to the expense of the ritual, this shaman told me, she was forced to reduce their frequency from two to one per annum and once had to mortgage her house to cover her costs.

7. Several local Cheju scholars have made a collective effort to transcribe most of the words from a *sin kut* conducted in 1994 (Mun 2001). The voluminous data lend credence to this assertion.

8. One of the shaman informants of Hyun-key Kim Hogarth compared the act of sponsoring *chinjŏk kut* sponsored by shamans to bring luck and prosperity to paying taxes to their tutelary spirits; many of her informants believed that misfortunes would befall them as a reprimand if they failed to sponsor such rituals over a long period of time (2009, 245).

9. Kim Seong-nae offers a detailed sociohistorical analysis of a *simbang* (1991b), and Mun provides succinct biographies of a dozen *simbang* (1998; 2005, 280–99). For life histories of mainland female shamans, see Byun 2014; Harvey 1979; Kendall 1988; Sarfati 2016; Sun 1991, 1992; and Walraven 2001.

10. This sum pales in comparison to the cost of the aforementioned three-day ritual that a Seoul-based shaman sponsored, given that on Cheju, a *sin kut* usually lasts about ten days. Several factors may explain the difference. Many mainland shamanic traditions require professional musicians in addition to assistant shamans. Moreover, shamans residing in Seoul usually rent commercial ritual halls (*kuttang*). In the first decade of the 2000s, I saw that catering was no longer part of the paid services provided by the *kuttang*, which means that lead shamans must hire cooks and delivery people in addition to the usual assistants and musicians. My observation was confirmed by Byun Jisun, who has been conducting research on *kut* in Seoul and Kyŏnggi Province for more than a decade, beginning in 2004. I am grateful to her for this information.

11. I suspect that paper money emerged for ritual use only after the monetary economy had begun to dominate and paper became readily available at a low price. However, this matter is beyond the scope of my research.

12. Unlike other small-scale rituals such as a *kosa* or a *pison*, which involve communication with the supernatural but do not necessarily require a shaman, this ritual, known as *munjŏn ch'ŏlgari*, typically is conducted on the island by a professional, making the beginning of the year one of the busiest times for *simbang*. I observed Simbang An performing as many as six in one day.

13. Escort services targeting Japanese men became popular beginning in the late 1970s in the Sin-Cheju area (Cho Miyoung 2005, 851–52).

14. The three-syllable name of one of the deceased.

15. *Sajang-nim* is an honorific term broadly used when addressing a business owner.

16. In order to convey a sense of rhythm, I have used line breaks throughout the book to indicate pauses in the *simbang's* recitation (Tedlock 1972) while at the same time taking syntactical structures into account in translation (Hymes 1981).

17. This litany has variations, a typical feature of oral tradition.

18. Similarly, I witnessed a cow worth 2 million won that a couple donated initially being rejected at a *kut* in Seoul in fall 2001. The lead shaman kept failing to balance the carcass on the prongs of the trident, a signal that the gods were not content with the enormous sacrifice. The shaman learned from the couple that they had disagreed over whether or not they should donate the cow and interpreted their qualms as a lack of sincerity on their part that was in turn a source of pollution (*pujŏng*) of the sacrifice. Only after the couple admitted their lack of sincerity and begged for the gods' forgiveness was the shaman able to move the ritual forward.

19. A *simbang's chŏngsŏng kŭllyang* can be compared with *sasŭl* or *sasil seugi* in rituals conducted by god-descended shamans following the regional traditions of Kyŏnggi and Hwanghae Provinces on the mainland. Shamans determine whether the gods are satisfied with offerings by balancing the carcass of a cow or a pig on the prongs of a trident; the shaman's inability to balance the carcass indicates the gods' dissatisfaction with the offering (e.g., Bruno 2007a, 55; Hogarth 2009, 87, 224; Chongho Kim 2003, 80).

20. One *kŭn* is the equivalent of 600 grams or 1.323 pounds.

21. The same motif is evident in the myths of Segyŏng and Ch'ilsŏng (Hyŏn Yongjun 1980a, 318, 419).

22. Unable to fully identify individuals' intentions in the face of rampant corruption involved in gift giving, often using subtle methods to avoid intervention by law enforcement authorities, the South Korean anti-bribery and anti-graft act that took effect on 28 September 2016, set a limit on the cash value of an acceptable gift (no more than 50,000 won, US$50). This has generated much confusion and frustration among those who care about sincere gifts as a means of managing human relationships.

23. See Grayson 2001, 352–53; and Walraven 1994; 2007a, 247–49; 2007b. For an exception, see Sorensen 1988.

24. For example, Chang 2001, 73–254; Chin Sŏng-gi 1968; Hyŏn Yongjun 1976, 1980a; Kim T'aegon 1979–80; and Son (1930) 2012.

25. Simbang and the laity of the island call this narrative "Samani ponp'uri." "Saman" (lit., "40,000") is the first name of the protagonist, and the "i" after the name is a suffix added to first names that end with consonants for euphonic effect.

26. The myth is also recited at the Menggam kosa, a small-scale fertility ritual sponsored by some Cheju residents at the beginning of each year (Yun Sunhŭi 2010). Menggam (or Myŏnggam) refers to "officials of the otherworld" to whom Saman makes sacrifices; thus, the myth is also referred to as Menggam ponp'uri. Walraven offers an English-language summary of this ponp'uri (1994, 102–3).

27. In Korea, the term chosang typically refers to ancestors, but in Cheju, it also means the tutelary gods of a family or clan (Hyŏn Yongjun 1992, 19; 1980a, 895–96). In Cheju mythology, the tutelary gods often were originally humans who have been transformed into deities. In this myth, the Skull Ancestor is a tutelary god of Saman.

28. Ch'asa is locally known as ch'ŏsŏ or ch'esa. The title also refers to an official sent by the government to arrest criminals during the Chosŏn dynasty.

29. According to the shamanic worldview and fortune-telling ideology in Korea, the destiny of each person is determined at the time of his or her birth (Dawnhee Yim Janelli 1979). Saman's wife was born at the same time on the same day as Saman, so they share the same fate.

30. Chŏngsŭng was a title referring to the prime minister in the Kingdom of Korea. Paek is a surname.

31. Here, the ponp'uri reinforces the central Confucian tenet of filial piety. Confucian ideology plays a pivotal role in other Cheju ponp'uri as well as in Korean shamanic discourse and practice in general (e.g., Janelli and Janelli 1982, 165–66; Kendall 1985a, 148–50; Sorensen 1988; Walraven 2007a, 244).

32. At the ritual of aengmaegi, a rooster is typically sacrificed in the hope of deterring the death of a family member.

33. In other versions of the myth, the judge of the otherworld explicitly accuses them of having accepted a bribe and/or the messengers themselves refer to the offerings they have received as a bribe when they persuade the secretaries (Hŏ et al. 2010, 329; 2015, 265; Kang, Kang, and Song 2008, 579; Mun 1998, 299; 2001, 565).

34. If a bird-shaped stroke is added on top of the Chinese character "ten" (十), the character becomes "thousand" (千).

35. The boxes are not only opened, but a few cigarettes are also pulled slightly out of them, in readiness for the messengers.

36. The term "meta-communication, coined by Gregory Bateson, means "communication about communication," that is, "explicit or implicit messages which carry instructions on how to interpret the other message(s) being communicated" (Ruesch and Bateson [1951] 1968, 209; Bauman 1977, 15).

37. These are the story of Kang T'aegong, the Tale of Sim Ch'ŏng, and the Tale of Kwakkwak and Chuyuk. Kang T'aegong is a mythic figure in the Cheju shamanic world who is believed to be a carpenter and who plays an important role in the *sŏngju p'uri*, a ritual performed for household gods after a new home is built.

38. Indeed, sincerity is also important in Confucian rituals (Walraven 1999a, 187, 192–94). Note that "Sincerity moves the gods" (Chisŏng kamsin) appears in Confucius's *Classic of History* (Shu ching), one of the Five Classics of Chinese antiquity. However, "Sincerity moves heaven" and "Piety brings charity" are not found in Confucian writings. For this information, I am indebted to Song Hyosup and Jang Sookpil.

39. *Sink'al* and *sanp'an* are divination tools made of bronze. *Sink'al* is a set of knives with white paper trim resembling a skirt, and *sanp'an* consists of five pieces: two small cups and coins (about 5 cm in diameter) with a shallow dish (about 15 cm in diameter).

40. See Brandt 1971; Chun 1984; Hogarth 2009, 220–31; Janelli with Yim 1993; and Jesook Song 2014, 52.

41. See Geschiere 2013; Keane 1994; LiPuma and Lee 2008; Mauss (1950) 1990; and Miyazaki 2004, 100.

42. Worse still, medical error is the third leading cause of death in the United States (*Washington Post*, 3 May 2016).

4. Skillful Performer or Greedy Animator?

1. For an exception, see Chongho Kim 2003.

2. *Mudang* is a rather derogatory term referring to Korean shamans in general regardless of their gender and region.

3. *Chilch'igi* is performed at *Siwang maji* (receiving the Ten Kings [of the otherworld]), *Yongwang maji* (receiving Dragon Kings), *Pultto maji* (receiving Birth Spirit Grandmother), and *kwiyang p'uri*, a ritual performed following the interment of a corpse. In terms of its ultimate goal, *chilch'igi* is equivalent to *Chinogwi kut* or *Ogu kut* (also called *Ogwi* or *Ogi kut*) in central Korea (Chungmoo Choi 1989; Kendall 1985b; Kister 1980; Kim Seong-nae 1991a, 20; Saeji 2018; Sorensen 1988) and *Ssikkim kut* of Chin Island, South Chŏlla Province (Bruno 2007c; Chun 1984, 108–11). Procedurally, however, *chilch'igi* is quite different from these other rituals. Eno Beuchelt provides a detailed description of *chilch'igi* (though he calls it *ch'ohon-gut*) that he observed while on Cheju Island in August 1962 (1975a).

4. I am following Kim Seong-nae's translation of the term (1989a, 1989b). *Yŏngge ullim* is also spelled *yŏnggue ullim*, but for the sake of consistency, I use *yŏngge ullim* throughout this work.

5. Collected at various moments during the *kut*, cash offerings are by no means exclusive to Cheju indigenous ritual tradition. On the mainland, these funds are

called *pyŏlbi* (Ch'oe Kil-sŏng 1981, 62) or *kajŏn* because they are collected in addition to the service fee. Some shamans include this extra money in the ritual fee and return it to the patron family who can offer it at the appropriate moments in the ritual process (Chungmoo Choi 1987, 194; Kendall 2008, 156; Kim Seong-nae 2002b, 72).

6. Some people sponsor a Buddhist ritual called *ch'ŏndoje* instead of hiring a shaman.

7. *Siwang maji* can also be performed before death, when a person is seriously ill and a *simbang* interprets the illness as a portent of the end of life, in order to implore the Ten Kings to get rid of the illness and lengthen the life (Hyŏn 1980a, 883). I have not had the opportunity to observe this kind of *Siwang maji*.

8. Most *simbang* conduct rituals in their clients' homes, except under special circumstances, when they perform the rituals at commercial ritual halls known as *kuttang*.

9. *Sot* is Cheju dialect for *kŭmjul*. For instance, people who have recently attended funerals are considered unclean.

10. The lead *simbang* receives the fee from the clients and distributes part of the money to the assistant *simbang*, typically when they return to the lead *simbang*'s home after a ritual. The amount the lead shaman distributes varies, and a stingy allotment could sour the relationship between the lead and assistant shamans (Chungmoo Choi 1987, 191–200).

11. Unlike in many mainland regions, where people visit shamans to have their fortunes read and are then often persuaded to sponsor a ritual (Bruno 2002, chap. 8; 2007a, 49; Chungmoo Choi 1987, 192–93; Kendall 1985a, 78–79), on Cheju, clients usually visit *simbang* after they have already decided to sponsor a ritual.

12. This is not unique to Cheju (cf. Chongho Kim 2003, 171–72; Sorensen 1988, 409). One day in early winter 2009, I accompanied a Korean American friend, Hyojŏng, as she visited a female shaman in Seoul. Hyojŏng was concerned about her siblings' situations and also a bit curious about the experience of consulting with a shaman. With great finesse the shaman provided an affective and comforting consultation for her new client and made her feel that a ritual for the family, especially for her sister, was of pressing urgency. Swayed by the shaman's persuasive words, Hyojŏng (who visited the shaman with no idea of what to expect) was willing to sponsor a one-day ritual on her sister's behalf, and the shaman instructed her on how to prepare for it. However, Hyojŏng was utterly astonished by the fee that the shaman requested at the end of the consultation: 10 million won (US$10,000). She obviously had not expected such an extravagant charge. Sensing her reluctance, the shaman asked how much she would be willing to spend, but Hyojŏng refused to respond, probably because of the large gap between what she could afford and what had actually been requested. After some consideration, she gave up the idea of sponsoring such a ritual.

13. For a detailed observation, see Chungmoo Choi 1987, 191–92.

14. Kim Tongsŏp, a researcher at the Folklore and Natural Museum of the Jeju Special Self-Governing Province at that time, kindly invited me to accompany him to

observe both of the rituals and provided the information about the ritual fee, for which I am most grateful.

15. Because the *simbang* did not "discount" his services until years after the economic crisis began, I suspect that the reduced fees might be a response to fewer ritual requests from cash-strapped potential clients.

16. Comparatively speaking, the market price for rituals performed by Cheju *simbang* is considerably lower than that for rituals performed by shamans in Seoul and nearby cities (see n. 12 here and n. 6 in chap. 3).

17. Some *simbang* do not actually shed tears—though according to my observations, this is rare—but they speak in a weeping voice and wipe their eyes as though they were shedding tears. These "[r]itual tears—both shed and unshed—are telling" (Ebersole 2000, 246). However, Simbang An criticized one such *simbang* as a perfunctory performer lacking in empathy.

18. Weeping is commonly seen among participants in Korean shaman ritual séances (Bruno 2002; Chungmoo Choi 1989, 240; Janelli and Janelli 1982, 153–54; Rhi 1970, 18).

19. Other scholars of shamanism have also emphasized the acquired and performative quality of medium speech (Bruno 2002, 84–85; Chungmoo Choi 1989; Kendall 2009, chap. 3; Schieffelin 1996).

20. One mainland shaman proudly told the Janellis about her ability to make an audience cry, which is a "major goal" in a séance and thus the mark of a successful performance (Janelli and Janelli 1982, 153–54).

21. This comment echoes the Kaluli term *sayalab*, capturing "the mélange of affect and cognition involved" that Steven Feld translated as "wept thoughts" (1990, 258).

22. Edward Schieffelin also observed this view at the Kaluli séance in Papua New Guinea (1996).

23. For representative works, see Abu-Lughod 1986; Bruno 2002, 158-80; Ebersole 2000; Feld 1990; Hochschild 2003; Kotthoff 2001; Lutz 1988; Lutz and Abu-Lughod 1990; Lutz and White 1986; Pritchard 2011; and Rosaldo 1984.

24. Richard Bauman discusses the differences between spirit mediumship, in which the spirit is "the source and author of the utterance, using the medium simply as an instrument of articulation," and mediational performances, in which a seer "communicate[s] with the ancestors who are the source" (2004, 138–39). *Yŏngge ullim* entails features of both in that spiritual inspiration and the *simbang*'s agency are indispensable for the successful delivery of the mediated speech.

25. Marilyn Ivy made similar observations about blind female spirit mediums, or *itako*, in Japan (1995, 175).

26. Erving Goffman (1974) and Stephen Levinson (1988) systemized terms referring to participant roles in speech events, while Bauman (2004) elaborated the role of inventory in his analysis of mediational performances.

27. An assistant *simbang* poured liquid into small cups for these alleged agents during Simbang Kim's recitation. This ritual segment is called *chujan kwŏnjan* (offering drinks).

28. The following is another example of this framing work: "The dear dead soul is going to give greetings [to you] by borrowing the mouth of the child of god [i.e., the *simbang*]" (Hyŏn Yongjun 1980a, 452).

29. "You" and "my" are implied personal pronouns. The frequent change of personal pronouns in oracles (*kongsu*) performed by god-descended shamans, challenges the notion that the words are a pure manifestation of spirits or gods without shamanic agency (e.g., Bruno 2002, chap. 3; Choi Chungmoo 1989, 243–45; Kim Seong-nae 1989a, 346–47, 357).

30. Beuchelt compared the *kut* he observed on Cheju in 1962 with a "group therapy session" that released "emotional tension in the individuals and the community" (1975a, 178). For the psychotherapeutic dimensions of Korean shamanic practice, see Kim Kwang-iel 1973; and Rhi 1970, 1977.

31. See also Ch'ŏlgi's greeting to his mother:

> Oh, my mother who bore me to live long beyond twenty-six,
> Oh, Mother, Mother,
> Oh, after I died,
> Having buried Ch'ŏlgi in your heart,
> How did you survive missing me?

32. According to Ch'ŏlgi's account, whereas his father shed tears only in private, his mother wept openly, which reflects the different expectations for men and women regarding the expression of emotions.

33. To his father, Ch'ŏlgi says, "Please stop thinking about me."

34. Developed by John Austin, the concept of illocutionary force describes the intended force of an utterance, as opposed to its semantic content per se ([1962] 1997).

35. See also Bruno 2002, 31, 64–83; Chungmoo Choi 1989, 236–41; Kendall 2009, 69; Kim Seong-nae 1991a, 20; and Walraven 2002, 98. Marveling at the *simbang*'s ability to improvise the *yŏngge ullim* and other ritual speeches even at a household where they had not previously performed, I once asked a *simbang* how they do it. "If you work for others, you will figure out how many spoons the household has," I was told. This comment suggests the importance of their experience and of their extraordinary intuition, called *nunch'i*, or "the ability to understand the context of a *kut* or the feelings of others and adapt one's own behavior accordingly" (Bruno 2007, 59).

36. Further, the ritual background, including Mr. Cho's family history and the family's reasons for sponsoring the ritual, had already been recited by the *simbang* as part of the ritual process, which undoubtedly helped set the stage for Simbang Kim's arresting performance of the *yŏngge ullim*.

37. I borrowed the terms "source" and "target" from Bauman's 2001 work.

38. The performer of insult poetry in Senegal, on the contrary, highlights the connections between an antecedent collusion and a subsequent performance in order to minimize the performer's responsibility for formulating the poetry (Irvine 1996).

39. Irvine's (1989) innovative call for understanding linguistic phenomena as verbal "goods" is noteworthy in this regard.

40. See Gates 1987; Kendall 1985b, 2009; Kwon 2007; McCreery 1990; Seaman 1982; Truitt 2013; and Yang 2000.

41. On the shamans' oratory, Chungmoo Choi suggests that they deliberately seek the emotional effect for profit (1989, 241).

42. This idea coincides with Buddhist beliefs.

43. Until the 50,000-won bill appeared in 2009, 10,000 won was the largest denomination and 5,000 won the second-largest denomination for legal tender. The smallest has been the 1,000-won note.

44. Mr. Kim, personal communication, 16 September 2010.

45. Mr. Kim, personal communication, 16 September 2010.

46. An Mi-jeong, personal communication, 31 December 2010.

5. A *Kut* as Heritage Goods with the UNESCO Brand

1. The gender of the deity is somewhat ambiguous. Some islanders refer to it as "Grandfather" (Tangherlini and Park 1990).

2. The organization was officially formed in 1986. For a detailed description of the shrine and the ritual, including a transcript of the *simbang*'s ritual speech, see Mun and Yi 2008.

3. *Cheju ilbo*, 23 February 2011, www.jejunews.com/news/articleView.html?idxno =820016 (accessed 10 July 2013). The Ministry of Culture, Sports, and Tourism is the current incarnation of the Ministry of Culture and Information and the Ministry of Culture and Information, the entities that formerly oversaw cultural activities in the Republic of Korea.

4. In 2010, UNESCO recognized six South Korean, two Japanese, and five Chinese elements. Three of the Chinese forms were added to the List of Intangible Cultural Heritage in Need of Urgent Safeguarding, the rest to the Representative List of the Intangible Cultural Heritage of Humanity.

5. As of 2016, out of the 342 elements on the UNESCO list, East Asian elements make up 71 (approximately 20 percent): 19 South Korean, 22 Japanese, and 30 Chinese elements. There were also disputes between China and South Korea over Tano, two different practices with the same name. *OhMyNews*, 7 October 2010, www.ohmynews .com/NWS_Web/view/at_pg.aspx?CNTN_CD=A0001413814 (accessed 10 July 2013). State delegations at the Intergovernmental Meeting of Experts on the Preliminary Draft Convention for the Safeguarding of the Intangible Cultural Heritage foresaw and discussed the competition the list system might generate in June 2003 (Hafstein 2009).

6. In 2007, UNESCO designated several World Natural Heritage sites on Cheju, the first and only areas that have earned this designation in South Korea, and named the island a Biosphere Reserve in 2002 and a Global Geopark in 2010. This information is widely advertised. For example, upon landing at Cheju International Airport, Korean Air now announces, "Ladies and gentlemen, we have arrived at the world natural heritage Cheju."

7. "UNESCO: Building Peace in the Minds of Men and Women," UNESCO, https://en
.unesco.org/70years/building_peace (accessed 28 May 2013).

8. "Functions of the Intergovernmental Committee for the Safeguarding of Intangible
Cultural Heritage," UNESCO, www.unesco.org/culture/ich/index.php?lg=en&pg
=00586 (accessed 15 October 2012).

9. Before it became independent in 1999, the Cultural Heritage Administration worked
under the Ministry of Culture, Sports, and Tourism.

10. Indeed, the committee acknowledged this national safeguarding measure as one of
five reasons for inscribing the rite on UNESCO's Representative List of the Intangible
Cultural Heritage of Humanity.

11. For example, see Foster 2011; Gilman 2015; and Noyes 2006.

12. "Jeju Chilmeoridang Yeongdeunggut," Consent of Communities, under Nomination
file No. 00187, UNESCO, https://ich.unesco.org/en/RL/jeju-chilmeoridang
-yeongdeunggut-00187/ (accessed 9 February 2019).

13. See Keith Howard 1998; Hwang Ru-shi 1988, 17, 128; Kendall 2009, 14; and
Tangherlini 1998.

14. Note the punning in the original Korean phrase *kut porŏ kaja* (굿 보러 가자), which
has been used for some time to advertise various traditional performance genres.
Here, *kut* (굿) is the transliteration of the English word "good" rather than "grand-
scale shamanic rituals."

15. See, for example, Keith Howard 1998; Kendall 2009; and Kyoim Yun 2006.

16. Keith Howard also observed perceived regional and generic hierarchies among
performers on Chin Island (Chin-do), where singers of work songs aspired to the
prestige of urban *p'ansori* singers and emulated their training system (1989, 212).

17. National Kugak Center, www.gugak.go.kr (accessed 15 September 2010).

18. Not all public rituals are performed as part of a heritage campaign. The Association
for the Ch'ilmŏri Shrine Yŏngdŭng Kut Preservation has also performed healing
rituals to console victims of tragic historical events, most notably the April Third
Events, at several venues (National Research Institute of Cultural Heritage 2008,
128–29). On 5 April 2002, for example, the *simbang* from the association performed
a ritual in front of a cave located in the Tarangshwi Orŭm, where eleven people
suffocated when the ROK police and military set a fire in the cave's entrance on 18
December 1948. During the ritual, both the *simbang* and the audience, including the
bereaved, shed tears. Other Korean shamans have also performed public healing
rituals for the victims of Korean and non-Korean tragedies (e.g., Kendall 2009, 23;
David Kim 2013).

19. See, for example, Hogarth 1999, 348–49; Kendall 2009, 32; Chongho Kim 2003, 215;
and Namhee Lee 2003, 572.

20. In contrast, see "Continuing Financial Deficit in Running the Cheju Diving
Women's Museum despite the UNESCO Recognition," which bemoans the lack of
economic benefits expected after UNESCO designated the diving women's culture
an Intangible Cultural Heritage of Humanity in 2016. *Yonhap News*, 6 January 2018.
www.yonhapnews.co.kr/bulletin/2018/01/05/0200000000AKR20180105131600056
.html (accessed 1 October 2018).

21. The total cost of the new structure was 2 billion won (about US$2 million), of which the Cultural Heritage Administration and the province each paid half (Kim Hoch'ŏn 2013).
22. The same is true for mainland shamans (e.g., Chongho Kim 2003, 99, 169).
23. This information was provided by a member of the association.
24. The new building officially opened on 17 June 2016.
25. See, for example, Kendall 2009; Kim Seong-nae 2000, 2002b; David Kim 2009; and Sarfati 2009.
26. I am grateful to Dorothy Noyes for drawing my attention to this reference.

Conclusion

1. For example, see Sang-Hun Choe 2016; *Financial Times*, 2 November 2016; Kim Hyosil 2016; Kim Myŏngjin 2016; and Tharoor 2016. For an academic discussion, see Doucette 2017, 853.
2. See, for instance, Kim Hyosil 2016; and Kim Myŏngjin 2016.
3. See Bruno 2007a; Chungmoo Choi 1989, 1991; Hogarth 2009,109; Kim Seong-nae 2002b; and Jun Hwan Park 2012.
4. See, for example, Byun 2014; Kendall 2009; Kim Seong-nae 2000, 2002b; and Sarfati 2009, 2016.
5. See, for example, Bruno 2002; Chungmoo Choi 1987, 1989; Kendall 2009, chap. 3; Kim Seong-nae 1989b; and Lévi-Strauss 1963.
6. See, for example, Asad 1993; Geertz 1973; Ong 1987, 1988; Romberg 2003; Rudnyckyj 2010; Stark 2006; Taussig 1980; and Weber (1946) 1958.

BIBLIOGRAPHY

Abu-Lughod, Lila. 1986. *Veiled Sentiments: Honor and Poetry in a Bedouin Society.* Berkeley: University of California Press.

Ahern, Emily M. 1981. *Chinese Ritual and Politics.* Cambridge: Cambridge University Press.

Akamatsu Chijō and Akiba Takashi. (1937–38) 1991. *Chosŏn musok ŭi yŏn'gu* [Study of Korean shamanism]. Translated by Shim Usŏng. Seoul: Tongmunsŏn.

Akiba Takashi. (1950) 1987. *Chosŏn musok ŭi hyŏnji yŏn'gu* [Ethnographic study of Korean shamanism]. Translated by Choe Kilsŏng. Taegu: Kyemyŏng University Press.

Allen, Chizuko T. 1990. "Northeast Asia Centered around Korea: Ch'oe Nam-sŏn's View of History." *Journal of Asian Studies* 49 (4): 789–806.

An Mi-jeong (Mijŏng). 2008. *Cheju chamsu ŭi padabat: Sahoe kwan'gye wa saengt'aejŏk chisok kanŭngsŏng ŭl wihan munhwajŏk silch'ŏn* [The maritime garden of Cheju woman divers: Social relations and cultural creativity for the sustainable environment]. Cheju: Cheju National University Press.

Anderson, Benedict. (1983) 1991. *Imagined Communities.* London: Verso.

Aono Masaaki. 1992. "Musok ŭi sunan kwa chŏhang: Chosŏn ch'ongdokpu ŭi misin t'ap'a e kwanhan yŏn'gu" [Suppression and persistance of Korean shamanism: A study of the anti-superstition campaign of the Government General of Korea]. In *Ilche sidae han ŏch'on ŭi munhwa pyŏnyong* [Cultural changes at one village during the Japanese colonial period] 1, edited by Ch'oe Kil-sŏng, 433–68. Seoul: Asea Munhwasa.

Appadurai, Arjun. 1986. "Introduction: Commodities and the Politics of Value." In *The Social Life of Things: Commodities in Cultural Perspective,* edited by Arjun Appadurai, 3–63. Cambridge: Cambridge University Press.

Armstrong, Robert Plant. 1971. "Affecting Things and Events." In *The Affecting Presence: An Essay in Humanistic Anthropology.* Urbana: University of Illinois Press.

Asad, Talal. 1993. *Genealogies of Religion: Discipline and Reasons of Power in Christianity and Islam.* Baltimore, Md.: Johns Hopkins University Press.

Association for the Ch'ilmŏri Shrine Yŏngdŭng Kut Preservation. 2005. *Param ŭi ch'ukche, Ch'ilmŏri-dang Yŏngdŭngkut* [The festival of wind, the Yŏngdŭng Kut at the Ch'ilmŏri Shrine]. With Mun Mubyŏng's transcriptions and explanations of the [oral] materials. Seoul: Gold Egg Publishing.

———. 2010. "The Ch'ilmŏri Shrine Yŏngdŭng Kut." Booklet. Cheju, The Association for the Ch'ilmŏri Shrine Yŏngdŭng Kut Preservation.

Atkins, Taylor E. 2010. *Koreana in the Japanese Colonial Gaze, 1910–1945.* Berkeley: University of California Press.

Austin, John L. (1962) 1997. *How to Do Things with Words.* Cambridge, Mass.: Harvard University Press.

Baik, Tae-Ung. 2007. "Justice Incomplete." In *Rethinking Historical Injustice and Reconciliation in Northeast Asia: The Korean Perspective,* edited by Gi-Wook Shin, Soon-won Park, and Daqing Yang, 94–113. New York: Routledge.

Baker, Don. 1998. "Christianity 'Koreanized.'" In *Nationalism and the Construction of Korean Identity,* edited by Hyung Il Pai and Timothy R. Tangherlini, 108–25. Berkeley: University of California Press.

———. 2007. Introduction to *Religions of Korea in Practice,* edited by Robert E. Buswell Jr., 1–31. Princeton, N.J.: Princeton University Press.

———. 2008. *Korean Spirituality.* Honolulu: University of Hawai'i Press.

Bauman, Richard. 1977. *Verbal Art as Performance.* Prospect Heights, Ill.: Waveland Press.

———. 1986. *Story, Performance, and Event.* Cambridge: Cambridge University Press.

———. 1992. "Contextualization, Tradition, and the Dialogue of Genres: Icelandic Legends of the *Kraftaskáld.*" In *Rethinking Context: Language as an Interactive Phenomenon,* edited by Alessandro Duranti and Charles Goodwin, 125–45. Cambridge: Cambridge University Press.

———. 2004. *A World of Others' Words: Cross-Cultural Perspectives on Intertextuality.* Malden, Mass.: Blackwell Publishing.

———. 2011. "'Better Than Any Monument': Envisioning Museums of the Spoken Word." *Museum Anthropology Review* 5 (1–2): 1–13.

Bauman, Richard, and Charles L. Briggs. 1990. "Poetics and Performance as Critical Perspectives on Language and Social Life." *Annual Review of Anthropology* 19: 59–88.

———. 2003. *Voices of Modernity: Language Ideologies and the Politics of Inequality.* Cambridge: Cambridge University Press.

Befu, Harumi. 1968. "Gift Giving in a Modernizing Japan." *Monumenta Nipponica* 23: 445–56.

Bendix, Regina. 1997. *In Search of Authenticity: The Formation of Folklore Studies.* Madison: University of Wisconsin Press.

———. 2009. "Heritage between Economy and Politics: An Assessment from the Perspective of Cultural Anthropology." In *Intangible Heritage,* edited by Laurajane Smith and Natsuko Akagawa, 253–69. New York: Routledge.

Beuchelt, Eno. 1963. "Cheju-do: Wandlungen in der Gesellschaftsordnung einer Koreanischen Inselkultur." *Sociologus* 13 (2): 150–68.

———. 1975a. "Die Rückrufen der Ahnen auf Cheju do (Süd Korea): Ein Ritual zur pychischen Stabilizierung." *Anthropos* 70: 145–79.

———. 1975b. "Zur Status-Persönlichkeit koreanischer Schamanen." *Sociologus* 25: 139–54.

Blacker, Carmen. 1975. *The Catalpa Bow: A Study of Shamanistic Practices in Japan.* London: George Allen & Unwin.

Blake, Janet. 2001. *Developing a New Standard-Setting Instrument for the Safeguarding of Intangible Cultural Heritage Elements for Consideration.* Paris: UNESCO.

Bourdieu, Pierre. 1977. *Outline of a Theory of Practice*. Cambridge: Cambridge University Press.

Brandt, Vincent S. R. 1971. *A Korean Village between Farm and Sea*. Cambridge, Mass.: Harvard University Press.

Bruner, Edward M., and Barbara Kirshenblatt-Gimblett. 1994. "Maasai on the Lawn: Tourist Realism in East Africa." *Cultural Anthropology* 9 (4): 435–70.

Bruno, Antonetta L. 2002. *The Gate of Words: Language in the Rituals of Korean Shamans*. Leiden, Netherlands: Research School of Asian, African and Amerindian Studies.

———. 2007a. "Transactions with the Realm of Spirits in Modern Korea." *Sungkyun Journal of East Asian Studies* 7 (1): 47–67.

———. 2007b. "Sending Away the Smallpox Gods." In *Religions of Korea in Practice*, edited by Robert E. Buswell Jr., 259–83. Princeton, N.J.: Princeton University Press.

———. 2007c. "A Shamanic Ritual for Sending On the Dead." In *Religions of Korea in Practice*, edited by Robert E. Buswell Jr., 325–52. Princeton, N.J.: Princeton University Press.

Buswell, Robert. 1998. "Imagining 'Korean Buddhism': The Invention of a National Religious Tradition." In *Nationalism and the Construction of Korean Identity*, edited by Hyung Il Pai and Timothy R. Tangherlini, 73–107. Berkeley: University of California Press.

———. 1999. "Buddhism under Confucian Domination: The Synthetic Vision of Sŏsan Hyujŏng." In *Culture and the State in Late Chosŏn Korea*, edited by JaHyun Kim Haboush and Martina Deuchler, 134–59. Cambridge, Mass.: Harvard University Asia Center.

Buyandelger, Manduhai. 2013. *Tragic Spirits: Shamanism, Memory, and Gender in Contemporary Mongolia*. Chicago: University of Chicago Press.

Byun Jisun [Pyŏn Chisŏn]. 2014. "Yŏsŏng musogin ŭi sam kwa musok" [Female shamans' lives and shamanism]. *Pigyo minsok hak* [Asian comparative folklore] 53: 377–412.

Cha, Ariana Eunjung. 2016. "Medical Errors Now Third Leading Cause of Death in United States." *Washington Post*, 3 May 2016. Accessed 1 November 2016. https://www.washingtonpost.com/news/to-your-health/wp/2016/05/03/researchers-medical-errors-now-third-leading-cause-of-death-in-united-states/.

Chang Chugŭn. 1983. "Kanginhan sam ŭi hyŏnjang, p'ungyo ŭi kiwŏn" [The resilient life, wishes for abundant harvest]. In *Han'guk ŭi kut 3, Chejudo Yŏngdŭng Kut* [Korean kut 3, Yŏngdŭng Kut of Cheju Island], edited by Chang Chugŭn and Yi Pohyŏng, 95–116. Seoul: Yŏlhwadang.

———. 2001. *Chejudo musok kwa sŏsa muga* [Cheju shamanism and shamanic epic songs]. Seoul: Yŏngnak.

———. 2007. "Chejudo musok yŏn'gu ŭi hoego" [A reflection on studying Cheju shamanism]. *Han'guk musokhak* [Korean shamanism] 14: 7–22.

Charyojip. See *Cheju pogŭm chŏllae paengnyŏn-sa charyojip*.

Chatterjee, Partha. 1986. *Nationalist Thought and the Colonial World: A Derivative Discourse*. Minneapolis: University of Minnesota Press.

Chau, Adam Yuet. 2006. *Miraculous Response: Doing Popular Religion in Contemporary China*. Stanford, Calif.: Stanford University Press.

Cheju Munhwawŏn. 2007. *Cheju kogi munjip* [A collection of old records of Cheju]. Translated and annotated by Cheju Munhwawŏn. Cheju: Cheju Munhwawŏn.

Cheju pogŭm chŏllae paengnyŏn-sa charyojip [A collection of materials for the 100-year history of spreading gospel in Chejudo]. 1997. 4 vols. Cheju: Ch'ŏnjugyo Cheju kyogu.

Chin Sŏng-gi. (1959) 1992. *Chejudo chŏnsŏl* [Traditional tales of Cheju Island]. Seoul: Paengnok.

———. 1968. *Namguk ŭi muga* [Shamanic songs of the southern country]. Cheju: Cheju Minsok Munhwa Yŏn'guso.

———. 1991. *Chejudo muga ponp'uri sajŏn* [Compilation of Cheju shamanic myths]. Seoul: Minsogwŏn.

Chin Sŏnhŭi. 2009. "Cheju-kut insik pakkwiŏssŭmyŏn" [Wishing for a change in people's attitude toward Cheju shamanic rituals]. *Halla ilbo*, 1 October 2009, 12.

Cho Hae-joang (Hyejŏng). 1983. "The Autonomous Women: Divers on Cheju Island." In *Korean Women: View from the Inner Room*, edited by Laurel Kendall and Mark Peterson, 81–95. New Haven, Conn.: East Rock Press.

———. 1988. *Han'guk ŭi yŏsŏng kwa namsŏng* [Women and men in South Korea]. Seoul: Munhak kwa Chisŏngsa.

Cho Hung-youn (Hŭng-yun). 1983. *Hanguk ŭi mu* [Korean shamanism]. Seoul: Chŏngŭmsa.

———. 1990. *Mu wa minjok munhwa* [Shamanism and national culture]. Seoul: Minjok Munhwasa.

———. 1997a. Han'guk mu ŭi segye [The world of Korean shamanism]. Seoul: Minjoksa.

———. 1997b. *Mu: Han'guk mu ŭi yŏksa wa hyŏnsang* [*Mu*: The history and present condition of Korean *mu*). Seoul: Minjoksa.

Cho Miyoung (Miyŏng). 2005. "Tabang, yuhŭk, orak" [Tearooms, pleasure, and entertainment]. In *Chejusi osipnyŏnsa* [The fifty-year history of Cheju City], Committee for the Publication of *The Fifty-Year History of Cheju City*, 839–56. Cheju: Cheju City.

Cho Sung-Youn (Sŏngyun). 1997. "19 segi Chejudo ŭi kukka chesa" [State rites on Cheju Island during the nineteenth century]. In *19 segi Cheju sahoe yŏn'gu* [Studies on nineteenth-century Cheju], edited by Kang Ch'angyong et al., 178–201. Seoul: Ilchisa.

———. 2003. "Chejusi ŭi mudang kwa yŏksurin" [Shamans and fortune-tellers in Cheju City]. In *Cheju chiyŏk min'gan sinang ŭi kujo wa pyŏnyong* [Structure and change of the folk beliefs on Cheju Island], edited by Cho Sung-Youn, Lee Sang-Cheol (Yi Sangch'ŏl), and Ha Soon-Ae (Ha Sunae), 279–395. Seoul: Paeksan Sŏdang.

Cho Sung-Youn and Pak Chan-Sik. 1998. "Chosŏn hugi Cheju chiyŏk ŭi chibae ch'eje wa chumin ŭi min'gan sinang" [The ruling systems and folk beliefs on Cheju Island during the late Chosŏn period]. *T'amna munhwa* [T'amna culture] 19: 199–218.

Ch'oe Kil-sŏng. 1974. "Chejudo purak sindang p'agoe wa misin t'ap'a" [The destruction of shamanic shrines and superstition in Cheju villages]. In *Han'guk minsok chonghap chosa pogosŏ Chejudo p'yŏn* [Report on a comprehensive survey of Korean folklore, Cheju Island], vol. 5, edited by Munhwajae Kwalliguk [Bureau of Cultural Property Preservation], 112–15. Seoul: Munhwajae Kwalliguk.

————. 1978. *Han'guk musok ŭi yŏn'gu: Tonghaean chiyŏk ŭl chungsim ŭro han sahoe illyuhakchŏk yŏn'gu* [A study of Korean shamanism: A socio-anthropological study focusing on the East Coast region]. Seoul: Asea Munhwasa.

————. 1981. *Han'guk ŭi mudang* [Korean shamans]. Seoul: Yŏlhwadang.

Ch'oe Nam-sŏn. 1973. *Yuktang Ch'oe Nam-sŏn chŏnjip* [Ch'oe Nam-sŏn's collected works]. Vol. 2. Seoul: Hyŏnamsa.

————. 2013. "Purham munhwaron; Salman'gyo ch'agi" [The theory of Purham culture; Notes on shamanism]. Translated by Chŏn Sŏng-gon. Seoul: Kyŏngin Munhwasa

Ch'oe Pu. (1488) 2004. *P'yohaerok* [A record of drifting across the sea]. Translated by Sŏ Inbŏm and Chu Sŏngji. P'aju, Korea: Han'gilsa.

Choe, Sang-Hun. 2016. "A Presidential Friendship Has Many South Koreans Crying Foul." *New York Times*, 27 October 2016. Accessed 30 October 2016.

Ch'oe Sŏnhong. 1935. "Chejudo haksal sakŏn kwa ponding yŏnhyŏk" [The Cheju massacre and a history of the church]. *Kat'olic yŏn'gu* 9/10: 177–82.

Choi, Chungmoo (Ch'oe Chŏngmu). 1987. "The Competence of Korean Shamans as Performers of Folklore." PhD diss., Indiana University, Bloomington.

————. 1989. "The Artistry and Ritual Aesthetics of Urban Korean Shamans." *Journal of Ritual Studies* 3 (2): 235–49.

————. 1991. "Nami, Ch'ae, and Oksun Superstar Shamans in Korea." In *Shamans of the 20th Century*, edited by Ruth-Inge Heinze, 51–61. New York: Irvington.

————. 1995. "The Minjung Culture Movement and the Construction of Popular Culture in Korea." In *South Korea's Minjung Movement: The Culture and Politics of Dissidence*, edited by Kenneth M. Wells, 105–18. Honolulu: University of Hawai'i Press.

Choi, Hyaeweol. 2009. *Gender and Mission Encounters in Korea: New Women, Old Ways*. Berkeley: University of California Press.

Choi Jong Seong (Ch'oe Chong-sŏng). 2002. *Chosŏnjo musok kukhaeng ŭirye yŏn'gu* [A study of national shamanic ceremonies during the Chosŏn dynasty]. Seoul: Ilchisa.

Choi Seok-Yeong (Ch'oe Sŏgyŏng). 1999. *Ilcheha musongnon kwa singminji kwŏllyŏk* [Theory of shamanism under Japanese rule and colonial power]. Seoul: Sŏgyŏng Munhwasa.

————. 2005. "Ilche ŭi Taehan cheguk kangjŏm chŏnhu Chosŏn musok e taehan sisŏn pyŏnhwa" [Changes in the viewpoint of Korean shamanism commissioned by the Taehan cheguk Japanese residency-general]. *Han'guk musokhak* [Korean shamanism] 9: 111–30.

————. 2008. "Haeje" [A bibliographical introduction]. In *Chōsen fuzoku no kenkyū* [Study of Korean shamanism], vol. 1, 1–16. Seoul: Minsogwŏn.

Choi Won-oh [Ch'oe Wŏno]. 2008. *An Illustrated Guide to Korean Mythology*. Folkestone: Global Oriental.

Chong, Kelly H. 2008. "Coping with Conflict, Confronting Resistance: Fieldwork Emotions and Identity Management in a South Korean Evangelical Community." *Qual Sociol* 31: 369–90.

Chŏng Yagyong. [1818] 2010. *Admonitions on Governing the People: Manual for All Administrators*. Translated by Choi Byonghyon. Berkeley: University of California Press.

Ch'ŏngdam Posal [Fortune salon]. 2010. DVD. Directed by Kim Chinyŏng. Seoul: PRE.GM.

Chŏngjo sillok [Veritable records of King Chŏngjo]. In *Chosŏn wangjo sillok.*

Chōsen sōtokufu. (1929) 1990. *Saenghwal sangt'ae chosa, Chejudo* [Social life and customs on Cheju Island]. Vol. 2. Seoul: Kyŏngin Munhwasa.

Chosŏn wangjo sillok [Veritable records of the kings of the Choson dynasty]. Translated and edited by Kuksa P'yŏnch'an Wiwŏnhoe. National Institute of Korean History (Kuksa P'yŏnch'an Wiwŏnhoe). http://sillok.history.go.kr.

Chun Kyung-soo (Chŏn Kyŏngsu). 1984. *Reciprocity and Korean Society: An Ethnography of Hasami.* Seoul: Seoul National University Press.

———. 2012. "'Musok' yŏn'gu paengnyŏn ŭi taegang kwa kulgok: Yi Nŭnghwa ihu" [History of shamanism studies and its misunderstanding in Korea: After Yi Nŭnghwa]. *Minsokhak yŏn'gu* [Korean journal of folk studies] 31: 15–44.

Chungjong sillok [Veritable records of King Chungjong]. In *Chosŏn wangjo sillok.*

Clark, Anthony E. 2015. *Heaven in Conflict: Franciscans and the Boxer Uprising in Shanxi.* Seattle: University of Washington Press.

Clark, Charles Allen. 1961. *Religions of Old Korea.* Seoul: Christian Literature Society of Korea.

Clark, Donald N. 1986. *Christianity in Modern Korea.* Lanham, Md.: University Press of America for the Asia Society.

Clifford, James. 1988. *The Predicament of Culture: Twentieth-Century Ethnography, Literature, and Art.* Cambridge, Mass.: Harvard University Press.

Chejudoji P'yŏnch'an Wiwŏnhoe (Committee for the Compilation of the *Chejudoji*). 2006. *Chejudoji 2: Yŏksa* [Gazetteer of Cheju 2: History]. Cheju: Cheju Provincial Government.

Cultural Heritage Administration of Korea. 2013a. "Munhwajaech'ŏng 2013 nyŏn saeng saeng munhwajae saŏp sŏnjŏng palp'yo" [CHA selects and announces the 2013 living cultural assets]. Cultural Heritage Administration of Korea. Accessed 15 November 2016. www.cha.go.kr/newsBbz/selectNewsBbzView.do?newsItemId =155698068&sectionId=b_sec_1&pageIndex=112&pageUnit=10&strWhere =&strValue=&sdate=&edate=&category=&mn=NS_01_02.

———. 2013b. "Munhwajaech'ŏng saeng saeng munhwajae saŏp, 3.3 pae ŭi kyŏngjaejŏk p'agŭp hyogwa ch'angch'ul" [CHA's living cultural assets project resulted in an economic jolt of as much as 3.3 times the original investment]. Cultural Heritage Administration of Korea. Accessed 15 November 2016. www.cha.go.kr/newsBbz /selectNewsBbzView.do?newsItemId=155698125&sectionId=b_sec_1&pageIndex =107&pageUnit=10&strWhere=&strValue=&sdate=&edate=&category=&mn=NS _01_02.

Cumings, Bruce. 2005. *Korea's Place in the Sun: A Modern History.* New York: W. W. Norton.

Deuchler, Martina. 1992. *The Confucian Transformation of Korea: A Study of Society and Ideology.* Cambridge, Mass.: Harvard University Press.

Doucette, Jamie. 2017. "The Occult of Personality: Korea's Candelight Protests and the Impeachment of Park Geun-hye." *Journal of Asian Studies* 76 (4): 851–60.

Duncan, John B. 2000. *The Origins of the Chosŏn Dynasty.* Seattle: University of Washington Press.

Dundes, Alan. 1969. "The Devolutionary Premise in Folklore Theory." *Journal of the Folklore Institute* 6: 5–19.

Duranti, Alessandro, and Charles Goodwin. 1992. *Rethinking Context: Language as an Interactive Phenomenon*. Cambridge: Cambridge University Press.

Durkheim, Émile. (1912) 1995. *Elementary Forms of the Religious Life*. New York: Free Press.

Ebersole, L. Gary. 2000. "The Function of Ritual Weeping Revisited: Affective Expression and Moral Discourse." *History of Religions* 39 (3): 211–46.

Eliade, Mircea. 1964. *Shamanism: Archaic Techniques of Ecstasy*. Translated by Willard R. Trask. New York: Pantheon Books.

Feld, Steven. 1990. "Wept Thoughts: The Voicing of Kaluli Memories." *Oral Tradition* 5 (2/3): 241–66.

Feuchtwang, Stephen. 2001. *Popular Religion in China: The Imperial Metaphor*. Richmond: Curzon.

Financial Times. 2016. "Park Should Come Clean over Seoul Svengali." 2 November 2016. Accessed 9 November 2016.

Foster, Michael D. 2011. "The UNESCO Effect: Confidence, Defamiliarization, and a New Element in the Discourse on a Japanese Island." *Journal of Folklore Research* 48 (1): 63–107.

———. 2015a. "Imagined UNESCOs: Interpreting Intangible Cultural Heritage on a Japanese Island." *Journal of Folklore Research* 52 (2–3): 217–32.

———. 2015b. "UNESCO on the Ground." *Journal of Folklore Research* 52 (2–3): 143–56.

Foster, Michael D., and Lisa Gilman, eds. 2015. *UNESCO on the Ground: Local Perspectives on Intangible Cultural Heritage*. Bloomington: Indiana University Press.

Gal, Susan. (1931) 1989. "Language and Political Economy." *Annual Review of Anthropology* 18: 345–67.

Gates, Hill. 1987. "Money for the Gods." *Modern China* 13 (3): 259–77.

Geertz, Clifford. 1973. *The Interpretation of Cultures*. New York: Basic Books.

Gell, Alfred. 1998. *Art and Agency: An Anthropological Theory*. Oxford: Clarendon Press.

Geschiere, Peter. 2013. *Witchcraft, Intimacy, and Trust: Africa in Comparison*. Chicago: University of Chicago Press.

Giddens, Anthony. 1994. "Living in a Post-traditional Society." In *Reflexive Modernization: Politics, Tradition and Aesthetics in the Modern Social Order*, edited by Ulrich Beck, Anthony Giddens, and Scott Lash, 56–109. Stanford, Calif.: Stanford University Press.

Gilman, Lisa. 2015. "Demonic or Cultural Treasure?: Local Perspectives on Vimbuza, Intangible Cultural Heritage, and UNESCO in Malawi." *Journal of Folklore Research* 52 (2–3): 199–216.

Goffman, Erving. 1974. *Frame Analysis*. New York: Harper and Row.

———. 1981. *Forms of Talk*. Philadelphia: University of Pennsylvania Press.

Grayson, James H. 2001. *Myths and Legends from Korea: An Annotated Compendium of Ancient and Modern Materials*. London and New York: Routledge.

Griffis, William E. 1889. *Corea, the Hermit Kingdom*. New York: Scribner's Sons.

Guyer, Jane I. 2004. *Marginal Gains: Monetary Transactions in Atlantic Africa*. Chicago: University of Chicago Press.

Ha Soon-Ae (Sunae). 2000. "18 segi ch'o Cheju-in ŭi sin'ang saenghwal kwa sindang p'agoe sakkŏn" [The religious lives of the Cheju people and the destruction of shamanic shrines in the early eighteenth century]. In *T'amna Sullyŏkto yŏn'gu nonch'ong*, edited by Committee for Studies of *T'amna Sullyŏkto*, 333–49. Cheju: Committee for Studies of *T'amna Sullyŏkto*.

———. 2003. "Chejudo mingan sin'ang ŭi kujo wa pyŏnhwasang" [Structure and change of folk beliefs on Cheju Island]. In *Cheju chiyŏk min'gan sinang ŭi kujo wa pyŏnyong* [Structure and change of the folk beliefs on Cheju Island], edited by Cho Sung-Youn, Lee Sang-Cheol (Yi Sangch'ŏl), and Ha Soon-Ae (Ha Sunae), 87–276. Seoul: Baiksan Publishing House.

Haboush, JaHyun Kim. 1991. "The Confucianization of Korean Society." In *East Asian Region: Confucian Heritage and Its Modern Adaptation*, edited by Gilbert Rozman, 84–110. Princeton, N.J.: Princeton Press.

Haboush, JaHyun Kim, and Martina Deuchler. 1999. Introduction to *Culture and the State in Late Chosŏn Korea*, edited by JaHyun Kim Haboush and Martina Deuchler, 1–13. Cambridge, Mass.: Harvard University Asia Center.

Hafstein, Valdimar Tr. 2009. "Intangible Heritage as a List: From the Masterpieces to Representation." In *Intangible Heritage*, edited by Laurajane Smith and Natsuko Akagawa, 93–111. New York: Routledge.

———. 2015. "Intangible Heritage as Diagnosis, Safeguarding as Treatment." *Journal of Folklore Research* 52 (2–3): 281–98.

Hamel, Hendrik. 2011. *Hamel's Journal and a Description of the Kingdom of Korea, 1653–1666*. Translated by Brother Jean-Paul Buys. 3rd rev. ed. Seoul: Royal Asiatic Society Korea Branch.

Han Do-Hyun. 1986. "1930 nyŏndae nongch'on chinhŭng undong ŭi sŏngkyŏk" [Characteristics of the rural revitalization campaign in the 1930s]. In *Han'guk kŭndae nongch'on sahoe wa Ilbon chejukchuŭi* [Rural Korea under Japanese imperialism], edited by Han'guk Sahoe Yŏn'guhoe, 233–77. Seoul: Munhak kwa Chisŏngsa.

———. 2000. "Shamanism, Superstition, and the Colonial Government." *Review of Korean Studies* 3 (1): 34–54.

Hardacre, Helen. 1997. *Marketing the Menacing Fetus in Japan*. Berkeley: University of California Press.

Harvey, Youngsook Kim. 1979. *Six Korean Women: The Socialization of Shamans*. Saint Paul, Minn.: West Publishing Co.

Healy, Kieran. 2006. *Last Best Gifts: Altruism and the Market for Human Blood and Organs*. Chicago: University of Chicago Press.

Hŏ Hojun. 2009. "Cheju Yŏngdŭng Kut segye yusan chijŏng 'tŏngsil'" [A Cheju Yŏngdŭng Kut designated World Heritage, "hurrah"]. *Han'gyŏre*, 2 October 2009, 11.

Hŏ Namch'un et al. 2009. *Yi Yongok simbang ponp'uri* [Ponp'uri recited by Simbang Yi Yongok]. Cheju: Tamla Culture Research Institute.

———. 2010. *Yang Ch'angbo simbang ponp'uri* [Ponp'uri recited by Simbang Yang Ch'angbo]. Cheju: Tamla Culture Research Institute.

———. 2013. *Ko Sunan simbang ponp'uri* [Ponp'uri recited by Simbang Ko Sunan]. Cheju: Tamla Culture Research Institute.

———. 2015. *Sŏ Sunsil simbang ponp'uri* [*Ponp'uri* recited by Simbang Sŏ Sunsil]. Cheju: Tamla Culture Research Institute.

Hobsbawm, Eric, and Terence Ranger, eds. 1983. *The Invention of Tradition*. Cambridge: Cambridge University Press.

Hochschild, Arlie. 2003. *The Managed Heart: Commercialization of Human Feeling with a New Afterword*. Berkeley: University of California Press.

Hogarth, Hyun-key Kim. 1999. *Korean Shamanism and Cultural Nationalism*. Seoul: Jimoondang.

———. 2009. *Gut, the Korean Shamanistic Rituals*. Seoul: Jimoondang.

Hong Sŏkjun. 2004. "Haenyŏ munhwa ch'ukche tŭng simŭi" (Discussion of the Haenyŏ Cultural Festival and other issues). *Jemin Ilbo*. 21 August 2004. Accessed 18 August 2005. www.jemin.com/news/articleView.html?idxno=118350.

Howard, Keith. 1989. *Bands, Songs, and Shamanistic Rituals: Folk Music in Korean Society*. Seoul: Royal Asiatic Society Korea Branch.

———. 1991. "Why Should Korean Shamans Be Women?" *Papers of the British Association for Korean Studies* 1: 75–95.

———. 1998. "Preserving the Spirits? Ritual, State Sponsorship, and Performance." In *Korean Shamanism Revivals, Survivals, and Change*, edited by Keith Howard, 187–217. Seoul: Seoul Press.

Howard, Peter. 2009. "The Rise of Heritage." *Asian Anthropology* 10: 1–28.

Hubert, Henri, and Marcel Mauss. (1899) 1964. *Sacrifice: Its Nature and Function*. Chicago: University of Chicago Press.

Hulbert, Homer B. 1906. *The Passing of Korea*. London: William Heineman.

Hwang, Kyung Moon. 2004. *Beyond Birth: Social Status in the Emergence of Modern Korea*. Cambridge, Mass.: Harvard University Asia Center.

Hwang, Merose. 2009. "The *Mudang*: Gendered Discourses on Shamanism in Colonial Korea." PhD diss., University of Toronto.

Hwang Kyŏng-gŭn. 2013. "'Cheju Ch'ilmŏri-dang Yŏngdŭngkut' chŏnsu hoegwan kŏllip hae pojon" ["'Cheju Ch'ilmŏri Shrine Yŏngdŭng Kut" will be safeguarded by building a preservation hall]. *Seoul sinmun*, 8 May, 27.

Hwang Ru-shi. 1988. *Han'gugin ŭi kut kwa mudang* [Shamans and shaman rituals of the Korean people]. Seoul: Munŭmsa.

———. 2000. *Hwang Ru-shi ŭi uri mudang iyagi* [Hwang Ru-shi on the subject of our shamans]. Seoul: P'ulppit.

Hwang Taegwŏn. 2016. "Shyamŏnijŭm ŭl yok toege hajimara" [Don't insult shamanism]. *Kyŏnghyang sinmun*, 7 November 2016.

Hymes, Dell. 1981. *"In Vain I Tried to Tell You": Essays in Native American Ethnopoetics*. Philadelphia: University of Pennsylvania Press.

Hyŏn Kirŏn. 1983. "Yŏksajŏk sasil kwa munhakchŏk insik—Yi Hyŏngsang moksa ŭi sindang ch'ŏlp'ye e taehan sŏrhwajŏk insik" [Historical facts and literary interpretation—understanding Governor Yi Hyongsang's destruction of shamanic shrines as a story]. *T'amna munhwa* [T'amla culture] 2: 95–125.

Hyŏn P'yŏngho et al. 1995. *Chejuŏ sajŏn* [A dictionary of the Cheju language]. Chejudo: Cheju Provincial Government.

Hyŏn Yongjun. 1969. "Chejudo ŭi Yŏngdŭng Kut" [The Yŏngdŭng Kut of Cheju Island]. *Han'guk minsokhak* [Korean folklore] 1: 117–35.

———. 1976. *Chejudo sinhwa* [Chejudo myth]. Seoul: Sŏmundang.

———. 1980a. *Chejudo musok charyo sajŏn* [Compilation of Cheju shamanic material]. Seoul: Sin'gu Munhwasa.

———. 1980b. "Yangmahŭi ko." In *Yŏnam Hyŏn P'yŏnghyo paksa hoegap kinyŏm nonch'ong* [A collection of treatises in memory of Dr. Yŏnam Hyŏn P'yŏnghyo's sixtieth birthday], 679–98. Seoul: Hyŏngsŏl Ch'ulp'ansa.

———. 1986. *Chejudo musok yŏn'gu* [A study of shamanism of Cheju Island]. Seoul: Chimmundang.

———. 1989. "Chugŭm kwa chaesaeng kŭrigo pingsin ch'ehŏm: Chejudo sin kut ŭi kusŏng kwa ŭimi" [Experiences of death, rebirth, and ecstasy: Composition and meaning of Cheju Sin Kut] In *Chejudo sin kut: Simbang ŭro tasi t'aeŏnam ŭl wihan kut* [*Cheju-do sin kut*: A ritual for being reborn as a *simbang*], edited by Hyŏn Yongjun and Yi Namdŏk, with photos and captions by Kim Sunam, 86–97. Seoul: Yŏlhwadang.

———. 1992. *Musok sinhwa wa munhŏn sinhwa* [Shamanic myths and literary myths]. Seoul: Chimmundang.

———. 2005. *Chejudo sinhwa ŭi susukkekki* [Mystery of Cheju myths]. P'aju: Chimmundang.

Hyŏn Yongjun and Kim Yŏngdon. 1983. *Han'guk kubi munhak taegye* [A survey of Korean oral literature]. Vol. 9(3) of *Cheju Sŏgwip'o-si, nam-Cheju kun* [Sŏgwip'o City and Southern Cheju County on Cheju Island]. Sŏngnam: Han'guk Chŏngsin Munhwa Yŏn'guwŏn.

Hyun Hye-Kyung (Hyŏn Hyekyŏng). 2005. "4.3 ŭi kiŏk kwa kut ŭi chaehyŏn" [Memory of the April Third Incident and its representation through *kut*]. *Minjujuŭi wa Inkkŏn* [Journal of democracy and human rights] 5 (1): 25–27.

———. 2008. "Formation and Structure of Memorial Ceremony for the Cheju April 3rd Incident." PhD diss., Chŏnnam National University.

Irvine, Judith T. 1990. "Registering Affect: Heteroglossia in the Linguistic Expression of Emotion." In *Language and the Politics of Emotion*, edited by Catherine A. Lutz and Lila Abu-Lughod, 126–61. Cambridge: Cambridge University Press.

Ivy, Marilyn. 1995. *Discourses of the Vanishing: Modernity, Phantasm, Japan*. Chicago: University of Chicago Press.

Izumi Seiichi. 2014. *Chejudo, 1935–65*. Translated by Kim Chong-ch'ŏl. Seoul: Yŏrŭm Ŏndŏk.

Jackson, Peter A. 1999. "Royal Spirits, Chinese Gods, and Magic Monks: Thailand's Boom-Time Religions of Prosperity." *South East Asia Research* 7 (3): 245–320.

Janelli, Dawnhee Yim. 1979. "Logical Contradictions in Korean Learned Fortunetelling." PhD diss., University of Pennsylvania.

———. 1982. "Faith, Fortunetelling, and Social Failure." In *Religions in Korea: Beliefs and Cultural Values*, edited by E. H. Phillips and E. Y. Yun, 59–69. Los Angeles: Center for Korean and Korean-American Studies, California State University.

———. 1984. "Strategic Manipulation of Social Relationships in Rural Korea." *Korea Journal* 24 (6): 27–39.

Janelli, Roger L. 1986. "The Origins of Korean Folklore Scholarship." *Journal of American Folklore* 99: 24–49.

Janelli, Roger L., and Dawnhee Yim Janelli. 1982. *Ancestor Worship and Korean Society*. Stanford, Calif.: Stanford University Press.

Janelli, Roger L., and Yim Dawnhee. 1997. "The Mutual Constitution of Confucianism and Capitalism in South Korea." In *Culture and Economy: The Shaping of Capitalism in Eastern Asia*, edited by Timothy Brook and Hy Van Luong, 107–204. Ann Arbor: University of Michigan Press.

———. 2002. "Ancestor Rites and Capitalist Industrialization in a South Korean Village." *Korea Journal* 42 (4): 298–328.

Janelli, Roger L., with Dawnhee Yim. 1993. *Making Capitalism: The Social and Cultural Construction of a South Korean Conglomerate*. Stanford, Calif.: Stanford University Press.

Jeju sinmun. 1969. "Abŏji nŭn pyŏnso kaeryang, ŏmŏni nŭn misin t'ap'a" [Fathers renovate privies; mothers work to eradicate superstition]. 4 February 1969.

———. 1972a. "'Halmang-dang' 11 kaeso ch'ŏlgŏ" [Destruction of 11 shamanic shrines]. 22 February 1972.

———. 1972b. "Mudang 3 myŏng ŭl sagi ipkkŏn" [The police booked three female shamans on charges of fraud]. 31 March 1972.

Jeju Special Self-Governing Province. 2013. Jeju Special Self-Governing Province (website). Accessed 30 October 2013. http://english.jeju.go.kr/.

Jeju Special Self-Governing Provincial Tourism Association. 2013. Jeju Special Self-Governing Province Tourism Association (website). Accessed 29 December 2013. www.hijeju.or.kr/korea/main.html.

Jeju Traditional Culture Research Institute. 2008–9. *Cheju sindang chosa* [Survey of Cheju shamanic shrines]. Cheju: Kak.

Jones, Charles. 2003. "Religion in Taiwan at the end of the Japanese Colonial Period." In *Religions in Modern Taiwan: Tradition and Innovation in a Changing Society*, edited by Philip Clart and Charles Jones, 10–35. Honolulu: University of Hawai'i Press.

Jones, George Heber. 1901. "The Spirit Worship of the Koreans." In *Transactions of the Korea Branch of the Royal Asiastic Society* 2 (1): 37–58.

Joralemon, Donald. 1990. "The Selling of the Shaman and the Problem of Informant Legitimacy." *Journal of Anthropological Research* 46 (2): 105–18.

JTBC *Nyusŭrum*. 2016. "Patkko chami omyŏn sŏnmul an omyŏn noemul" [If you can sleep well after receiving something, that is a gift; if not, a bribe]. "Anchor Briefing." 30 August 2016.

———. 2016. "Shyamŏnijŭm ŭl yok toege hajimara" [Don't insult shamanism]. "Anchor Briefing." 9 November 2016.

Kang Jung-sik (Chŏng-sik), Kang So-Jeon (Sojŏn), and Song Chŏnghi. 2008. *Tongbok Chŏng Pyŏngch'un taek Siwang maji* [The ritual of *Siwang maji* for the family of Chŏng Pyŏngch'un of Tongbok-ri]. Seoul: Pogosa.

Kang Kyŏngsŏn. 2003. "Cheju chiyŏk nongŏp ŭi kwagŏ, hyŏnjae kŏmt'o wa chŏn'gae panghyang" [An examination of the past and present of the Cheju region's agriculture and directions for the future]. In *Chŏnhwan'gi Chejudo chiyŏk kaebal chŏngch'aek ŭi sŏngch'al kwa panghyang* [Reflection on development policies of the

Cheju region during a transitional period and discussion of future directions],
edited by Cheju Pulgyo Sahoe Munhwawŏn, 81–127. Cheju: Kak.

Kang So-Jeon (Sojŏn). 2004. "Cheju 4.3 haewŏn sangsaeng-kut ŭi chae chomyŏng"
[Reexamining the Cheju 4.3 ritual for releasing grief and promoting coexistence].
Tamla munwha 25: 1–24.

———. 2005. "Chejudo chamsu kut yŏn'gu: Focusing on the Case of Tong Kimnyŏng-ni,
Kujwa-ŭp, Puk Cheju-gun." MA thesis, Cheju National University.

———. 2006. "Chejudo kut ŭi mugu 'kime' e taehan koch'al" [A study of the uses of
kime in Cheju *kut*]. *Han'guk musokhak* [Korean shamanism] 13: 103–41.

Kapchan, Deborah A. 1995. "Performance." *Journal of American Folklore* 108 (430):
479–508.

Keane, Webb. 1994. "The Value of Words and the Meaning of Things in Eastern
Indonesian Exchange." *Man* 29: 605–29.

———. 2001. "Money Is No Object: Morality, Desire, and Modernity in an Indonesian
Society." In *The Empire of Things: Regimes of Value and Material Culture*, edited by
Fred R. Myers, 65–90. Santa Fe, N.M.: School of American Research Press.

Kendall, Laurel. 1985a. *Shamans, Housewives, and Other Restless Spirits: Women in
Korean Ritual Life*. Honolulu: University of Hawai'i Press.

———. 1985b. "Death and Taxes: A Korean Approach to Hell." *Transactions of the Royal
Asiatic Society, Korea Branch*, 60: 1–14.

———. 1988. *The Life and Hard Times of a Korean Shaman*. Honolulu: University of
Hawai'i Press.

———. 2003. "Gods, Markets, and the IMF in the Korean Spirit World." In *Transparency
and Conspiracy: Ethnographies of Suspicion in the New World Order*, edited by
Harry G. West and Todd Sanders, 38–64. Durham, N.C.: Duke University Press.

———. 2008. "Of Hungry Ghosts and Other Matters of Consumption." *American
Ethnologist* 35 (1): 154–70.

———. 2009. *Shamans, Nostalgias, and the IMF: South Korean Popular Religion in
Motion*. Honolulu: University of Hawai'i Press.

Keyes, Charles, Laurel Kendall, and Helen Hardacre, eds. 1994. *Asian Visions of
Authority: Religion and Modern States of East and South-East Asia*. Honolulu:
University of Hawai'i Press.

Kim, Chongho. 2003. *Korean Shamanism: The Cultural Paradox*. Burlington, Vt.: Ashgate.

Kim, David J. 2009. "Divining Capital: Spectral Returns and the Commodifications of
Fate in South Korea." PhD diss., Columbia University, New York.

———. 2013. "Critical Mediations: Haewŏn Chinhon Kut, a Shamanic Ritual for Korean
'Comfort Women.'" *Positions: East Asia Cultures Critique* 21 (3): 725–54.

Kim, Dong Kyu. 2012. "Looping Effects between Images and Realities: Understanding the
Plurality of Korean Shamanism." PhD diss., University of British Columbia, Vancouver.

Kim, Hun Joon. 2014. *The Massacres at Mt. Halla: Sixty Years of Truth Seeking in South
Korea*. Ithaca, N.Y.: Cornell University Press.

Kim, Kwang-iel (Kwang-il). 1973. "Shamanist Healing Ceremonies in Seoul." *Korea
Journal* 13 (4): 41–47.

Kim, Kwang-Ok. 1994. "Rituals of Resistance: The Manipulation of Shamanism in
Contemporary Korea." In *Asian Visions of Authority: Religion and the Modern States*

of East and Southeast Asia, edited by Charles F. Keyes, Laurel Kendall, and Helen Hardacre, 195–219. Honolulu: University of Hawai'i Press.

———. 2013. "Colonial Body and Indigenous Soul: Religion as a Contested Terrain of Culture." In *Colonial Rule and Social Changes in Korea, 1910–1945*, edited by Hong Yung Lee, Clark W. Sorensen, and Yong-Chool Ha, 264–313. Seattle: University of Washington Press.

Kim, Sun Joo. 2008. "Fragmented: The T'ongch'ŏng Movements by Marginalized Status Groups in Late Chosŏn Korea." *Harvard Journal of Asian Studies* 68 (1): 135–68.

———. 2010. *The Northern Region of Korea: History, Identity, and Culture*. Seattle: University of Washington Press.

Kim Ch'anhŭp. 2002. *Chejusa inmyŏng sajŏn* (Biographical dictionary of Cheju historical personages). Cheju: Cheju Culture Center.

Kim Dong Jeon [Tongjŏn]. 1991. *Chosŏn sidae Chejudo ŭi kunhyŏn kujo wa chibae ch'eje* [Structure of *kun hyŏn* and governing system in Cheju during the Chosŏn period]. *Chejudo sa yŏn'gu* 1: 45–69.

Kim Eun-kyung. 2009. "1950 nyŏndae sinsaenghwal undong yŏn'gu" [A study of the New Life Movement in the 1950s]. *Yŏsŏng kwa yŏksa* 11: 203–40.

Kim Hoch'ŏn. 2013. "Illyu Yusan Cheju Ch'ilmŏri-dang Yŏngdŭng Kut chŏnsu hoegwan kŏllip toenda" [The preservation hall will be built for the World Heritage Yŏngdŭng Kut at the Ch'ilmŏri Shrine]. *Yŏnhap News*, 21 February 2013. Accessed 15 July 2013. www.yonhapnews.co.kr/culture/2013/02/21 /0906000000AKR20130221093000056.html.

Kim Hyŏnjong. 2009. "Cheju sin'ang kut 'segye-yusan' toeda" [A Cheju shamanic ritual has become world heritage]. *Cheju Daily*, 2 October 2009.

Kim Hyosil. 2016. "Ch'oe T'aemin Ch'oe Sunsil mudang anida" [Ch'oe T'aemin and Ch'oe Sunsil are not *mudang*]. *Han'gyŏrye 21*, 10 November 2016. Accessed 10 November 2016. http://h21.hani.co.kr/arti/culture/culture_general/42618.html.

Kim Inhoe. 1982. "Han'guk musok yŏn'gusa" [A history of Korean shamanism studies]. In *Han'guk musok ŭi chonghapchŏk koch'al* [A comprehensive study of Korean shamanism], 1–30. Seoul: Koryŏ Taehakkyo Minjok Munhwa Yŏn'guso.

Kim Iru. 2000. *Koryŏ sidae T'amnasa yŏn'gu* [Study of T'amna history of the Koryŏ period]. Seoul: Sinsŏwŏn.

———. 2007. Annotation of *Cheju p'ungt'orok* [Cheju topography]. In *Cheju kogi munjip* [A collection of old records of Cheju]. Translated and annotated by Cheju Munhwawŏn, 11–14. Cheju: Cheju Munhwawŏn. Kim Kŭmhwa. 1995. *Kim Kŭmhwa ŭi mugajip* [Kim Kŭmhwa ŭi collected shaman songs]. Seoul: Munŭmsa.

Kim Myŏngjin. 2016. "Mudang ŭn ŏgulhada" [*Mudang* feel it is unfair]. *Han'gyŏrye*, 17 November 2016. Accessed 17 November 2016. http://v.media.daum.net/v /20161117115651049?d=y.

Kim Okhŭi. 1980. *Chejudo sinch'uk-nyŏn kyonansa* [A history of the Catholic persecution in the year of *sinch'uk* on Cheju Island]. Cheju: Ch'ŏnjukyo Cheju kyogu.

Kim Paeksun. 2000. *P'yŏl mich'in nyŏn ta pwanne* [What a crazy bitch!]. Seoul: Hanpit.

Kim Pong-ok. 2000. *Chŭngbo Cheju t'ongsa* [Cheju history, revised and enlarged]. Cheju: Serim.

Kim Sanghŏn. (1601)1992. *Namsarok* [Travel writings on Cheju Island]. Translated by
Kim Hŭidong. Seoul: Yŏngga Munhwasa.

Kim Seong-nae. 1989a. "Chronicle of Violence, Ritual of Mourning: Cheju Shamanism
in Korea." PhD diss., University of Michigan.

———. 1989b. "Lamentations of the Dead: The Historical Imagery of Violence on Cheju
Island, South Korea." *Journal of Ritual Studies* 3 (2): 251–85.

———. 1990. "Musok chŏnt'ong ŭi tamnon punsŏk" [An analysis of discourse in the
musok tradition]. *Han'guk munhwa illyuhak* [Korean cultural anthropology] 22: 211–43.

———. 1991a. "Cheju musok: P'ongnyŏk ŭi yŏksajŏk tamnon" [Cheju shamanism:
Historical discourse of violence]. *Chonggyo sinhak yŏn'gu* [Journal of religion and
theology] 4: 9–28.

———. 1991b. "Han'guk musok e nat'anan yŏsŏng ch'ehŏm: Kusul saengaesa sŏsa
punsŏk" [Women's experience in Korean shamanism: Narrative analysis of life
history]. *Han'guk yŏsŏnghak* [Journal of Korean women's studies] 7: 7–37.

———. 1998. "Problems in Defining Shaman Types and Local Variations." In *Korean
Shamanism Revivals, Survivals, and Change*, edited by Keith Howard, 15–31. Seoul:
Royal Asiatic Society.

———. 2000. "Korean Shamanic Heritage in Cyber Culture." *Syamŏnijŭm yŏn'gu*
[Shamanism studies] 3: 269–95.

———. 2002a. "Han'guk mugyo ŭi chŏngch'esŏng kwa chonggyosŏng: Chaengchŏm
punsŏk" [The essence and religiosity of Korean *mugyo*: A critical analysis].
Shyamŏnijŭm yŏn'gu [Shamanism studies] 4: 359–94.

———. 2002b. "Kibok sinang ŭi yulli wa chabonjuŭi munhwa" [The ethics of shamanic
fortune belief in the Korean capitalist culture]. *Chonggyo yŏn'gu* [Studies in religion]
27: 61–86.

———. 2004. "Shamanic Epics and Narrative Construction of Identity on Cheju Island."
Asian Folklore Studies 63: 57–78.

Kim Sunam. 1983. "Ch'ilmŏri-dang Yŏngdŭng Kut" [The Yŏngdŭng Kut at the
Ch'ilmŏri Shrine]. In *Han'guk ŭi Kut 3, Chejudo Yŏngdŭng Kut*, edited by Chang
Chugŭn and Yi Pohyŏng, 15–54. Seoul: Yŏlhwadang.

Kim T'aegon. 1966. *Hwangch'ŏn muga yŏn'gu* [A study of shaman songs of the land of
the dead]. Seoul: Ch'angusa.

———. 1972. "Components of Korean Shamanism." *Korea Journal* 12 (12): 17–27.

———. 1971–80. *Han'guk mugajip* [A collection of Korean shamanic songs]. 4 vols.
Seoul: Chimmundang.

———. 1981. *Han'guk musok yŏn'gu* [A study on Korean shamanism]. Seoul:
Chimmundang.

Kim Taewŏn. 1998. "18 segi min'gan ŭiryo ŭi sŏngjang" [Development of popular
medical treatment in the 18th century]. *Han'guk saron* [Studies of Korean history]
39: 187–238.

Kim Tubong. 1936. *Chejudo silgi* [True records of Cheju Island]. Taep'an, Japan: Cheju
Silchŏk Yŏn'gusa.

Kim Wŏnyŏng. 1900. *Susin yŏngyak* [Miraculous remedy for human body and mind].
Reprint. Cheju: Cheju Tongmun Church.

Kim Yŏl-gyu. 1977. *Han'guk sinhwa wa musok yŏn'gu* [A study of Korean myth and shamanism]. Seoul: Ilchogak.

Kim Yŏngdon. 2000. *Chejudo, Cheju saram* [Cheju Island and the Cheju people]. Seoul: Minsogwŏn.

Kim Yunsik. 1996. Translated by Kim Iksu. *Sok Ŭmch'ŏngsa* [History of clear and cloudy days, continued]. Cheju: Cheju Culture Center.

Kipnis, Andrew B. 1997. *Producing Guanxi: Sentiment, Self, and Subculture in a North China Village*. Durham, N.C.: Duke University Press.

Kirshenblatt-Gimblett, Barbara. 1998. *Destination Culture: Tourism, Museums, and Heritage*. Berkeley: University of California Press.

———. 2004. "Intangible Heritage as Metacultural Production." *Museum International* 56 (1–2): 52–65.

Kister, A. Daniel. 1980. "Korean Mudang Rites for the Dead and the Traditional Catholic Requiem: A Comparative Study." In *Customs and Manners in Korea*, edited by Shin-yong Chun, 44–54. Seoul: International Cultural Foundation.

———. 1995. "Dramatic Characteristics of Korean Shaman Ritual." *Shaman* 3 (1): 15–40.

Kleeman, Terry F. 1994. "Licentious Cults and Bloody Victuals: Sacrifice, Reciprocity, and Violence in Traditional China." *Asia Major* 7: 185–211.

Koh, Hea-Kyoung (Ko Hyegyŏng). 2001. "The Goddesses of Cheju Island: A Study of the Myths of a Korean Egalitarian Culture." PhD diss., Pacifica Graduate Institute.

Ko Taekyŏng. 1997. *Sindŭl ŭi kohyang* [Homeland of gods]. Seoul: Chungmyŏng.

Kopytoff, Igor. 1986. "The Cultural Biography of Things." In *The Social Life of Things: Commodities in Cultural Perspective*, edited by Arjun Appadurai, 64–91. Cambridge: Cambridge University Press.

Kotthoff, Helga. 2001. "Aesthetic Dimensions of Georgian Grief Rituals: On the Artful Display of Emotions in Lamentation." In *Verbal Art across Cultures: The Aesthetics and Proto-aesthetics of Communication*, edited by Helga Kotthoff and Hubert Knobaluch, 167–94. Tübingen: Gunter Narr Verlag.

Kwon, Gwisook. 2013. "Remembering 4/3 and Resisting the Remilitarisation of Jeju: Building an International Peace Movement." In *Under Occupation: Resistance and Struggle in a Militarised Asia-Pacific*, edited by Daniel Broudy, Peter Simpson, and Makoto Arakaki, 238–70. Newcastle upon Tyne, UK: Cambridge Scholars Publishing.

Kwon, Heonik. 2007. "The Dollarization of Vietnamese Ghost Money." *Journal of the Royal Anthropological Institute* 13 (1): 73–90.

———. 2009. "Healing the Wounds of War: New Ancestral Shrines in Korea." *Asia-Pacific Journal: Japan Focus* 7, no. 24: 1–16. Accessed 10 November 2009. www .japanfocus.org/-Heonik-Kwon/3172.

Kwŏn T'aehyo. 2005. "Chejudo Maengam Ponp'uri ŭi hyŏngsŏng e mich'in tang-shin ponp'uri ŭi yŏnghyang kwa ŭimi" [Influence that myths of village tutelary gods had on Cheju Maenggam Ponp'uri's formation and its meanings]. In *Han'guk kujŏn shinhwa ŭi segye* [The world of Korean oral myths], 49–97. Seoul: Chisik Sanŏpsa.

Kwŏn Yŏngch'ŏl. 1978. *Pyŏngwa Yi Hyŏngsang yŏn'gu* [A study of Pyongwa Yi Hyŏngsang]. Seoul: Han'guk Yŏn'guwŏn.

Laderman, Carol. 1997. "The Limits of Magic." *American Anthropologist* 99 (2): 333–41.

Landis, Eli Barr. 1895. "Notes on the Exorcism of Spirits in Korea." *China Review* 21 (6): 399–404.

Lebra, William P. 1966. *Okinawan Religion: Belief, Ritual, and Social Structure.* Honolulu: University of Hawai'i Press.

Lee, Nam-hee. 2003. "Between Interminacy and Radical Critique: Madang-guk, Ritual, and Protest." *Positions: East Asia Cultures Critique* 11 (3): 555–84.

Lee, Peter H. 1993. *Sourcebook of Korean Civilization.* Vol. 1, *From Early Times to the Sixteenth Century.* New York: Columbia University Press.

———. 1989. *A Korean Storyteller's Miscellany: The P'aegwan chapki of Ŏ Sukkwŏn.* Princeton, N.J.: Princeton University.

Lee Du-hyun (Yi Tu-hyŏn). 1969. "On the Conservation of Intangible Folklore and Cultural Properties." *Korea Journal* 9 (7): 21–24.

———. 2003. *Han'guk yŏn'gŭksa* [History of Korean drama]. Seoul: Hagyŏnsa.

Lee Ki-baik. 1984. *A New History of Korea.* Translated by Edward W. Wagner and Edward J. Shultz. Cambridge, Mass.: Harvard University Press.

Lee Wook. 2008. "Chosŏn hugi chegwan ch'ajŏng ŭi kaltŭng ŭl t'ong hae pon kukka sajŏn ŭi pyŏnhwa" [Changes in national religious service regulation, examined through the conflict over assigning service managers in the late Chosŏn]. *Chonggyo yŏn'gu* [Studies in religion] 53: 113–43.

———. 2009. *Chosŏn sidae chaenan kwa kukga ŭirye* [Calamities and national rites of the Chosŏn period]. P'aju, Korea: Ch'angjak kwa Pip'yŏngsa.

Levinson, Stephen C. 1988. "Putting Linguistics on a Proper Footing." In *Erving Goffman: Exploring the Interaction Order,* edited by Paul Drew and Anthony Wootton, 161–227. Boston: Northeastern University Press.

Lévi-Strauss, Claude. 1963. *Structural Anthropology.* Garden City, N.Y.: Anchor Books.

LiPuma, Edward, and Benjamin Lee. 2008. "The Performativity of Ritual Exchange: A Melanesian Example." In *Exchange and Sacrifice,* edited by Pamela J. Stewart and Andrew Strathern, 95–137. Durham, N.C.: Carolina Academic Press.

Lowthorp, Leah. 2015. "Voices on the Ground: Kutiyattam, UNESCO, and the Heritage of Humanity." *Journal of Folklore Research* 52 (2–3): 157–80.

Luckmann, Thomas. 1996. "The Privatization of Religion and Morality." In *Detraditionalization: Critical Reflections on Authority and Identity,* edited by Paul Heelas, Scott Lash, and Paul Morris, 72–86. Cambridge, Mass.: Blackwell Publishers.

Lutz, Catherine. 1986. "Emotion, Thought, and Estrangement: Emotion as a Cultural Category." *Cultural Anthropology* 1 (3): 287–309.

———. 1988. *Unnatural Emotions: Everyday Sentiments on a Micronesian Atoll and Their Challenges to Western Studies.* Chicago: University of Chicago Press.

Lutz, Catherine A., and Lila Abu-Lughod. 1990. *Language and the Politics of Emotion.* Cambridge: Cambridge University Press.

Lutz, Catherine A., and Geoffrey M. White. 1986. "The Anthropology of Emotions." *Annual Review of Anthropology* 15: 405–36.

MacCannell, Dean. 1999. *The Tourist: A New Theory of the Leisure Class.* Berkeley: University of California Press.

Maeil sinbo. 1937. "Chŏnsŏl ŭi T'osan-dang ch'ŏrhwe" [Destruction of the legendary T'osan-dang]. 12 November 1937.

Martel, Emile. 1901. "The Disturbances on Quelepart." *Korea Review* 1 (12): 539–42.

Marty, Martin E. 1993. "Churches as Winners, Losers." *Christian Century* 110: 88–89.

Maurer, Bill. 2006. "The Anthropology of Money." *Annual Review of Anthropology* 35: 15–36.

Mauss, Marcel. (1950) 1990. *The Gift: The Form and Reason for Exchange in Archaic Societies*. Translated by W. D. Halls. New York: W. W. Norton.

McBride, D. Richard, II. 2006. "What Is the Ancient Korean Religion?" *Acta Koreana* 9 (2): 1–30.

———. 2007. "Yi Kyubo's 'Lay of the Old Shaman.'" In *Religions of Korea in Practice*, edited by Robert E. Buswell, 233–43. Princeton, N.J.: Princeton University Press.

McCreery, John. 1990. "Why Don't We See Some Real Money Here? Offerings in Chinese Religion." *Journal of Chinese Religions* 18: 1–24.

Merrill, John. 1980. "The Cheju-do Rebellion." *Journal of Korean Studies* 2: 139–97.

Miller, Daniel. 1995. "Consumption and Commodities." *Annual Review of Anthropology* 24: 141–61.

———. 2001. "Alienable Gifts and Inalienable Commodities." In *The Empire of Things: Regimes of Value and Material Culture*, edited by Fred R. Myers, 91–115. Santa Fe, N.M.: School of American Research Press.

Mills, Simon. 2007. *Healing Rhythms: The World of South Korea's East Coast Hereditary Shamans*. Burlington, Vt.: Ashgate.

Min Chŏnghŭi. 2000. "Chosŏn chŏn'gi ŭi musok kwa chŏngbu chŏngch'aek" [Government policies on shamanic practice during the early Chosŏn period]. *Hangnim* 21: 1–46.

Miyazaki, Hirokazu. 2004. *The Method of Hope: Anthropology, Philosophy, and Fijian Knowledge*. Stanford, Calif.: Stanford University Press.

Mizuno, Naoki. 2007. "Singminjigi Chosŏn ŭi ilbonŏ sinmun" [The Japanese newspaper in colonial Korea]. *Yŏksa munje yŏn'gu* 18: 253–66.

Monaghan, John. 2008. "Liturgical Forms of Economic Allocations" In *Dimensions of Ritual Economy*. Research in Economic Anthropology Series, vol. 27, 19–35. Bingley, UK: Emerald Group Publishing Limited.

Moose, Robert. 1911. *Village Life in Korea*. Nashville, Tenn: Publishing House of the M. E. Church, South Smith and Lamar, Agents.

Mudang naeryŏk [*Mudang* chronicles]. 1996. Seoul: Kyujanggak Institute.

Mun Mubyŏng. 1987a. "Chejudo kut undong ŭi silch'ŏn kwaje" [Practical strategies for the *kut* movement on Cheju Island]. In *Minjok kwa kut* [Nation and *kut*], edited by Minjok Kut Hoe, 185–218. Seoul: Hangminsa.

———. 1987b. "Nallang chukkŏn takpat-e mudŏng . . ." [When I die, bury me under the mulberry tree . . ."] In *Minjok kwa kut* [Nation and *kut*], edited by Minjok Kut Hoe, 270–307. Seoul: Hangminsa.

———. 1998. *Chejudo musok sinhwa: Yŏltu ponp'uri charyojip* [Shamanic myths on Cheju Island: Materials of twelve *ponp'uri*]. Cheju: Ch'ilmŏri-dang Kut Pojonhoe.

———. 1999. "Chejudo musok sinwha wa sin'gut" [The myth of Cheju shamanic ancestors and *sin kut*]. *Pigyo munhwa yŏn'gu* [Cross-cultural studies] 5: 87–108.

————. 2001. *Chejudo k'ŭn kut charyo* [Transcription of a Cheju grand-scale *kut*]. Cheju: Cheju Provincial Government and Institute of Cheju Traditional Culture.

————. 2005. *Param ŭi ch'ukche Ch'ilmŏri-dang Yŏngdŭngkut* [A festival of wind: Yŏngdŭng Kut at the Ch'ilmŏri Shrine]. Seoul: Gold Egg Publishing Company.

————. 2009a. "Cheju kut ŭi kippal kwa chongi mugu" [Banners and paper decorations in Cheju shamanic rituals]. *Pulhwigong* 2: 61–76.

————. 2009b. "Cheju ŭi param ch'ukche Ch'ilmŏri-dang Yŏngdŭng Kut" [Cheju Island's festival of wind, the Yŏngdŭng Kut of the Ch'ilmŏri Shrine]. *Halla Daily*, 1 October 2009, 15.

Mun Mubyŏng and Yi Myŏngjin. 2008. *Cheju Ch'ilmŏri-dang Yŏngdŭng Kut* [Cheju Ch'ilmŏri Shrine Yŏngdŭng Kut]. Seoul: Minsogwŏn.

Murayama Chijun. (1929) 1990. *Chosŏn ŭi kwisin* (Spirits of Korea). Translated by No Sŏng-hwan. Seoul: Minŭmsa.

————. (1932) 2014. *Chosŏn ŭi mugyŏk* (Korean shamans). Translated by Ch'oe Kilsŏng and Park Howŏn. Seoul: Minsogwŏn.

Munjong sillok [Veritable records of King Munjong]. In *Chosŏn wangjo sillok*.

Munn, Nancy D. 1983. "Gawan Kula: Spatiotemporal Control and the Symbolism of Influence." In *The Kula: New Perspectives on Massim Exchange*, edited by J. W. Leach and E. Leach, 277–308. Cambridge: Cambridge University Press.

Myers, Fred R. 2001. "Introduction: The Empire of Things." In *The Empire of Things*, edited by Fred R. Myers, 3–61. Santa Fe, N.M.: School of American Research Press.

Nam Kun-Wu [Kŭnu]. 2006. "Chosŏn ŭi mosongron kwa singminjuŭi, Akiba Takasi ŭi *Chosŏn minjokchi* yŏn'gu" [Discourse on Korean shamanism and colonialism: A study of Akiba Takasi's *Ethnology of Korea*]. In *Cheguk Ilboni kŭrin Chosŏn minsok* [Korean ethnology written by imperial Japan], edited by Chu Youngha, Yim Kyŏngt'aek, and Nam Kun-Wu, 199–236. Sŏngnam: Academy of Korean Studies.

————. 2008. "Minsok ŭi munhwajaehwa wa kwan'gwang chawŏnhwa" [Folk culture between cultural property and tourism: Gangneung Dano Festival appropriated]. In *Tongasia ŭi kŭndae wa minsokhak ŭi ch'angch'ul* [Modernity and creation of folkloristics in East Asia], edited by Nam Kun-Wu, 321–60. Seoul: Minsogwŏn.

Nas, Peter J. M. 2002. "Masterpieces of Oral and Intangible Culture: Reflections on the World Heritage List." *Cultural Anthropology* 43 (1): 139–48.

National Kugak Center. 2010a. "2010 T'oyo Myŏngp'um Kongyŏn Sirij" [The 2010 Saturday Premium Performances Series]. Brochure. Seoul: National Kugak Center.

————. 2010b. "Sŏul esŏ Cheju Ch'ilmŏri-dang Yŏngdŭngkut ŭl kyŏnghŏmhae poseyo" [Experience the Cheju Ch'ilmŏri Yŏngdŭng Kut in Seoul]. *NewsWire*, 2010. Accessed 13 July 2013. www.newswire.co.kr/newsRead.php?no=496643.

National Research Institute of Cultural Heritage. 2008. *Mu, kut kwa ŭmsik* [Shamanism, shamanic ritual, and food]. Taejŏn: National Research Institute of Cultural Heritage.

Neimeyer, Robert A., Holly G. Prigerson, and Betty Davies. 2002. "Mourning and Meaning." *American Behavioral Scientist* 46 (2): 235–51.

Nelson, Laura C. 2000. *Measured Excess: Status, Gender, and Consumer Nationalism in South Korea*. New York: Columbia University Press.

Nemeth, David J., Jr. 1984. "Cheju Island Peasant Landscape: An Architecture of Neo-Confucian Ideology." PhD diss., University of California, Los Angeles.

Noonan, John T., Jr. 1984. *Bribes*. New York: Macmillan.

Noyes, Dorothy. 2003. *Fire in the Plaça: Catalan Festival Politics after Franco*. Philadelphia: University of Pennsylvania Press.

———. 2006. "The Judgment of Solomon: Global Protections for Tradition and the Problem of Community Ownership." *Cultural Analysis* 5: 27–56.

Oak, Sung-Deuk. 2013. *The Making of Korean Christianity: Protestant Encounters with Korean Religions, 1876–1910*. Waco, Tex.: Baylor University Press.

Oh, Youjeong. 2014. "Korean Television Dramas and the Political Economy of City Promotion." *International Journal of Urban and Regional Research* 38 (6): 2141–55.

Olwig, Karen Fog. 1999. "The Burden of Heritage: Claiming a Place for a West Indian Culture." *American Ethnologist* 26 (2): 370–88.

Ong, Aihwa. 1987. *Spirits of Resistance and Capitalist Discipline: Factory Women in Malaysia*. Albany: State University of New York Press.

———. 1988. "The Production of Possession: Spirits and the Multinational Corporation in Malaysia." *American Ethnologist* 15 (1): 28–42.

Oppenheim, Robert. 2005. "'The West' and the Anthropology of Other People's Colonialism: Frederick Starr in Korea, 1911–1930." *Journal of Asian Studies* 64 (3): 677–703.

———. 2011. "Crafting the Consumability of Place: *Tapsa* and *Paenang Yŏhaeng* as Travel Goods." In *Consuming Korean Tradition in Early and Late Modernity: Commodification, Tourism, and Performance*, edited by Laurel Kendall, 105–28. Honolulu: University of Hawai'i Press.

Pai, Hyung Il. 2000. *Constructing "Korean" Origins: A Critical Review of Archaeology, Historiography, and Racial Myth in Korean State-Formation Theories*. Cambridge, Mass.: Harvard University Press.

———. 2013. *Heritage Management in Korea and Japan: The Politics of Antiquity and Identity*. Seattle: University of Washington Press.

Pak Chongch'an. 2011. "Cheju '400 ŏk' chŏnhwa yogŭm naeya 7 tae kyŏnggwan sŏnjŏng?" [Cheju can be designated a seventh wonder of the world only after paying the 40-billion-won phone fee]. *Han'gyŏre*. Accessed 10 July 2013. www.hani.co.kr /arti/society/society_general/509915.html.

Palais, James B. (1975) 1991. *Politics and Policy in Traditional Korea*. Cambridge, Mass.: Harvard University Press.

Park, Jun Hwan. 2012. "'Money Is the Filial Child. But, at the Same Time It Is Also the Enemy!': Korean Shamanic Rituals for Luck and Fortune." *Journal of Korean Religions* 3 (2): 39–72.

Park Chan-Sik (Pak Ch'anshik). 2013. *1901 nyŏn Cheju Millan yŏn'gu: Kŭndae oerae munhwa wa t'ochak munhwa ŭi kanttŭng* [A study of the 1901 Cheju Rebellion: A conflict between foreign and native cultures in modern Korea]. Cheju: Kak.

Park Il-Young [Iryŏng]. 1990. "Musok ŭi taedong chanch'i" [Communitas of Korean shamanism]. *Chonggyo sinhak yŏn'gu* [Journal of religion and theology] 3: 115–40.

Park Kyŏnghun. 2013. "Minjok kwangdae, Minjung Simbang Chŏng Kongch'ŏl t'agye" (The death of Chŏng Kongch'ŏl, a clown and shaman for the subaltern people). *Cheju ŭi sori*, 14 June 2013. Accessed 30 June 2015. www.jejusori.net/?mod =news&act=articleView&idxno=130588.

Parry, Jonathan. 1989. "On the Moral Perils of Exchange," In *Money and the Morality of Exchange*, edited by Jonathan Parry and Maurice Bloch, 64–93. Cambridge: Cambridge University Press.

Pedersen, Morten A. 2011. *Not Quite Shamans: Spirit Worlds and Political Lives in Northern Mongolia*. Ithaca, N.Y.: Cornell University Press.

Pettid, Michael J. 2000a. "Reshaping History: The Creation of the Myth of the Three Surnames, the Foundation Myth of the T'amna Kingdom." *Review of Korean Studies* 3 (1): 157–77.

———. 2000b. "Late Chosŏn Society as Reflected in a Shamanistic Narrative: An Analysis of the 'Pari kongju muga.'" *Korean Studies* 24: 113–41.

———. 2001. "Vengeful Gods and Shrewd Men: Responses to the Loss of Sovereignty on Cheju Island." *East Asian History* 22: 171–86.

Pihl, Marshall R. 1994. *The Korean Singer of Tales*. Cambridge, Mass.: Harvard University Press.

Pritchard, Mauren. 2011. "Creativity and Sorrow in Kyrgyzstan." *Journal of Folklore Research* 48 (2): 167–96.

P'ungsok mum. 1994. Vol. 2. Cheju: T'amna Munhwa Yŏn'guso.

Rhi, Bou-yong (Yi Puyŏng). 1970. "Psychological Aspects of Korean Shamanism." *Korea Journal* 10 (9): 15–21.

———. 1977. "Psychological Problems among Korean Women." In *Virtues in Conflict: Tradition and the Korean Woman Today*, edited by S. Mattielli, 129–46. Seoul: Samhwa.

Rim Haksŏng. 1993. "Chosŏn sidae ŭi muse chedo wa kŭ silt'ae" [The shamanic tax system and its reality during the Chosŏn period]. *Yŏksa minsokhak* [The journal of Korean historical folklife] 3: 90–126.

Robinson, James C. 1969. *Okinawa: A People and Their Gods*. Rutland, Vt.: Charles E. Tuttle.

Robinson, Michael E. 1988. *Cultural Nationalism in Colonial Korea, 1920–1925*. Seattle: University of Washington Press.

Rockhill, Woodville. 1891. "Notes on Some of the Laws, Customs, and Superstitions of Korea." *American Anthropologist* 4 (2): 177–88.

Roh Minyŏng. 1988. *Chamdŭlji annŭn namdo* [Sleepless southern island]. Seoul: Onnuri.

Romberg, Raquel. 2003. *Witchcraft and Welfare: Spiritual Capital and the Business of Magic in Modern Puerto Rico*. Austin: University of Texas Press.

Roodenburg, Herman. 2002. "Making an Island in Time: Dutch Folklore Studies, Painting, Tourism, and Craniometry around 1900." *Journal of Folklore Research* 39 (1): 173–99.

Rosaldo, Michelle. 1984. "Toward an Anthropology of Self and Feeling." In *Culture Theory: Essays on Mind, Self, and Emotion*, edited by Richard A. Shweder and Robert A. LeVine, 137–57. New York: Cambridge University Press.

Rudnyckyj, Daromir. 2010. *Spiritual Economies: Islam, Globalization, and the Afterlife of Development*. Ithaca, N.Y.: Cornell University Press.

Ruesch, Jurgen, and Gregory Bateson. (1951) 1968. *Commnication: The Social Matrix of Psychiatry*. New York: Norton.

Rupp, Katherine. 2003. *Gift-Giving in Japan: Cash, Connections, Cosmologies*. Stanford, Calif.: Stanford University Press.

Rutt, Richard. 1964. *Korean Works and Days: Notes from the Diary of a Country Priest*. Rutland, Vt.: Charles E. Tuttle.

Ryang, Sonia. 2000. "Osaka's Transnational Town: An Ethnography." In "Koreans in Japan: New Dimensions of Hybrid and Diverse Communities," edited by Sonia Ryang. Special issue, *Korean and Korean American Studies Bulletin* 11 (1): J71–93.

Ryu, Dae Young. 2003. "Treaties, Extraterritorial Rights, and American Protestant Missions in Late Joseon Korea." *Korea Journal* 43 (1): 174–203.

Saeji, CedarBough. 2018. "Replacing Faith in Spirits with Faith in Heritage: A Story of the Management of the Gangneung Danoje Festival." In *Safeguarding Intangible Heritage: Practices and Policies*, edited by Laurajane Smith and Natsuko Akagawa, 155–73. London: Routledge.

Said, Edward. 1978. *Orientalism*. New York: Vintage Books.

Sands, William Franklin. (1904) 1931. *Undiplomatic Memories: The Far East 1896–1904*. London: J. Hamilton.

Sandstrom, Alan R. 2008. "Ritual Economy among the Nahua of Northern Veracruz, Mexico." In *Dimensions of Ritual Economy*. Research in Economic Anthropology Series, vol. 27, 93–119. Bingley, UK: Emerald Group Publishing Limited.

Sarfati, Liora. 2009. "Objects of Worship: Material Culture in the Production of Shamanic Rituals in South Korea." PhD diss., Indiana University, Bloomington.

———. 2016. "Shifting Agencies through New Media: New Social Statuses for Female South Korean Shamans." *Journal of Korean Studies* 21 (1): 179–211.

Schechner, Richard. 1982. "Collective Reflexivity: Restoration of Behavior." In *Crack in the Mirror: Reflexive Perspective in Anthropology*, edited by J. Ruby, 39–81. Philadelphia: University of Pennsylvania Press.

Schein, Louisa. 2000. *Minority Rules: The Miao and the Feminine in China's Cultural Politics*. Durham, N.C.: Duke University Press.

Scher, Philip. 2002. "Copyright Heritage: Preservation, Carnival and the State in Trinidad." *Anthropological Quarterly* 75 (3): 453–84.

———. 2010. "UNESCO Conventions and Culture as a Resource." *Journal of Folklore Research* 47 (1–2): 197–202.

Schieffelin, Edward. 1996. "On Failure and Performance: Throwing the Medium Out of the Séance." In *The Performance of Healing*, edited by Carol Laderman and Marina Roseman, 59–89. New York: Routledge.

Schmid, Andre. 2002. *Korea between Empires 1895–1919*. New York: Columbia University Press.

Seaman, Gary. 1982. "Spirit Money: An Interpretation." *Journal of Chinese Religions* 10(1): 80–91.

Sejong sillok [Veritable records of King Sejong]. In *Chosŏn wangjo sillok*.

Seo, Maria. 2002. *Hanyang Kut: Korean Shaman Ritual Music from Seoul*. New York: Routledge.

Seo Dae-seok [Sŏ Taesŏk]. 1996. "*Mudang naeryŏk* haeje" [A bibliographical introdution to *Mudang naeryŏk*], 3–25. Seoul: Kyujanggak Institute.

Seo Dae-seok and Peter H. Lee. 2000. *Myths of Korea*. Seoul: Jimoondang.

Sherzer, Joel. 1987. "A Diversity of Voices: Men's and Women's Speech in Ethnographic Perspective." In *Language, Gender, and Sex in Comparative Perspective*, edited by Susan U. Phillips, Susan Steele, and Christine Tanz, 95–120. Cambridge: Cambridge University Press.

Shields, M. James. 2017. *Against Harmony: Progressive and Radical Buddhism in Modern Japan*. New York: Oxford University Press.

Shim, Doobo. 2008. "The Growth of Korean Cultural Industries and the Korean Wave." In *The Growth of Korean Cultural Industries and the Korean Wave*, edited by Chu Beng Huat and Koichi Iwabuchi, 15–31. Hong Kong: Hong Kong University Press.

Shin, Gi-Wook. 2003. "The Paradox of Korean Globalization." Working paper. Stanford, Calif.: Walter H. Shorenstein Asia-Pacific Research Center.

Shin, Gi-Wook, and Han Do-Hyun. 1999. "Colonial Corporatism: The Rural Revitalization Campaign, 1932–1940." In *Colonial Modernity in Korea*, edited by Gi-Wook Shin and Michael Robinson, 70–96. Cambridge, Mass.: Harvard University Press.

Shin, Gi-Wook, and Michael Robinson, eds. 1999. *Colonial Modernity in Korea*. Cambridge, Mass.: Harvard University Press.

Simmel, George. (1900) 1978. *The Philosophy of Money*. Translated by Tom Bottomore and David Frisby. London: Routledge and Kegan Paul.

Sin Myŏnggi. 2001. *Ch'ŏn Pokhwa Mudang naerŏk* [*Mudang* chronicles of Ch'ŏn Pokhwa]. Seoul: Minsogwŏn.

Sinjŭng Tongguk yŏji sŭngnam [Augmented survey of the geography of Korea]. (1530) 1969. 7 vols. Compiled and revised by Yi Haeng et al. Reprinted and translated by Minjokmunhwa Ch'ujinhoe. Seoul: Minjokmunhwa Ch'ujinhoe.

Smith, Laurajane. 2006. *Uses of Heritage*. New York: Routledge.

Smith, Laurajane, and Natsuko Akagawa, eds. 2009. *Intangible Heritage*. New York: Routledge.

Smith, S. G. F. (Samuel George Frederick). 1970. *Dictionary of Comparative Religion*. New York: Scribner.

Sŏgwip'o Citrus Museum. Accessed 30 December 2013. www.citrusmuseum.com/index .php/contents/story/history/derive/derive_01 (site discontinued).

Sokol, A. E. 1948. "The Name of Quelpaert Island." *History of Science Society* 38 (3/4): 231–35.

Sŏl Sŏng-gyŏng. 1973. "Legends of Wind Spirits in Korea." *Korea Journal* 13 (9): 24–30.

Son, Cheolbae (Ch'ŏlbae). 2006. "The Ordinary Reaction by Koreans against the Foreign Penetration, 1876 to 1910." PhD diss., University of Washington, Seattle.

Son Chint'ae. 1981. *Son Chint'ae sŏnsaeng chŏnjip* [Son Chint'ae's collected works]. 6 vols. Seoul: T'aehaksa.

———. (1930) 2012. *Chosŏn sin'ga yup'yŏn* [The remaining shaman songs of Korea]. Seoul: Pagijŏng.

Song, Jesook. 2014. *Living on Your Own: Single Women, Rental Housing, and Postrevolutionary Affect in Contemporary South Korea*. Albany: State University of New York Press.

Song Chaeho. 2002. *Cheju kwan'gwang ŭi ihae* [Understanding Cheju tourism]. Cheju: Kak.

Song Sŏkha. 1960. *Han'guk minsokko* [A study of Korean folklore]. Seoul: Ilsinsa.

Sorensen, Clark. 1988. "The Myth of Princess Pari and the Self Image of Korean Women." *Anthropos* 83: 403–19.

———. 1995. "Folk Religion and Political Commitment in South Korea in the 1980s." In *Render unto Caesar: The Religious Sphere in World Politics*, edited by Sabrina Petra Ramet and Donald W. Treadgold, 325–53. Washington, DC: The American University Press.

Stark, Rodney. 2006. "Economics of Religion." In *The Blackwell Companion to the Study of Religion*, edited by Robert A. Segal, 47–67. Malden, Mass.: Blackwell.

Statistics of Korea. http://kostat.go.kr/eng/.

Stewart, Pamela J., and Andrew Strathern, eds. 2008. *Exchange and Sacrifice*. Durham, NC: Carolina Academic Press.

Strathern, Marilyn. 1988. *The Gender of the Gift: Problems with Women and Problems with Society in Melanesia*. Berkeley: University of California Press.

Sukchong sillok [Veritable records of King Sukchong]. In *Chosŏn wangjo sillok*.

Sun, Soon-Hwa. 1991. "Women, Religion, and Power: A Comparative Study of Korean Shamans and Women Ministers." PhD diss., Dew University.

———. 1992. "The Vocational Socialization of the Korean Shaman." *Korea Journal* 32 (3): 86–102.

T'aejo sillok [Veritable records of King T'aejo]. In *Chosŏn wangjo sillok*.

Tangherlini, Timothy R. 1998. "Students, Shamans, and the State: Politics and the Enactment of Culture in South Korea, 1987–88." In *Nationalism and the Construction of Korean Identity*, edited by Hyung Il Pai and Timothy R. Tangherlini, 126–47. Berkeley: University of California Press.

———. 2008. "Chosŏn Memories: Spectatorship, Ideology, and the Korean Folk Village." In *Sitings: Critical Approaches to Korean Geography*, edited by Timothy R. Tangherlini and Sallie Yea, 61–82. Honolulu: University of Hawai'i Press.

Tangherlini, Timothy R., and So Yong Park (Pak So-Yŏng). 1988. "The Ritual Landscape of Sunshine Village, Cheju-do Island at Lunar New Year." *Korea Journal* 28 (5): 21–36.

———. 1990. "The Comings and Goings of a Korean Grandfather: The Yŏngdŭng Kut Sequence of a Cheju Island Village." *Korean Studies* 14: 84–97.

Taussig, Michael. 1980. *The Devil and Commodity Fetishism in South America*. Chapel Hill: University of North Carolina Press.

———. 1991. *Shamanism, Colonialism, and the Wild Man: A Study in Terror and Healing*. Chicago: University of Chicago Press.

Tedlock, Barbara. 2006. "Toward a Theory of Divination Practice." *Anthropology of Consciousness* 17 (2): 62–77.

Tedlock, Dennis. 1972. *Finding the Center: Narrative Poetry of the Zuñi Indians*. New York: Dial Press.

Tharoor, Ishan. 2016. "South Korea's President Is Hardly the Only Leader to Turn to Mystics and Shamans." *Washington Post*, 2 November 2016. Accessed 7 November 2016. https://www.washingtonpost.com/news/worldviews/wp/2016/11/02/south-koreas-president-is-hardly-the-only-leader-to-turn-to-mystics-and-shamans/?noredirect=on&utm_term=.8a47f8f6a7d4.

Tonga ilbo. 1922. "Ojo ch'ŏngnyŏn ŭi il saŏp" [A project of the Ojo youth]. 26 September 1922, 4.

Tonga ilbo. 1932. "Misin hoenghaeng" [Rampant superstition]. 30 December 1932, 3.

Torii Ryūjō. (1913) 1976. "Chōsen no fugeki" (Korean shamans). In *Torii Ryūjōshū*, vol. 7, 347–54. Tokyo: Asahi Shimbunsha.

———. (1920) 1974. "Ni-senjin wa 'tōgen' nari" (Korean-Japanese have the "same" origin). In *Torii Ryūjōshū*, vol. 6, 538–39. Tokyo: Tsukijishokan.

Tran, Tommy. 2015. "Imagining Urban Community: Contested Geographies and Parallax Urban Dreams on Cheju Island, South Korea." *Cross-Currents: East Asian History and Culture Review* 17. E-journal. Accessed 29 January 2016. http://cross -currents.berkeley.edu/e-journal/issue-17.

Truitt, Allison J. 2013. *Dreaming of Money in Ho Chi Minh City.* Seattle: University of Washington Press.

Walraven, Boudewijn. 1991. "Confucians and Shamans." *Cahiers d'Extrême-Asie* 6: 21–44.

———. 1993. "Our Shamanistic Past: The Korean Government, Shamans, and Shamanism." *Copenhagen Papers in East and Southeast Asian Studies* 8: 5–25.

———. 1994. *Songs of the Shaman: The Ritual Chants of the Korean Mudang.* London: Kegan Paul.

———. 1995. "Shamans and Popular Religion around 1900." *Religions in Traditional Korea,* edited by Henrik H. Sørensen, 107–30. Copenhagen: Seminar for Buddhist Studies.

———. 1998. "Interpretations and Reinterpretations of Popular Religion in the Last Decades of the Chosŏn Dynasty." In *Korean Shamanism: Revivals, Survivals, and Change,* edited by Keith Howard, 55–72. Seoul: Royal Asiatic Society, Korea Branch.

———. 1999a. "Popular Religion in a Confucianized Society." In *Culture and the State in Late Chosŏn Korea,* edited by JaHyun Kim Haboush and Martina Deuchler, 160–98. Cambridge, Mass.: Harvard University Asia Center.

———. 1999b. "The Natives Next-Door: Ethnology in Colonial Korea." In *Anthropology and Colonialism in Asia and Oceania,* edited by Jan van Bremen and Akitoshi Shimizu, 219–44. Surrey, England: Curzon Press.

———. 2001. "Opening the Gate of Writing: Literate Shamans in Modern Korea." In *The Concept of Shamanism: Uses and Abuses,* edited by Henri-Paul Francfort and Roberte N. Hamayon, 331–48. Budapest: Akadémiai Kiadó.

———. 2002. "Weavers of Ritual: How Shamans Achieve Their Aims." *Review of Korean Studies* 5 (1): 85–104.

———. 2007a. "The Creation of the World and Human Suffering." In *Religions of Korea in Practice,* edited by Robert E. Buswell, 244–58. Princeton, N.J.: Princeton University Press.

———. 2007b. "Village Deities of Cheju Island." In *Religions of Korea in Practice,* edited by Robert E. Buswell, 284–305. Princeton, N.J.: Princeton University Press.

———. 2007c. "Shamans, the Family, and Women." In *Religions of Korea in Practice,* edited by Robert E. Buswell, 306–24. Princeton, N.J.: Princeton University Press.

———. 2009. "Cheju Island 1901: Records, Memories and Current Concerns." *Korean Histories* 1 (1): 3–24.

Weber, Max. (1946) 1958. *From Max Weber: Essays in Sociology.* Translated and edited by H. H. Gerth and C. Wright Mills. New York: Oxford University Press.

Weller, Robert P. 1994. "Capitalism, Community, and the Rise of Amoral Cults in Taiwan." In *Asian Visions of Authority: Religion and the Modern States of East and Southeast Asia*, edited by Charles F. Keyes, Laurel Kendall, and Helen Hardacre, 141–64. Honolulu: University of Hawai'i Press.

Wells, Christian E., and McAnany Patricia, eds. 2008. *Dimensions of Ritual Economy*. Bingley, UK: JAI.

Wells, Kenneth M. 1990. *New God, New Nation: Protestants and Self-reconstruction Nationalism in Korea, 1896–1937*. Honolulu: University of Hawai'i Press.

Whisnant, David. 1983. *All That Is Native and Fine: The Politics of Culture in an American Region*. Chapel Hill: University of North Carolina Press.

Yang, Jongsung. 2003. *Cultural Protection Policy in Korea: Intangible Cultural Properties and Living National Treasures*. Edison, N.J., and Seoul: Jimoondang International.

———. 2004. "Kangsinmu, sesŭpmu yuhyŏngnon e ttarŭn musok yŏn'gu kŏmt'o: Kim T'ae-gon, Ch'oe Kil-sŏng ŭl chungsim ŭro" [An examination of *musok* studies dealing with the typology of *kangsin mu* and *sesŭp mu* and focusing on the theories of Kim T'aegon and Ch'oe Kil-sŏng]. *Han'guk musokhak* 8: 9–36.

Yang, Mayfair Mei-hui. 1994. *Gifts, Favors, and Banquets: The Art of Social Relationships in China*. Ithaca, N.Y.: Cornell University Press.

———. 2000. "Putting Global Capitalism in Its Place: Economic Hybridity, Bataille, and Ritual Expenditure." *Current Anthropology* 41 (4): 540–60.

———. 2008. Introduction to *Chinese Religiosities: Afflictions of Modernity and State Formation*, 1–40. Berkeley: University of California Press.

Yeo, Andrew. 2013. "A Base for (In)security?: The Jeju Naval Base and Competing Visions of Peace on the Korean Peninsula." In *Under Occupation: Resistance and Struggle in a Militarised Asia-Pacific*, edited by Daniel Broudy, Peter Simpson, and Makoto Arakaki, 224–37. Newcastle upon Tyne, UK: Cambridge Scholars Publishing.

Yi Hyŏngsang. (1703) 2004. *T'amna Sullyŏkto* [Illustrated records of the T'amna inspections]. Cheju: Cheju City Publisher.

———. (1704) 2009. *Namhwan pangmul* [Various things observed in the South]. Translated and annotated by Yi Sang-gyu and O Ch'ang-myŏng. Seoul: P'urŭn Yŏksa.

———. 1990. *Pyŏngwa chip* [A collection of Pyŏngwa]. Vol. 3. Translated by Han'guk Chŏngsin Munhwa Yŏn'guwŏn. Sŏngnam: Han'guk Chŏngsin Munhwa Yŏn'guwŏn.

Yi Ik. 1977–84. *Sŏnghosasŏl* [Collected works of Sŏngho]. 12 vols. Translated by Minjok Munhwa Ch'ujinhoe. Seoul: Minjok Munhwa Ch'ujinhoe.

Yi Kyŏng-hŭi. 2009. "Kanggang sullae, Ch'ŏyongmu segye muhyŏng yusan twaetta" [Kangkang sullae and Ch'ŏyongmu have been added to the world's intangible cultural heritage]. *Jungang Daily*, 1 October 2009, 28.

Yi Nŭnghwa. 1923. "Chosŏn sin'gyo wŏllyuko" [The history of *sin'gyo* in Korea]. *Shirin* 8 (1): 135–44.

———. (1927) 2008. *Chosŏn musokko* [Treatise on Korean shamanism]. Translated by Sŏ Yŏngdae. P'aju: Ch'angbisa.

Yi Sang-gyu. 2009. "Haeje" [A bibliographical introduction]. In *Namhwan pangmul* [Various things observed in the South], translated and annotated by Yi Sang-gyu and O Ch'ang-myŏng, 5–17. Seoul: P'urŭn Yŏksa.

Yi Sugil. 2008. *Pyŏngwa Yi Hyŏngsang ŭi sam kwa hangmun* [Life and scholarship of Pyŏngwa Yi Hyŏngsang]. Pusan: Sejong Ch'ulp'an.

Yi Suja. 2004. *Chejudo musok ŭl t'onghaesŏ pon k'ŭn kut yŏltu kŏri ŭi kujojŏk wŏnhyŏng kwa shinhwa* [Structural archetype and myths of the grand-scale ritual's twelve sessions examined through Cheju shamanism]. Seoul: Chimmundang.

Yi Sŭngnok. 2011. "UNESCO Illyu Yusan 'Cheju ŭi kut' i misin iran marinya" [Who calls the UNESCO Intangible Cultural Heritage of Humanity a superstition?]. *Cheju ŭi sori.* Accessed 14 May 2014. www.jejusori.net/news/articleView.html?idxno=96945.

Yi Wŏnjin. (1653) 2002. *T'amnaji.* Translated by Kim Ch'anhŭp, Ko Changsŏk, Kim Hyeu, Kim Sangok, Cho Sŏngyun, Kang Ch'angyong, O Ch'angmyŏng, and O Sujŏng. Seoul: P'urŭn Yŏksa.

Yi Yong-Bhum [Yong-bŏm]. 2005. "Musok e taehan kŭndae Han'guk sahoe ŭi pujŏngjŏk sigak e taehan koch'al" [An examination of the negative viewpoint on *musok* in modern Korea]. *Han'guk musokhak* [Korean shamanism] 9: 151–79.

Yi Yŏnggwŏn. 2005. *Saero ssŭnŭn Cheju-sa* [Rewriting Cheju history]. Seoul: Hyumŏnisŭt'ŭ.

———. 2008. *Cheju Yŏksa kihaeng* [Historical trips on Cheju]. Seoul: Han'gyŏrye Shinmunsa.

Yim Suk-jay [Im Sŏkchae]. 1970. "Han'guk musok yŏn'gu sŏsŏl I" [Introduction to Korean shamanism I]. *Asesa yŏsŏng yŏn'gu* [Journal of Asian women] 9: 73–90.

———. 1971. "Han'guk musok yŏn'gu sŏsŏl II" [Introduction to Korean Shamanism II]. *Asesa yŏsŏng yŏn'gu* [Journal of Asian women] 10: 161–224.

Yim Suk-jay, Roger L. Janelli, and Dawnhee Yim Janelli. 1989. "Korean Religion." In *The Religious Traditions of Asia*, edited by Joseph M. Kitagawa, 333–46. New York: Macmillan. [Reprint of entry in vol. 8 of *The Encyclopedia of Religion*, edited by Mircea Eliade, published in 1987.]

———. 1993. "Toward a Political Economy of Korean Shamanism." In *Shamans and Cultures: The Regional Aspects of Shamanism*, edited by M. Hoppál and K. Howard, 52–60. Budapest: Korrekt Ltd.

Yoo Cheol-In [Yu Ch'ŏrin]. 1986. "Cheju saramdŭl ŭi munhwajŏk chŏngch'egam" [The cultural identity of the Cheju people]. *T'amna munhwa* [T'amna culture] 5: 71–93.

———. 2000. "Cheju saramdŭl ŭi saenghwal segye esŏ pon 'ilbon'" [The meaning of Japan in the life-world of Cheju people]. *Han'guk munhwa illyuhak* [Korean cultural anthropology] 33 (2): 361–78.

Yu Hongjun. 2012. *Na ŭi munhwa yusan tapsagi 7* [The chronicle of my field study of cultural remains 7]. P'aju: Ch'angjak kwa Pip'yŏngsa.

Yu Hongyŏl. 1962. *Kojong ch'iha ŭi sŏhak sunan ŭi yŏn'gu* [Studies on Catholic persecutions during King Kojong's reign]. Seoul: Ŭlyu Munhwasa.

Yu Tongsik. 1975. *Han'guk mugyo ŭi yŏksa wa kujo* [History and structure of Korean shamanism]. Seoul: Yonsei University Press.

Yúdice, George. 2003. *The Expediency of Culture: Uses of Culture in the Global Era.* Durham, N.C.: Duke University Press.

Yun, Kyoim. 2006. "The 2002 World Cup and a Local Festival in Cheju: Global Dreams and the Commodification of Shamanism." *Journal of Korean Studies* 11: 7–40.

———. 2011. "Negotiating a Korean National Myth: Dialogic Interplay and Entextualization in an Ethnographic Encounter." *Journal of American Folklore* 124, no. 494 (2011): 295–316.

———. 2015. "The Economic Imperative of UNESCO Recognition: A South Korean Shamanic Ritual." *Journal of Folklore Research* 52 (2–3): 181–98.

———. 2016. "Spiritual Entrepreneurship: Negotiating the Ritual Marketplace on Contemporary Cheju Island, South Korea." *Journal of Ritual Studies* 30 (2): 53–65.

Yun Ihŭm. 2002. "Koryŏ chonggyo sasang ŭi t'ŭksŏng kwa hŭrŭm" [Characteristics and changes of religious thoughts of Koryŏ]. In *Koryŏ sidae ŭi chonggyo wa munhwa* [Religions and culture of the Koryŏ period], 15–65. Seoul: Seoul National University Press.

Yun Ihŭm, Kim Ilkwŏn, and Choi Chongsŭng. 2002. *Koryŏ sidae ŭi chonggyo munhwa* [Religious culture of the Koryŏ period]. Seoul: Seoul National University Press.

Yun Sunhŭi. 2010. "Chejudo wasan-ri Menggam-je yŏn'gu" [A study of Menggam-je of Wasan-ni, Chejudo]. MA thesis, Cheju National University.

Yun Yong-bŏm. 2005. "Musok e taehan kŭndae Han'guk sahoe ŭi pujŏngjŏk sigak e tahan koch'al" [An examination of the negative viewpoint on *musok* in modern Korea]. *Han'guk musokhak* [Korean shamanism] 9: 151–79.

Zelizer, Viviana. 1994. *The Social Meaning of Money: Pin Money, Paychecks, Poor Relief and Other Currencies*. New York: BasicBooks.

Zulaika, Joseba. 2005. "Desiring Bilbao: The Krensification of the Museum and Its Discontents." In *Learning from the Bilbao Guggenheim*, edited by Anna Maria Guasch and Joseba Zulaika, 149–70. Reno: University of Nevada Center for Basque Studies.

INDEX

A

aengmaegi (ritual sequence for forestalling misfortune), 3, 90, 95–99, 194n32
Akamatsu Chijō, 67; *Study of Korean
Shamanism*, 62, 190n24
Akiba Takahashi, 22, 61–64, 66, 67,
189n10; *Study of Korean Shamanism*,
62, 190n24
altars, 13, 82, 96, 138
An, Simbang: on offerings, 89; on reason
for conducting *kut*, 96; on value of
shamans' services, 84; and ritual fees,
109–10, 113; on ritual tears, 197n17;
rituals performed by, 85–86, 193n12;
on sponsoring *sin kut*, 100
An Mi-jeong, 133
An Sain, Simbang (1928–1990), 158
anthropologists. *See* ethnographic research
anti-bribery act, 194n22
anti-superstition campaigns, 50, 54–56,
65, 66, 69, 71, 73, 146, 153
April Third Events (Sasam Sakkŏn),
17–18, 73, 80, 106, 155, 158, 200n18
Association for the Ch'ilmŏri Yŏngdŭng
Kut Preservation: collaboration with
Mun, 149, 153; formation of, 199n2;
members of, 81, 144; office managers
of, 142, 158; performances by, 70, 138,
150–51, 200n18; and UNESCO
recognition, 154–55, 157–59, 160. *See
also* Kim, Manager
Atkins, Taylor E., 30, 34
Austin, John L., 95–96, 198n34
authenticity: concern for, 111; of
contemporary shamanism, 24, 59; of
hereditary shamans, 19–20; in heritage
events, 151; island authenticity, 139,

144, 145–46, 150, 167–68; politics of,
158; and ritual economy, 13, 64, 162;
and traditionalization, 97; in *yŏngge
ullim*, 114–15, 117, 122, 170
Ayukai Fusanosin, 57

B

Bateson, Gregory, 195n36
Bauman, Richard, 120, 197nn24,26, 198n37
Beuchelt, Eno, 22, 198n30
Boxers, 188n3
bribes, 9, 11, 194nn22,33
Bruner, Edward M., 148
Bruno, Antonetta, 85–86
Buddhism, 186n16, 187n28, 196n6
Byun Jisun, 193n10

C

capitalism, 12, 14, 100, 102, 167, 170
Catholics: converts, 52–53, 189n7;
missionaries, 50–53, 74, 163, 188n3
censorship, 189n11
Ch'agwi, 31
Ch'agwi Shrine, 34
chakttu kŏri ritual, 144
chamnyŏ (women divers), 16. *See also*
diving women
Chang Chugŭn, 67–68; "Recollection on
Studies of Cheju Shamanism," 67
changgye, 35. *See also under* Yi Hyŏngsang
Chau, Adam Yuet, *Miraculous Response*,
12
Cheju: administration of, 28–29, 29*fig.*,
139–40, 182n20; as Chosŏn's periphery,
27–31, 184n4; Confucianization of, 22;
emigration ban, 17; governors of, 28,
30, 33, 34, 38, 46, 47, 184n4, 186n20,